ROUTLEDGE LIBRARY EDITIONS: 18TH CENTURY PHILOSOPHY

Volume 17

VOLTAIRE

VOLTAIRE

RICHARD ALDINGTON

LONDON AND NEW YORK

First published in 1925 by George Routledge & Sons, Ltd.
Second Impression (Revised) in 1929

This edition first published in 2019
by Routledge
2 Park Square, Milton Park, Abingdon, Oxon OX14 4RN

and by Routledge
52 Vanderbilt Avenue, New York, NY 10017

Routledge is an imprint of the Taylor & Francis Group, an informa business

© 1929 George Routledge & Sons, Ltd.

All rights reserved. No part of this book may be reprinted or reproduced or utilised in any form or by any electronic, mechanical, or other means, now known or hereafter invented, including photocopying and recording, or in any information storage or retrieval system, without permission in writing from the publishers.

Trademark notice: Product or corporate names may be trademarks or registered trademarks, and are used only for identification and explanation without intent to infringe.

British Library Cataloguing in Publication Data
A catalogue record for this book is available from the British Library

ISBN: 978-0-367-13518-8 (Set)
ISBN: 978-0-429-02691-1 (Set) (ebk)
ISBN: 978-0-367-13574-4 (Volume 17) (hbk)
ISBN: 978-0-367-13581-2 (Volume 17) (pbk)
ISBN: 978-0-429-02727-7 (Volume 17) (ebk)

Publisher's Note
The publisher has gone to great lengths to ensure the quality of this reprint but points out that some imperfections in the original copies may be apparent.

Disclaimer
The publisher has made every effort to trace copyright holders and would welcome correspondence from those they have been unable to trace.

VOLTAIRE

By
Richard Aldington

LONDON
GEORGE ROUTLEDGE & SONS, LTD.
NEW YORK: E. P. DUTTON & CO.

First Edition : 1925
Second Impression (Revised) : 1929

Printed in Great Britain by
M. F. Robinson & Co., Ltd., The Library Press, Lowestoft.

CONTENTS

PART I

		Page
I	"Voltaire"	5
II	Early life, 1694-1726	9
III	Voltaire in England, 1726-1729	24
IV	Paris to Cirey, 1729-1734	34
V	Cirey, 1734-1744	48
VI	Madame du Châtelet and the King of Prussia	61
VII	Voltaire at Court—Death of Madame du Châtelet, 1744-1749	68
VIII	Frederick, 1749-1753	78
IX	The Patriarch of Ferney, 1753-1778	102
X	The Last Journey, 1778	119

PART II

XI	Voltaire's Works	133
XII	Voltaire as Poet	137
XIII	Voltaire as Dramatist	155
XIV	Voltaire as Literary Critic	167
XV	Voltaire as Historian and Biographer	175
XVI	"Le Philosophe"	194
XVII	Novels and Pamphlets	213
XVIII	Correspondence	233
XIX	Conclusion	247
Appendix	Chronological List of Works	251
	English Translations	264
	Bibliography	267
Index		269

VOLTAIRE
PART I

A CHARACTER OF VOLTAIRE

Titus gets up in the winter alone and without a fire; when his servants come in they find there is already a pile of letters for post on the table. He begins simultaneously several works which he finishes with inconceivable rapidity, while his impatient genius does not allow him to polish them. Whatever he undertakes it is impossible for him to linger over; any business he delayed would trouble him until he could take it up again. Though occupied with such serious exertions, he is to be met with in society like the idlest of men. He does not enclose himself in one group, he cultivates several at once; he has innumerable acquaintances within and outside the Kingdom. He has travelled, he has written, he has been to court and to war; he excels in several occupations, and knows everybody and has read everything. He spends the hours he is in company in forming intrigues and cultivating friends; he cannot understand how men can talk for the sake of talking, act for the sake of acting, and it is plain his mind suffers when he is uselessly detained by necessity and politeness. If he is seeking some pleasure, he employs as much finesse as in the most serious business; and the use he makes of his mind occupies him more vividly than the very pleasure he is pursuing. He retains the same activity in health and in sickness, he goes to solicit in a law-case on the day he has taken medicine, and writes verses when he has a fever. When he is told to take care of himself he answers: "Why! how can I? You see how overwhelmed I am with business!" Although as a matter of fact there is not one of these affairs but is voluntary. He is attacked by a more dangerous illness and has himself dressed to put his papers in order; he remembers the words of the emperor Vespasian, and, like that emperor, wishes to die standing upright.

MARQUIS DE VAUVENARGUES

VOLTAIRE

PART I: LIFE

I

"VOLTAIRE"

Everyone who takes an interest in literature and the changes of the human mind knows the name of Voltaire, and has at least a vague idea of his personality and work. Voltaire, we say, was a " European figure " or " Voltaire is the eighteenth century ". There was indeed a time when the word " Voltaire " was the intellectual battle-cry of half Europe ; when the philosophy of M. de Voltaire, the wit, the charm, the enlightenment, the glory of M. de Voltaire were the delight and guiding power of innumerable people in twenty countries ; when, on the other hand, " the detestable opinions of the ignoble Voltaire " caused deep concern to the orthodox defenders of Christianity and privilege. What is left of " so much glory that once filled the world with its sound " ? A few echoes, a few vague memories, remain in the public mind ; a few of Voltaire's numerous books are still commonly read. But the Europe of to-day does not know and love or hate Voltaire as he was known and loved or hated by the Europe of 1825 or of 1775.

Like all men of real eminence, Voltaire has acquired a certain traditional reputation, a *légende.* It is not

VOLTAIRE

easy to say exactly what is the shape of this *légende* in England, what associations are generally evoked by the word "Voltaire". It is something like this. First, as a kind of general symbol of his personality, Voltaire is the famous smile of Houdon's statue, an enigmatic smile, sharp and yet kindly, mocking but wise, the smile of a Pan with a Jesuit education. Next, Voltaire is the "precursor of the Revolution" and the violent (but now discredited) opponent of Christianity; sometimes he is the "defender of rationalism", of Deism, and the Calas family. Then there are echoes of that extraordinary novel, his life—his early satires and the beating he received from the Chevalier de Rohan's servants, his Bastille days, the visit to England (where of course he acted as a "French spy"), his skirmishes with the French government and the persecution he endured for trying to introduce the ignorant French people to some of the perfection of English life and politics, his flights and concealments, his life with Mme du Châtelet at Cirey, his flirtation with Frederick and the years at Potsdam and Berlin, "Dr Akakia", his old age at Lausanne and Ferney, Mme Denis and the Calas family, his immense fortune, his "meanness and treachery", his squabbles with petty writers, "Fréron and Piron", the last journey to Paris, the apotheosis at the Comédie Française, his death and the difficulties in obtaining Christian burial, the final translation of his remains to the Panthéon during the Revolution. Then, though their general excellence is rarely allowed, come Voltaire's Works—*Candide* and a few other novels of the same type, the letters on England, the philosophical dictionary, the "reprehensible *La Pucelle*", the "unreadable *Henriade*", the "dreary tragedies" and "unimportant minor poems", the *Age*

VOLTAIRE

of Louis XIV and the *History of Charles XII*, the letters, and " other miscellaneous writings " . . .

That is approximately the English *légende* of Voltaire, distorted by Carlyle's prejudices, narrowed by Lord Morley's puritanism, minimised by national incomprehension, enlivened in recent years by the intelligence and malice of Mr Lytton Strachey—himself no unworthy descendant of the great master of irony. Voltaire found partisans and enjoyed great praise in England, but those who best understood him were not popular in the semi-puritan society of the last century[1] and some who have written effectively about him were too severe to his faults as a man and writer or have praised him for political motives. In France the *légende* is a different one, errs perhaps on the side of admiration and uncritical praise ; but then a large section of the French bourgeoisie is still Voltairean in temperament and in prejudice.

The purpose of the present book is limited. It does not pretend to original research or original views. There exists in France an enormous body of Voltaire literature ; the gigantic work of Desnoiresterres and his successors[2] contains detailed information about Voltaire's life ; the short study of M. Gustave Lanson is a model of critical appreciation. To compete successfully with such writers is hardly possible. What can be attempted is to put before the reader, as impartially as one can, the results of research and investigation ; to base oneself, in other words, upon critical science and not upon fantasy, to make a bridge between the mass of existing Voltaire knowledge and the people who would like to know the

[1] Lord Chesterfield, for example, urbanely described by Wordsworth as " a false-hearted Frenchified coxcomb ".
[2] Churton Collins has excellently supplemented Desnoiresterres on *Voltaire in England*.

VOLTAIRE

essence of it, yet have neither time nor desire to make a close study. Voltaire—life, personality, writings, influence—is an immense subject; the aim of the writer is to provide a guide-book to the continent of Voltaire. This is a series devoted to men of letters; therefore, Voltaire will be investigated more as a man of letters, as an artist in words, and less as a political and social influence, though of course these aspects will not be ignored. For the facts of biography one must rely upon the researches of others, but all literary comment will be based upon a direct contact with Voltaire's writings. To promise more than that at this date would be misleading; whatever new facts may be discovered about Voltaire's life cannot be very important; the main outline is firmly established; the available material has been collected, arranged, sifted by generations of commentators. His complex and contradictory personality is well known, and to attempt some wholly new interpretation is merely adding an unneeded heresy; one can but try to tell what seems to be the truth as clearly as possible. His writings are a different matter; while the facts of biography and personality are immutable, the writings change as we change and cannot mean quite the same to us as to other generations. It may not be altogether useless, then, while avoiding personal crochets to the limit of possibility, to say how Voltaire's writings appear to a twentieth-century reader.

II

EARLY LIFE

1694-1726

(From Birth to Exile in England)

On the 24th of November, 1694, a certain Pierre Bailly wrote from Paris to his father : " Our cousins have another boy, born three days ago ; Madame Arouet . . . was very ill, but it is hoped she will be better. The child does not look well, having suffered by the mother's fall." This child, born the 21st of November, 1694, in the parish of Saint-Pierre André des Arcs in Paris, was François Marie Arouet, known to the world as Voltaire.

Voltaire's life, like Fontenelle's, began with the doctor's expectation that he would not live a day ; he lived to be eighty-four. His constitution was strong, but he was thin, cadaverous, always dieting, always in the hands of doctors and charlatans. He had a passion for drugs and stole Mme de Rumpelmonde's pills from pure gluttony. This valetudinarianism is an important part of Voltaire's life. It deprived him of the placidity of serene good health ; he lived in a pretended expectation of death, nervous, irritable, excitable, restless, labouring with feverish energy to achieve something before he died, yet not dying until he reached extreme old age ; supported by a fiery spirit, calmed by a smiling philosophy

VOLTAIRE

of reasonable enjoyment. But when we read of absurd quarrels prolonged beyond the verge of an ordinary anger, sudden gusts of ill-humour, a sometimes venomous malice, undignified cunning, turnings and wheelings among a maze of lies, we must recollect that these are in part the infirmities of a sick man, all nerves and susceptibilities, even more apt to take offence and to seek prompt revenge than those "exceeding hot fiery whoresons", his countrymen generally.

The childhood and adolescence of most men leave important traces in their later life; these early influences to impress the mind that they are seldom wholly erased. It is a commonplace. This was particularly the case with Voltaire, a child of extraordinary precocity and quickness of apprehension. In a sense, it is not untrue to say that he was always the bourgeois son of Maître Arouet, a ways the disciple of the Abbé de Châteauneuf and the society of the Temple, always the brilliant pupil of the Jesuits.[1] No man escapes these vivid early impressions; he acknowledges their power even by revolt, and often the old spirit remains under a new manner. There is the Jesuit-trained mind in Voltaire even when he is bitterly attacking the Jesuits; much as the puritan mind remains with some English rationalists when they denounce the faith they have rejected without being able to divest themselves of its narrow spirit.

In the mass of facts, more or less authentic anecdotes, rumours and calumnies, certain main influences in Voltaire's early life can be detected. There are his father and his father's friends and clients. Arouet *père* was a lawyer, first *notaire du Châtelet*, later *payeur des épices*. It is perhaps a trivial fact, but curious, that his

[1] Lanson, *Voltaire*.

EARLY LIFE

lodgings as *payeur des épices* were opposite La Sainte Chapelle, that symbol of Christianity and chivalry which Voltaire afterwards attacked so persistently, above all in his pamphlets and *La Pucelle*. The Arouet family was of decent bourgeoisie and can be traced back to Poitou in 1525 ; Voltaire's grandfather was a successful linen-draper. Maître Arouet had distinguished friends and some taste for literature. He was solicitor to the family of Saint-Simon, which the memoir-writing Duke does not fail to record in his contemptuous way. He was also in touch with the Richelieu family (later so friendly to Voltaire) with other aristocratic and legal families of eminence ; he knew Corneille, and Boileau lived as next-door neighbour to the Arouets when Voltaire was seven. Too much must not be made of this ; but at least we can see that this milieu of distinguished clients and friends was of use to Voltaire as he grew up and that his father's interest in literature may have served him. But Arouet *père's* influence was more important in the choice of education, in a certain bourgeois training of prudence and common-sense, particularly in money matters, which are supposedly so defective in poets and are so marked in Voltaire.

Voltaire's mother (*née* Marguerite Daumard) died when he was seven. Not much is known about her. She was a friend of Ninon de Lanclos, which fact has been responsible for the unprovable assertion that Voltaire was really the child of Rochebrune or the Abbé de Châteauneuf. However this may be, it is certain that Voltaire remembered very little of his mother and hardly ever mentioned her ; it is equally certain that the Abbé du Châteauneuf took a great interest in the child and, personally and by introducing him to others, was an important

VOLTAIRE

early influence. There may be more legend than truth in the story that Châteauneuf (one of those delightful Epicurean abbés, whose " only weakness was that they did not believe in God ") taught Voltaire at the age of three to repeat from memory passages of an irreligious poem called the *Moïsade*, attributed to J. B. Rousseau[1] ; in any case it makes an amusing story. Châteauneuf enjoyed the impertinence of this infant prodigy and would sometimes provoke a dispute between him and his elder brother, whom the infant Voltaire always vanquished in these premature wit-combats. We shall see later how the abbé introduced him to " The Temple '.

Arouet *père* was a moderate Jansenist. His elder son, educated by the Jansenists, grew up a " fanatic " ; not the least cause of his later disagreements with Voltaire. But the credit of the Jansenists declined, Maître Arouet swam with the current, and, to the great gain of the world, Voltaire was entrusted to the more tolerant and lively Jesuits, who were admirable masters of literary education. In October, 1704, at the age of ten, Voltaire entered the Collège de Louis le Grand. What the Jansenists would have made of him we cannot guess ; the Jesuits certainly did not succeed in making him a Christian, though they gave him their taste for belles lettres and bon gout, their interest in the drama, their indulgence. Probably he owed his clear easy style to their lessons. The Jesuits took great delight in the talents of their pupil ; at a prize-giving ceremony, we are told, Voltaire was pointed out to J. B. Rousseau by one of the Fathers as a boy " with an astounding faculty for writing verse ". At twelve he had made translations from the *Anacreontea* and the *Anthology* ; he also wrote a tragedy of *Amulius and*

The real author was Lourdet.

EARLY LIFE

Numitor, and, while still a schoolboy, rhymed a supplication to the Dauphin on behalf of an old soldier. In recreation hours, we hear, he deserted the games of the other boys to walk and talk with one or other of the Fathers—particularly Father Porée—discussing poetry and asking eager questions upon contemporary history and politics. Already we see in this schoolboy the first sketch of Voltaire; he is there even to the awkward questions about religion and the impertinences. The Fathers smiled at the impertinences which were often at the expense of the Jansenists; they still hoped to plant the seed of the true faith in this fertile but rebellious soil; they were indulgent to the caprices and impudences of a young talent which might hereafter be ably directed A M D G.

A man of letters could have no more fortunate education than that of learned priests, particularly of the Jesuit Fathers; in them the dignity of the priest is enhanced by the prestige of scholarship, the austerity of virtue is softened by a kindly indulgence, while they have that superior unworldliness which is often lacking to secular instructors harassed by pecuniary and marital exigences. Voltaire repaid the care and interest of the Jesuits with a genuine affection.[1] In later years he exempts the Jesuit tutors from his satire. For thirty years he kept an affectionate memory of Fathers Tournemine and Porée, sent them declarations of orthodoxy for them to show their Superior so that the commerce might not be interrupted; and the Jesuits defended their old pupil until the breach between him and the Church became irreparable.

There is another scarcely less important influence in the Abbé de Châteauneuf and his friends of " The

[1] Correspondance (*Œuvres*, vol. 29, Letter 102).

VOLTAIRE

Temple." They were the survivors or descendants of the seventeenth century "Libertins", among whom Molière was for a time numbered, while Cyrano de Bergerac and Saint-Evremond were wholly of the party. The Libertins were of many shades, but they were all free-thinkers and free-livers, a kind of hidden current of paganism in the stream of Christianity; their ideas were derived from Epicurus and Lucretius, Gassendi[1] and Montaigne. There was nothing austere and pedantic about them, none of the repulsive dryness of modern rationalism; they sought to recapture the smiling wisdom of the more indulgent ancient philosophers. Zeno and Epictetus were not for them. Their philosophy was borrowed from poets rather than from thinkers; they might talk about atoms and the first cause, but wine, verse, and the "charming fair" were what they really understood. Ninon de Lanclos was the Muse of the Libertins in the seventeenth century. She was not submerged in the deluge of religion à la Maintenon and lived into the eighteenth century; Voltaire is supposed to have been introduced to her when he was a child and she a wrinkled hag of eighty-five—touching hands as it were with the apostolic tradition of unbelief. It is almost certain that she left him 2,000 livres to buy books.

As early as 1706 Châteauneuf had introduced his infant prodigy to "The Temple" society. The Temple was a thirteenth century castle of Paris, in a district that enjoyed privileges similar to those of the Alsatia of old London. At the head of this society was Philippe de Vendôme, younger son of Laura Mancini, grand prior of the Knights of Malta, an amiable and cultured

[1] Gassendi did not deny the Supreme Being; as to Montaigne's belief—que sçais-je?

EARLY LIFE

"atheist" who is heavily abused by Saint-Simon. Before he was exiled he entertained regularly at the Temple a set of passing and temporary guests, many of them poets, nearly all of them Libertins. Among the more important were La Fontaine, J. B. Rousseau, and Chaulieu. Ninon, Mme Des Houlières, Mme de Bouillon, Mme Dunoyer (with whose daughter Voltaire afterwards fell in love), the Duchesse du Maine and Fontenelle had all been guests at the Temple, where they reasoned glass in hand and sang odes to Venus and Bacchus rather than to more austere deities. Most of the Temple *habitués* were amiable old men when Voltaire knew them ; infidel abbés with large benefices, who held that the sanction for life was pleasure regulated by reason, that the terrors of religion were vain, that Lucretius had said the final word about God. Courtin and Chaulieu especially influenced the young Voltaire as a freethinker and as a poet.[1] It must be insisted that Voltaire's free thought was originally derived from the Libertins of the Temple, not from the English Deists, whose writings only strengthened and modified an already existing conviction.

At school Voltaire made several friendships to which he was very loyal. There were the d'Argensons, afterwards so powerful and so useful to him, Cideville the subsequent magistrate of Rouen ; and there were others less fortunate in life, whom Voltaire more than once aided with money, influence, and kindness.

In 1710, when he was sixteen, the usual parental war began. Voltaire told his father he wanted to be a man of letters ; Arouet *père* thought a lawyer's life preferable. But how lodge on an office stool this precocious sparkling youth, whose early poems had already made some stir,

[1] See Correspondance (*Œuvres*, vol. 29, Letters 16, 17, 21, 22).

VOLTAIRE

this poet who was already the privileged companion of well-known authors and great nobles? There is a legend that the youthful Voltaire received a hundred louis for a poem from the Duchesse de Richelieu. A more authentic story informs us that Maître Arouet sent word that some legal post would be bought for him, if he wished ; Voltaire is said to have answered : "Tell my father I do not want a bought position, I will make one that costs nothing for myself." He had written an Ode in competition for the Academy prize and had begun his tragedy of *Oedipe*, but his life in Paris was displeasing to the prudent respectability of Arouet *père*, who doubtless viewed the pagan wisdom of the Temple with some suspicion, and arranged with the Marquis de Châteauneuf to take the young man on a diplomatic mission to the Hague. This was in 1713.

Voltaire was interested in Dutch life, struck by its prosperity and freedom ; but, if this lesson of commercial republicanism afterwards was of use to him, he neglected it at first by falling in love with " Pimpette " Dunoyer. Voltaire's letters to her are preserved and show him already with all his habitual ardour and restlessness. Mme Dunoyer, who had other plans for her daughter, complained to the ambassador and he confined Voltaire to the Embassy ; Pimpette, who was an amorous creature, disguised herself to visit her imprisoned Romeo. The ambassador sent Voltaire back to Paris and informed Maître Arouet of what had occurred. Voltaire tried to plan an elopement, and secured the help of the Jesuits in " winning back this soul from heresy to the Faith ". His letters of directions to Pimpette are amusing for the effrontery with which he proposed to make a Bishop their unsuspecting go-between. Fortunately or unfortu-

EARLY LIFE

nately, Pimpette fell in love with someone else, so this wonderful project was never carried out.[1] Maître Arouet was so angry that he secured a *lettre de cachet* against his son—Voltaire's first. For a time the poet lay in hiding ; then capitulated and went into a lawyer's office where he met his life-long friend, Thiériot, and learned the business methods he afterwards used so effectively.

It was not easy for this young man to keep out of mischief and publicity. In 1714 his satire, *Le Bourbier* and another poem, *L'Anti-Giton* caused some disturbance. Maître Arouet was in despair, and had thoughts of sending his son to the French colonies. Fortunately, M. de Caumartin, an old nobleman of literary tastes, had become interested in Voltaire and invited him to Saint-Ange, near Fontainebleau. Voltaire was naturally enchanted to get away from his father and the office. M. de Caumartin, Marquis de Saint-Ange, had seen the reign of Louis XIV from the inside ; through him Voltaire obtained the suggestion for his *Siècle de Louis XIV*, and many details of the reign ; and it was M. de Caumartin's enthusiasm for Henri IV which gave the poet his plan for *La Henriade*.

Louis XIV died in September, 1715. One of the first acts of the Regent was to recall M de Vendôme and the Abbé Servien from abroad ; the fêtes of the Temple were enlivened by their presence and by rejoicings at the death of the " old bigot ". Voltaire shared the general intoxication, dined with great lords,—" Are we all princes or all poets ? " he asked the Prince de Conti—haunted the dressing-rooms of the actresses at the Opera and the

[1] Voltaire did not forget her and in later life tried to help her with money.

VOLTAIRE

Comédie Française; for he had a tragedy to produce and "*hommages*" to express. He was not very successful with these ladies, who even then were less sensitive to wit then to other attractions.

There was a fashion at this time for venomous satires on the government, particularly on the Duc d'Orléans and his family; some of the things they were accused of they had done, others they had not. The Regent (May, 1716) exiled Voltaire from Paris for writing two poems which Voltaire swore he did not write; but these were Voltaire's continual tactics in those days of *lettres de cachets* and Bastilles—at the threat of persecution he denied his works with vigour and veracity. Voltaire found this exile pleasant enough; he was sent to relatives at Sulli-sur-Loire, but we soon discover him installed at the Duc de Sulli's Château, writing verses for the ladies, letters to his friends, and working at *Oedipe*, his first tragedy. Though he complained of his woes and his ill-health, Voltaire usually made the best of life; it was one of the lessons of the Temple. But he was soon in trouble again. Two satires, *J'ai vu* and *Puro rgnante* were circulating in Paris and he was accused of writing them; Voltaire was guilty of the second but not of the first. He was arrested on the 16th of May, 1717, and remained in the Bastille eleven months, until the 11th of April, 1718. In prison he read Virgil and Homer, composed a poem *La Bastille* and several cantos of *La Henriade*, written in pencil between the lines of a book.

On his release he was exiled to Chateney[1] but soon returned to Paris. The multiple occupations of this restless little demon of a man now elude narration. One

[1] After imprisonment in the Bastille, a sort of period of purification in the provinces was exacted of the victim.

EARLY LIFE

looks aghast at his activities between his leaving the Bastille (1718) and the exile to England (1726.) The mere list of his friends and acquaintances is startling ; in addition to those already mentioned it includes the Abbé de Bussi, Cardinal de Polignac, the Président d'Hénault, M. de Maisons, Lord Bolingbroke, the Marquise de Mimeure, the Marquise de Bernières, M. et Mme. de Villars, the financiers Paris, the banker Hoguère, Crébillon the tragic dramatist, Grècourt, Piron—the list is endless. We see him at great country houses, Richelieu, Vaux, Maisons, Sceaux ; here he is taking the waters at Forges with the Duc de Richelieu (1724), feeling better at first ; then ill, feverish, despairing, when back in Paris. Before that, he is nearly dead of small-pox at Maisons, is only saved by Gervasi's strange treatment of " two hundred pints of lemonade ". Here he is again, the new tragic poet ; *Oedipe*, his first attack on despotism and the clergy,[1] is an immense success, runs for forty-five nights, and is supposed to have reconciled Voltaire with his father. It is dedicated to Madame (here the signature " Voltaire " first occurs) and contains prefatory letters with impertinent remarks on Sophocles and Corneille. *Artémire* is a complete failure ; is immediately withdrawn and rewritten ; then runs for eight nights. In 1724 *Marianne* has a like failure, is taken off, recast, and reappears, to be an immense success. Meanwhile the

---

[1] For example : Act I, scene II,
 " Qu'eussé-je été sans lui ? *rien que le fils d'un roi,
 Rien qu'un prince vulgaire*, et je serais peut-être
 Esclave de mes sens, dont il m'a rendu maitre."
and Act iv, scene I,
 " Nos prêtres ne sont point ce qu'un vain peuple pense ;
 Notre crédulité fait toute leur science."
There were several such passages, which were vigorously applauded.

VOLTAIRE

first version of *La Henriade* (" La Ligue ") is written ; there are trips (one with a lady) to the Hague and Rouen to arrange for it to be printed ; the privilege is refused and there is the charming task of getting the poem printed at Rouen and smuggled into Paris (1724).

Turn the glass again and look at Voltaire as a lover. He fails with the actress Duclos, succeeds with the charming Lecouvreur. He and Suzanne de Livry pass their days together ; he obtains parts for her in his plays ; she is a bad actress ; hence disturbances. He introduces her to his friend Genonville, who supplants him. Voltaire bears no ill-will, is reconciled with both, and writes a witty poem about it—happy effect of Lucretius and the Temple ! In 1719, he is wildly in love with the Maréchale de Villars, who is coquettish but cruel. In 1722, he takes a six-weeks tour from Paris to the Hague, via Cambrai, tête-à-tête with Madame de Rumpelmonde. Later he is innocently flirting by letter with Mme. de Bernières. But our poet and amorist does not forget that fame and love must be fed. He secures pensions from the Regent ; 1,200 livres in 1718, 2,000 livres in 1722 ; from the Queen, 1,500 livres in 1725. On the death of Maître Arouet in 1722, he inherits an income of 4,500 livres and is involved in a long law-suit with his Jansenist brother. In 1722 he has already saved 5,000 francs in notes, has three shares in the Compagnie des Indes, is speculating in financial operations, and laying the foundations of his vast wealth. Greatest tribute of all to his financial sense, he avoids Law's Mississippi scheme.

Lastly—ignoring a multitude of other details—we have the category of misfortunes and feuds. Voltaire's vanity and irritability, the vivacity of his feelings, his determination to assert the dignity of a man of letters and to raise it to a level with that of the aristocracy, involved him in numerous affairs all his life. Often he began a quarrel in the right and pursued his vengeance so bitterly that he put himself in the wrong; sometimes he has all our sympathy, sometimes we feel him incredibly paltry. It must be admitted that he was not modest; and one of the worst humiliations of his life came indirectly from political hopes and ambitions soaring into arrogance.

In this period of eight years (1718-1726) we find him quarrelling with the comedian Poisson about Suzanne, exiled from Paris once more under suspicion of having written La Grage Chancel's *Philippiques*, attacking old J. B Rousseau after some quarrel with his former " cher maître ",[1] sparring with the witty and amusing Piron. Then comes the more serious affair with Beauregard, the officer who had betrayed the authorship of *Puero regnante* to the Regent and had accused Voltaire of seditious talk. Voltaire insults Beauregard in the streets, is beaten by him, starts a law-suit which he pursues with implacable energy, and finally succeeds in overcoming Beauregard's influential protectors; his enemy is imprisoned for a time in the Châtelet.

Yet Voltaire had excellent impulses of friendship. When the Abbé Desfontaines was accused of sodomy and imprisoned, Voltaire, suspecting injustice and persecution, used his influence indefatigably to secure the Abbé's release. Desfontaines repaid him with ingratitude, though it must be admitted Voltaire behaved as if he had purchased the Abbé's submission and praise for life. Voltaire laboured to secure Thiériot a secretaryship to

---

[1] Voltaire is supposed to have said of J. B. Rousseau's *Ode to Posterity*: "Ah, maître, I'm afraid it will never reach its address."

VOLTAIRE

the Duc de Richelieu and bore Thiériot's hesitations and evasions angelically, though they had compromised him (Voltaire) with Richelieu. Again, when Genonville (the friend who stole Suzanne) died, Voltaire was desolated ; we find him writing affectionately and regretfully of Genonville ten years after his death. It is a fact to be noticed that his friends were almost always more to him than his mistresses.

Voltaire's political ambitions have been mentioned. In 1722 he was in touch with Cardinal Dubois and tried to obtain a political mission ; in 1725, at the time of the King's marriage, he was at Fontainebleau, in great favour with the Queen (who called him " Mon pauvre Voltaire ") and with Mme. de Prie, the prime minister's mistress. *Oedipe, Marianne,* and his comedy, *L'Indiscret*, were received with applause at Court ; Voltaire obtained another pension and dreamed of " gloire ". He saw wonderful prospects of power opening before him ; the Abbé Dubois had been a nobody ; why should not Voltaire become a *philosophe* prime minister ? In December, 1725, his chimaeras were harshly dispelled. He talked about his success in public with exultation and perhaps with arrogance. He was deliberately insulted at the Comédie Française by the Chevalier de Rohan-Chabot and replied tartly ; Rohan lifted his cane, Voltaire clapped his hand to his (alas ! unready) sword ; Mlle. Lecouvreur obligingly fainted to prevent a fracas.[1] A few days later Voltaire was dining with the Duc de Sulli ; he received a message that someone wished to

---

[1] There were two rows between Voltaire and Rohan, one at the Opera, the other at the Comédie Française ; two days elapsed between them. The attack on Voltaire occurred several days later, (early 1726).

EARLY LIFE

speak to him, went down calmly and, outside the door, was attacked and beaten by valets, while the brave Rohan in the background encouraged them—" Don't hurt his head, there may be some good in it." Voltaire rushed back into the house exclaiming that he was "assassiné", called upon Sulli to aid him, to make a deposition to secure vengeance; the Duke refused. What was the honour of a man of genius compared with the whim and safety of a Rohan?

Voltaire was in despair, enraged, furious. He, a born poltroon, was determined to cross swords with Rohan; he took arduous fencing lessons, consorted with bullies, longed for bloody vengeance. The Rohans were concerned; the little poet could not take his beating as a court jester should; apparently he meant to bite. Voltaire was dogged by police spies, who sent in alarmist reports; he was "living in the company of ruffians", "learning to fight", "changing his dwelling-place continually". The relatives of "le brave Chevalier de Rohan" now grew seriously alarmed and applied to the minister for protection. On the 17th of April, 1726, Voltaire was once again in the Bastille. Fifteen days later he was released on condition that he left France. A police officer accompanied him to Calais; he was there on the 5th of May; a few weeks later he was at Greenwich and slept that night in London at the house of his friend, Lord Bolingbroke.[1] The ancien régime had made an enemy of a man who was far more dangerous than it guessed; "I have no sceptre", said Voltaire, "but I have a pen."[2]

[1] Probably 30th of May, 1726. See Churton Collins.
[2] Œuvres, vol. 32, Letter 1908.

III

VOLTAIRE IN ENGLAND
1726-1729

Voltaire's exile in England is an important episode in his life. If it has been over-estimated by English writers anxious to claim for their own country the credit of Voltaire's genius, it has been almost as much under-estimated by Frenchmen either from a similarly absurd nationalism or from real ignorance of English life and literature. The truth would seem to lie somewhere between the complacence of Morley and Churton Collins, the disparagement of Desnoiresterres, and the reticences of M. Lanson. Certainly, Voltaire himself always retained an affection for England and Englishmen, was surrounded with English classics at Ferney, always greeted English visitors with courtesy, and repeatedly acknowledged his debt to the English. One or two of his best works were wholly or in part written in this country; the effect of English thought and literature on his subsequent writings is considerable. Moreover, the money he made in England, if not the foundation of his wealth, was a great assistance towards it.

On the boat, Voltaire was occupied with "gloomy thoughts"—of the Chevalier de Rohan, we may surmise, of Bastilles and suspended pensions, of wrecked literary and political ambitions, of liberty and genius oppressed; for with all his self-seeking, there was in

VOLTAIRE IN ENGLAND

Voltaire a streak of generous impulse and philanthropy. The change when he reached Greenwich was complete. Voltaire has sketched his first impressions of England in two letters (one fragmentary) written with his customary wit and sharpness of observation.[1] The day of his arrival was fair with a soft west wind and a cloudless sky. The Thames between its green banks was lined by two rows of merchant vessels over a space of six miles, with all sails set in honour of the King, who went by in the State Barge[2] preceded by musicians and followed by a fleet of smaller boats rowed by Thames watermen in their gala costume. In Greenwich Park Voltaire saw horse and foot races and was struck by the number of pretty girls. In the crowd he met some merchants to whom he had letters of introduction ; they greeted him, cordially, lent him a horse, obtained him refreshments and found him a place where he could see both the races and the spectacle of the river. Voltaire was delighted ; he thought himself at the Olympic games ; more, he blushed to compare this beauty, this crowd of vessels, the immensity of London, with anything so paltry as ancient Greece. A courier from Denmark who, like himself, had just arrived in England was filled with joy and astonishment ; he thought the nation was always gay ; that all the women were handsome and lively, that the sky of England was always pure and serene, that the English thought of nothing but pleasure, that every day was like that day.

It is a charming picture of an old English holiday and a happy moment for a foreigner to arrive. But (Voltaire

[1] A M * * * (1727). *Œuvres*, vol. 22.
[2] It was the King's birthday procession. Voltaire talks about the Queen too, but that is a mistake.

VOLTAIRE

goes on) the Danish courier was lucky enough to leave that night and to retain the vision. That same evening Voltaire was introduced to certain " ladies of the Court "[1] in London. He thought they were the same ladies he had seen riding so gracefully ; yet he was surprised to see that they did not look as if they had been enjoying themselves, that they were frigid and reserved, drank tea, made a great clatter with their fans, and said nothing or talked scandal ; some were playing cards, others reading the *Gazette*. Finally, one of them informed him that " Society "[2] never condescended to be present at these " popular gatherings ", that his fair ladies of the Park were servants and village girls ; and the horsemen apprentices and schoolboys on hired hacks. Voltaire felt " really angry " with the woman and determined to go back to the city to find the merchants who had greeted him so cordially.

Next morning he found most of these gentlemen in a " dirty, badly furnished, badly served, badly lighted " coffeehouse ; none of them recognised him when he ventured to address them ; he received only monosyllables in reply. Voltaire wondered what enormity he had committed and finally asked them " with a vivacity which seemed to them very strange " why they were so gloomy ? " Because there's an east wind ! " At that moment another man came in and said in an indifferent tone : " Molly cut her throat this morning ; her lover found her dead in her room with a bloody razor beside her." (This Molly was a pretty and rich girl who was about to be married). The company received the news without any

---

[1] At Bolingbroke's house, presumably
[2] " *Le beau monde* "— one can hear the tone of voice.

VOLTAIRE IN ENGLAND

emotion. Someone asked what had become of the lover? "He bought the razor."

Voltaire went off to Court, persuaded he would find gaiety there at least, but everyone was dull and depressed, even the maids of honour. On confiding in a celebrated doctor Voltaire was informed that the bad weather in England, especially during March and November, actually made people ill and spread melancholy through the whole nation. "Never ask any favour at Court when there is an east wind", he was told.

This little sketch, for all its exaggeration, gives humourously several traits of English society and the English people. The observer who saw so much and so clearly in two days was to make further discoveries, the recital of which was not without effect upon Europe generally. Voltaire set about his task of investigating England, if not methodically, at least with characteristic energy, good sense, and impetuosity. He had brought letters from the British ambassador at Versailles (Horatio Walpole, the elder) to the Duke of Newcastle, Bubb Dodington, and the Duc de Broglie. He knew Lord Bolingbroke and his second wife (who was a Frenchwoman) intimately; had read them parts of *La Ligue* when Bolingbroke himself was in exile, and (as we have seen) was welcomed by them on his arrival. His first few months in England, however, were marked by some misfortunes and were chiefly spent in retirement. In June, 1726, he appears to have made a secret journey, lasting about a month, to Paris, in search of the Chevalier de Rohan, whom he failed to find. He was back in England in July. Meanwhile a Jewish banker, on whom he had a letter of credit for a considerable sum, went bankrupt, leaving him in some embarrassment financially. An "English gentleman"

VOLTAIRE

(believed to be King George) sent him a hundred guineas on hearing of this. Then his sister died, and the news " plunged him into an agony of grief ". A letter to Thiériot, written in English, gives an account of this period :

" At my coming to England I found my damned Jew was broken. I was without a penny, sick to death of a violent ague, a stranger, alone, helpless, in the midst of a city wherein I was known to nobody. My Lord and my Lady Bolingbroke were in the country. I could not make bold to see our ambassador in so wretched a condition. I had never undergone such distress ; but I am born to run through all the misfortunes of life. In these circumstances, my star that, among all its direful influences, pours always on me some kind refreshment, sent to me an English gentleman unknown to me, who forced me to receive some money that I wanted. An other London citizen that I had seen but once at Paris carried me to his own country house wherein I lead an obscure and charming life since that time, without going to London, and quite given over to the pleasures of indolence and of friendship. The true and generous affection of this man who soothes the bitterness of my life, brings me to love you more and more."[1]

Most of the autumn of 1726 was spent with Falkener[2]

---

[1] Churton Collins, *Appendix*. This letter must have been written some time later, since Voltaire's English is already good.

[2] Mr., afterwards, Sir Everard Falkener, ambassador to Constantinople and secretary to the Duke of Cumberland. Voltaire corresponded with him in English for many years (See *Lettres Inédits*, vol. I, 1865.) Voltaire always expresses gratitude and warm friendship to Falkener. In 1774 Voltaire welcomed Falkener's son with enthusiasm at Ferney. (See Mason's letter to La Harpe, 1780).

VOLTAIRE IN ENGLAND

(the "other London citizen") at Wandsworth, in writing, in study, and in learning English. There is an interesting legend that Voltaire went to Drury Lane Theatre every night when he was in London and followed the play from the prompter's copy, to improve his English. In January, 1727, he was presented at Court and rapidly made the acquaintance of English noble families and men of letters. He stayed three months at Lord Peterborough's where he met Swift.[1]

He met the Duchess of Marlborough, Lord and Lady Hervey,[2] Pulteney, Walpole, Lady Sundon, Pope, Gay, Young, Congreve, Berkeley, Samuel Clarke, Dr Henry Pemberton (the expositor of Newton), and Newton's relatives, the Conduitts. Voltaire was greatly impressed by the funeral of Newton, at Westminster Abbey, and by the spectacle of the greatest aristocrats in England contending for the honour of bearing his pall.

The story of Voltaire's visit to Congreve is well known. Congreve at that time had abandoned literature for grandeur and the Duchess of Marlborough; he begged Voltaire not to look upon him as a writer but as a "gentleman"; to which Voltaire very properly replied that if Congreve had been "only a gentleman" he should not have taken the trouble to call. Pope mistrusted Voltaire, though he admired his works. When Voltaire said farewell to Pope, he used these words: "I am come to bid farewell to a man who never treated

---

[1] There are several letters from Voltaire to Swift, in one of which Voltaire asks him to get subscribers for the English edition of *La Henriade*. Voltaire was one of the first critics to point out the peculiar quality of Swift's poetry—see *Lettres Philosophiques*, Lettre XXII.

[2] He wrote an eight line poem to her, beginning "Hervey, would you know the passion."

VOLTAIRE

me seriously from the first hour of my acquaintance with him to the present moment." Nevertheless, Voltaire is always generous in his praise of Pope's poetry. It is noticeable that two of the stories to the discredit of Voltaire in England are traceable to Pope ; one is the charge that Voltaire was a "spy", the other given currency by Johnson[1] that he "talked so grossly" at table that Mrs Pope was forced to leave the room. The evidence for these is slight and seldom accepted by French commentators ; possibly Voltaire betrayed Pope's confidence about the authorship of a political squib ; possibly a French anecdote expressed in a too popular turn of phrase, frightened the chaste Mrs Pope. But Voltaire was notoriously polite and charming in conversation. The story about embezzling money from Lord Peterborough is the merest scandal of the kind so frequently applied to Voltaire.[2]

Much more important than these little tales and social acquaintances are Voltaire's work in England, his study of the language, institutions, and literature, and their effect upon him. Some of his best-known works were composed or begun in England : *Brutus*, *Mort de César*, *Lettres Philosophiques*, *Siècle de Louis XIV* ; (materials), *Histoire de Charles XII*. As usual Voltaire laboured persistently. He took pains to acquaint himself with English life in all classes and in many aspects, while

---

[1] Johnson disliked Voltaire and cannot be depended upon to turn an anecdote in his favour.

[2] Voltaire's friendship with Young is worth noting. At a discussion of Milton's episode of Death and Sin, Young made this impromptu epigram on Voltaire :
  " You are so witty, profligate ,and thin,
    At once we think you Milton, Death, and Sin."
His *Sea-Piece* is dedicated to Voltaire.

VOLTAIRE IN ENGLAND

he made himself so much a master of our language that he saved himself from an angry anti-French mob by a ready harangue, and composed an essay on epic poetry in a style, says Professor Collins expansively, which would " have reflected no discredit on Dryden or Swift " ; and indeed it is good English prose. Voltaire (in the same letter to M. A. . .) speaks of conversing freely with Whigs and Tories ; of dining with a Bishop and supping with a Quaker[1] ; of going on Saturday to the Synagogue, on Sunday to Saint Paul's ; of hearing a sermon in the morning and a play in the afternoon ; of going from the Court to the Exchange and " above all " ! of not being repelled by the " icy and disdainful " air of the English ladies at the " beginning of one's intercourse ". He was informed that at Newmarket he would find once more the " Olympic games " of Greenwich which had so delighted him ; he found only " jockeys of quality " betting against each other, and saw " more swindling than magnificence ".

The English publication of *La Henriade* in 1728 was a considerable event in French literature. The poem was dedicated to Queen Caroline instead of Louis XV, as Voltaire had first intended ; Duplessis-Mornay was substituted for Sulli as second hero.[2] All the " quality " of England subscribed for it and Voltaire is thought to have cleared about £2,000, though the faithful Thiériot lost or embezzled eighty French subscriptions. The poem was greatly admired. Chesterfield writes of it in terms which seem to us now almost insane. It is not

---

[1] The account of his visit to the Quaker, Andrew Pitt, at Hampstead, is as amusing as anything in *Candide*.

[2] As revenge for the conduct of the Duc de Sulli in the Rohan affair.

quite true to say that the money made from the English edition of *La Henriade* was " the foundation of Voltaire's fortune "; he had other money before, but £2,000 changed into livres was a pleasant sum and useful for speculations, which with Voltaire were almost invariably successful.

The *Lettres Philosophiques*—which will be examined in more detail in their place—give proof of the profound effect of England on Voltaire's mind. He was here at a time when an interesting and valuable discussion between freethinkers and Christians was in progress. That liberty of thought and expression should be permitted to this extent filled Voltaire with admiration for England, just as the rights of the subject under the *Habeas Corpus* made him envious of English political liberty. England was the political model Voltaire presented to the French during nearly half a century of pamphleteering. But he owed more than this to his stay in England. Locke and Newton, Clarke, Woolston, and Collins gave him a far firmer basis, furnished him with much better arguments for his rationalising Deism than were dreamed of in the society of the Temple. These English thinkers and writers cared for truth ; the Temple " philosophers " were interested in thought, but chiefly wanted excuses for self-indulgence. They cared little or nothing about other men ; the English did, and so did Voltaire. For him Locke's writings became a kind of " philosophical gospel " ; he never progressed much beyond Locke. In these studies Clarke was his guide and for a time seduced him into metaphysics, but Voltaire soon returned from these airy nothings, this " art of reasoning about that which we do not know ", to more solid ground. His knowledge of Newton was derived largely from Pemberton ; he read Hobbes but obviously not much of

VOLTAIRE IN ENGLAND

Bacon whom he praised by hearsay. He admired Berkeley, but did not agree with him.[1]

In literature, Bolingbroke was his preceptor. The *Lettres Philosophiques* show the limits to his appreciation of English literature. He read Shakespeare and Ben Jonson, but not the other early dramatists apparently[2]; he read most of the great English contemporaries, and had a real admiration for Pope and Swift ; he liked Burnet and " Hudibras " Butler, Dryden, Rochester, Addison, Thomson and others among the late 17th and early 18th century English authors. His critical remarks on these writers, while strictly limited by French eighteenth century *bon goût*, are acute and show knowledge and appreciation of our literature. On the whole one may say without exaggeration that the years in England were probably the most stimulating and valuable experience in Voltaire's life. " It may be," he wrote Thiériot, " French folly is pleasanter than English madness, but, by God, English wisdom and English honesty is above yours."

[1] There is a (very poor) refutation of subjective idealism in Voltaire's *Traité de Métaphysique* (1734).

[2] He must have seen some of them on the stage. Destouches, who " discovered " the English drama several years before Voltaire's visit, shows traces of the influence of Beaumont and Fletcher, and Middleton, as well as of all the principal Restoration dramatists.

IV

PARIS TO CIREY
1729-1734

It was in fact a different Monsieur de Voltaire who returned to France in the spring of 1729.[1] If we may judge from his letters, he had suffered in health from his residence in England ; but we know that Voltaire's health was not always so bad as he constantly believed or represented it to be. The change in him was mental ; not yet perhaps quite clear to himself. He was now thirty-five, in the plenitude of those intellectual powers which he retained almost unimpaired for nearly half a century ; and the English edition of *La Henriade* had given him a superior position among the poets, not only of France, but of Europe. If this dissemination of his fame in England, in Italy, in Germany, were in part due to the intellectual hegemony of France, it was also due to a widespread and spontaneous admiration for his talents. *La Henriade* gave him the foundations of his European influence as well as the most appreciable addition to his early fortune ; for, though he was well known in Paris as a writer of tragedy and a most accomplished poet in light verse, such achievements were too common to

[1] Voltaire, malheureux pour la première fois, s'exila en Angleterre, il y étudia le gouvernement, les moeurs publiques, l'esprit philosophique, la littérature, et il revint de là tout entier formé et avec sa trempe dernière." Sainte-Beuve.

PARIS TO CIREY

attract great attention. The eighteenth century, which knew nothing of the *Chanson de Roland,* despised Ronsard, and never troubled to read Agrippa d'Aubigné, thought that *La Henriade* really had given France its missing epic poem; even less prejudiced foreigners thought the *Henriade* worthy to be compared with Homer and Virgil, superior to Tasso and Milton. Voltaire, then, had by this time (1729) an enviable fame as a poet, and it was as a poet that he was admired for many years. This did not content him; his prodigiously active and versatile mind, so perpetually alert to discovery, so widely interested, had already set him at work upon a series of prose-writings which have sustained his posthumous reputation more effectually than his poetry. But there was something more than this working within him, something more than the desire for fame and money and self-expression. He had a definite purpose, vitiated no doubt by resentment and vanity, but not wholly selfish. He desired that men should live together comfortably, more rationally, with more personal liberty. He saw three great enemies to this object: they were religion, despotism, and the spirit of military conquest. Voltaire was not what we should call a good democrat; he believed in capitalism, in superior rights and rewards for superior merit, and, though he was not unfriendly to the common people, he despised their ignorance, their stupidity, and their levity— "a yoke and a goad is what they need". But in the France of 1729 Voltaire's programme was a formidable one, enlightened and greatly daring.

Up to 1726 and the amenities of the Chevalier de Rohan, with their resultant humiliations and demonstration of aristocratic indifference to a " mere " poet of bourgeois rank, Voltaire may have been an agitator;

he was not then a genuine reformer. At that time he wanted liberty, for himself perhaps, but scarcely for others—indeed, we shall meet later with some survivals of this spirit—and his dislike for the Church was partly instinctive, partly annoyance at interference with his pleasures. In England he had seen something different from the spiritual and political despotism of Church and King in France ; he saw religion, powerful indeed, but subject to the state ; he saw a monarchy and an aristocracy, but a monarchy limited by the two chambers, an aristocracy enlightened and open to newcomers ; above all he saw a successful cultivation of commerce which was certainly of benefit to the fine arts and literature. He could not foresee that commerce would become so dominant an interest that it would almost destroy them. Granted that the *Lettres Philosophiques* were rather a satire upon France than a panegyric of England, it is easy to see from them what Voltaire wanted : limitation or suppression of the power of the Church, freedom of thought and of expression, modification of absolutism by juster laws, abolition of oppressive privileges and legal injustices, destruction of aristocratic prejudices against commerce, a complete alteration in a system of taxation which took half his earnings from the peasant and nothing at all from the duke—these are some of his proposed reforms.

These reforms, which to us appear so obvious that we find it difficult to believe that the abuses existed, were tolerated, were defended—these reforms could only be proposed in eighteenth century France with the utmost caution and even then with danger to the proposer. What we are to contemplate in the remaining years of Voltaire's life is a contest, a battle between a pen and the strongest

PARIS TO CIREY

absolute government in western Europe. The *Lettres Philosophiques* made the first serious attack on the ancien régime ; it was not the beginning of an aimless Fronde, it was the first word in the prologue to the Revolution. In returning to the details of Voltaire's life, we must not forget that this life is a contest with Church and State ; though there is a danger of exaggerating his belligerence.

We shall find plenty of inconsistencies, vanities, disavowals, temporary capitulatons, paltry squabbles and vengeances ; but the contest will be there, the objective will never be wholly forgotten. In the battle between the pen and the régime, we shall see the pen commit errors, weaknesses, baseness, which we cannot but regret. We must not forget that Voltaire's fight had generosity[1] and philanthropy in it ; that few men live eighty years in the world without committing follies, stupidities, and even base actions ; and, if we are to estimate correctly Voltaire's courage and virtue, we must remember that we write in comparative political freedom while he wrote under oppression.

Voltaire saw that he needed allies in this warfare ; money, invested abroad, to keep him above the necessity of government pensions and of writing for his living ; money again to give him freedom of movement, to enable him to fly from France at a moment's notice ; money, once more, to enable him to print, if necessary, without profit to himself. He needed powerful friends —governmental and legal—he needed a safe retreat to

[1] His first impulses were often generous and disinterested, but his amour-propre and susceptibilities so often destroyed them. It was generous to aid a stranger like Desfontaines ; it was weak to expect perpetual gratitude and submission ; it was base to squabble with him and twit him with past benefits.

VOLTAIRE

work in, a faithful woman companion to encourage him. And he needed constant advertisement, a necessity which he understood before almost all his contemporaries. We shall see how he obtained these as we watch the progress of the Philosopher's War.

It is immediately after the date of his return to France that Voltaire's letters suddenly become so numerous, another proof of the general esteem for the *Henriade* ; his correspondents were now anxious to preserve the letters of so famous a poet. But this fame did not soften the hostility of the government ; on the contrary. At first he was not even allowed into Paris, but lay in a sort of hiding at Saint-Germain-en-Laye, whence he wrote for and obtained permission from Maurepas to go to Paris ; still full of ideas about English liberty, he calls Maurepas a " vizier " in a letter to Thiériot. He took up his abode in the Rue du Cloître-Saint-Médéric, but his restlessness, his plans, his dangers, kept him constantly on the move. Between 1729 and 1734 he was at Paris, at Plombières, at Rouen, in Lorraine, at Court ; even in Paris, he was always shifting lodgings, now at the house of Mme. de Fontaine-Martel, now living with one Demoulin, under whose name he indulged in speculation.

These money-making schemes of Voltaire's are infinitely amusing and ingenious. One day at table, the conversation turned upon a lottery arranged by the Minister of Finance in order to extinguish certain *rentes* payable by the town of Paris ; the tickets in the lottery could only be bought by a scrip of the rentes ; the prizes were in cash. Someone remarked casually that the difference between the market price of the rentes and the cash value of the prizes was so considerable that if someone could buy all the tickets he would clear a large sum.

PARIS TO CIREY

Voltaire heard this, found out that it was true, rushed about Paris interesting financiers in the "company" he had created, succeeded in obtaining their attention, and their money; and his "company" made over a million livres, in which doubtless Voltaire had a reasonable share. This artful manoeuvre so irritated the Minister that Voltaire for a time thought of retiring to England again; instead, he went to Richelieu at Plombières. There he heard of another lottery in Lorraine, the terms of which were so advantageous that foreigners were not allowed to buy tickets. Nevertheless Voltaire posted off to Lorraine, was at first refused the tickets, "but" (he writes to the President Hénault) "in spite of their blackguard jests, after pressing entreaties they allowed me to subscribe for fifty shares, which were delivered to me a week later because of the lucky similarity of my name to that of a Gentleman of His Royal Highness's; for no foreigner was allowed to have them. I profited at once by the demand for this paper; I tripled my gold. . ."[1]

Later, he did not disdain to make money by picture dealing and speculations in jewels, though in the case of the pictures he was gratifying his life-long delight in painting. There are numerous letters of his about pictures to an expert, and another correspondence, now lost, was occupied with a scheme for making paper out of straw. Again, he speculated in the sale of grain through Demoulin who acted as his agent; Demoulin some years later cheated him of 24,000 livres, but Voltaire, with that odd generosity of his, forgave the man on his writing a letter of apology and paying about a tenth of the debt. Though he lost in that particular affair, he was then able to afford it; there is a good authority for believing that by 1736

[1] Œuvres, vol. 29, Letter 108.

VOLTAIRE

he possessed an income of 28,000 livres, and this steadily increased in spite of occasional losses and the poet's lamentations that he " is ruined ". Voltaire's ruin was like his dying, indefinitely postponed ; neither prevented his working ; for his usual state was like that reported by Mme. du Châtelet in a letter to Richelieu (1732), " Voltaire has been ill for three weeks—he has written two Operas ".

Voltaire's energy in writing and publishing in this, as in other, periods, was only equalled by the disturbance and persecution it brought upon him. There was a strong hostile party watching him and even his skill in lying (which he constantly recommended to his friends as a safeguard in life) could not always extricate him from the awkward positions into which he plunged himself, either by his freedom of speech or by some imprudence or impudence. Even his small poems were received with a degree of opposition, anger, disapprobation, which would be incredible, were it not that one knows that disparagement and moral indignation are the tributes paid by mediocrity to abilities.

The amusing *Le Tu et le Vous* only made an enemy of his former mistress, Suzanne, who by a strange turn of fortune became a Marquise ; when Voltaire called to pay his ironic respects to the happy couple, he was refused admission by the porter, and avenged himself with this poem, a little masterpiece in its genre. More serious agitations afflicted the poet when he learned that the public had possession of his poem on the death of another mistress, Adrienne Lecouvreur. She had persisted in acting when ill, grew suddenly worse during the night, and died in Voltaire's arms. The odious ecclesiastical prejudices of the age refused legal burial to an " impure

PARIS TO CIREY

actress" who had also been the mistress of Voltaire. Her body was taken away and buried in a piece of wasteland at night. The public indignation was considerable, and Voltaire, with a warmth of feeling which did credit to his humanity and friendship, wrote his poem, containing these denunciatory lines :

> " Ah ! verrai-je toujours ma faible nation
> Incertaine en ses voeux, flétrir ce qu'elle admire ;
> Nos moeurs avec nos lois toujours se contredire ;
> Et le Français volage endormi sous l'empire
>   De la superstition ?
>   Quoi ! n'est-ce donc en Angleterre
>   Que les mortels osent penser ?
> O rivale d'Athène, o Londre ! heureuse terre !
> Ainsi que les tyrans vous avez su chasser
> Les préjugés honteux qui vous livraient la guerre.
> C'est là qu'on sait tout dire, et tout recompenser ;
> Nul art n'est méprisé, tout succès a sa gloire. . ."

It is easy to see how such words might offend the prejudices of the age ; but the authorities were too wise to persecute the poet when public opinion was so obviously on his side, and Voltaire escaped with nothing worse than his fears. But not long afterwards a more serious scrape came along, again apropos a short poem. Someone had obtained and made public the *Pour et le Contre*, written ten years before to Mme. de Rumpelmonde who required a statement for and against Christianity ; Voltaire expounded both sides, but naturally the " against " was a more powerful plea than the " for ". The publication caused an uproar of religious rage ; the Archbishop of Paris complained, Voltaire was summoned before the court, lied with effrontery, and said the poem had been written by Chaulieu (then dead). Voltaire was not believed, but escaped with a warning. This poem, as Morley remarks, would scarcely be objected to by anyone now; in 1732 it was a storm-centre for weeks and religious poets deluged the author with vituperation. As an example of the conventional mentality, take this anecdote: The Chancellor Anguesseau asked his secretary what he thought of the poem and received the reply, " Monseigneur, Voltaire ought to be shut up in a place where there is neither pen, ink, nor paper. By the turn of his mind the man could ruin the state." Even the completely harmless *Temple du Goût*, a sort of mild *Dunciad* in prose and verse, was received with execration —" a nasty little author who ought to be made to cross the sea again " is one of the many urbane remarks aroused by this mild defence of " bon goût ".

The death of Lecouvreur was followed by those of de Maisons in 1731 and of Mme de Fontaine-Martel, in whose house Voltaire was living, in 1733. In the case of the Comtesse (a free-thinker), Voltaire had the additional distress of knowing that if she died without confession he would be made the scape-goat; the Comtesse sent for a priest, chiefly to shield Voltaire. The death of de Maisons upset Voltaire completely and his letter[1] to Cideville describing it is gloomy and poignant—" I have lost my friend, my support, my father." It is curious how often the supposedly hard-hearted and avaricious Voltaire can be proved tender and generous. His regrets for Génonville and de Maisons are genuine. Again, he frequently performed acts of kindness to poor young authors; among several may be mentioned Linant and Lefèbre, whom he took into his own house, fed, dressed, lodged, " treated as gentlemen "; and when Linant,

[1] *Œuvres*, vol. 29, Letter 133.

PARIS TO CIREY

after living in idleness on Voltaire for years, repaid him with base ingratitude, Voltaire only asked a friend to tell Linant that " this was hardly the fit return for friendship and an expenditure of 1,600 livres a year ", and continued to help him.

The most important events of these years (1729-1734) are (as usual) Voltaire's industry and contests with authority, and the meeting with Mme du Châtelet. When at Rouen, disguised as an English " milord " to supervise Jore's clandestine publication of *Charles XII*[1], Voltaire re-wrote the last part of that work, supervised a new edition of *La Henriade*, and composed two tragedies, all in the space of three months, during which time he was rather seriously ill. His new tragedies were influenced by " his Shakespeare ", as some abbé contemptuously called the author of *Macbeth*.[2] The republican *Brutus* (1730) did not maintain its first success, only due perhaps to some surprisingly bold lines against despotism. *La Mort de César*, imitated from *Julius Caesar*,[3] was utterly rejected by the French players, chiefly because it had no love-plot ; later it was privately played by a school. *Eriphyle* (1732) was a failure, and Voltaire later turned it into *Sémiramis*. Immediately after the withdrawal of this play, when some of Voltaire's friends kindly advised him not to write any more tragedies, he produced in a surprisingly short time his greatest dramatic success, *Zaïre* (1732). Voltaire was applauded on entering the

---

[1] The privilege was refused on the ground that Voltaire's biography was offensive to one of the kings of Poland.

[2] The same enlightened critic tried to prove that Grévin was as great a dramatist as Shakespeare ! Whatever we think of Voltaire's criticism, we must remember that he was the first great foreign writer to realise Shakespeare's genius.

[3] But possibly from Grévin's *César* (1561).

VOLTAIRE

theatre during the fourth performance. " Vous pleurez, Zaïre ? " long remained one of the " clous " of the French tragic stage. *Adélaïde du Guesclin* was too romantic and Shakespearean for this generation, but achieved a huge success when revived thirty years later. This extraordinary fertility could only be sustained by incessant labour and by the fact that Voltaire always had five or six different works on hand ; his industry remains a great and stimulating spectacle, for, in addition to these productions, he was engaged in arduous historical and philosophical studies, kept up a wide correspondence, and yet found time to be an excellent business man, to go out into society, to see all the new plays, scan all the new books, and fall in love with Mme du Châtelet.

Voltaire was thirty-nine and she twenty-seven when they fell in love. Mme du Châtelet was not beautiful[1] ; she was tall, rather thin, a little bony, with an olive complexion, rather bad teeth, clear green eyes, and a high intelligent forehead. " Mme du Châtelet ", says M. Lanson, " was certainly a coquette, liked clothes, was of an ardent temperament, and boldly, aristocratically immodest." She did not care much for her husband, and had several lovers before and after meeting Voltaire, but their liaison endured, with sundry shocks, absences, and quarrels, until her death. It was a durable passion, founded upon esteem and intellectual sympathy. Voltaire's gifts we know—his charm, his witty malice, his immense intellectual activity, his universal curiosity. Mme du Châtelet understood Latin, Italian, English ; she delighted

---

[1] There is a pitilessly malignant " portrait " of her by Mme du Deffand ; I have preferred the more amiable account by Desnoiresterres. It is certain that Voltaire was attracted by something besides physical beauty, but it is unlikely that he would love a hag.

in mathematics, physics, and metaphysics.[1] She read Newton and Leibnitz ; Maupertuis and Clairaut were among her friends. She was not a female pedant ; she merely preferred to use her mind instead of wasting it in frivolities ; and she was not a Christian. What more could Voltaire ask?

Voltaire took refuge at her Château de Cirey from the tempest roused by the *Lettres Philosophiques* and the "affaire Jore". The bookseller was undoubtedly ruined by printing this work, but his "factum" against Voltaire was envenomed by Desfontaines, who wrote it. However foolish Voltaire's behaviour may have been, it is certain that Jore betrayed him very readily, that Voltaire had once obtained his release from the Bastille, that Jore did not win his case, and that Voltaire subsequently gave the indigent printer money, was in fact blackmailed by him. Voltaire was fully awake to the danger of even a clandestine edition of the *Lettres Philosophiques*, hence the visit to Rouen in disguise, the veils of mystery, the exhortations to Jore not to produce the work until Voltaire gave the word, and the preliminary trial of an English translation published in London by Thiériot, who was allowed to keep all the profits. Among other imprudences Voltaire gave Jore a copy of his remarks on Pascal, a brilliant critique of that formidable Christian apologist. In the spring of 1734, when Voltaire was in the country at the marriage of the Duc de Richelieu and Mlle de Guise (which he had himself "arranged", to his own great satisfaction, but to no one else's), news came that an edition of the *Lettres Philosophiques* with the remarks on Pascal was being sold in Paris, that the scandal was great, that the edition

---

[1] "And understood them", adds Lanson.

VOLTAIRE

had been seized, that Jore was in the Bastille, that Voltaire's papers had been seized.[1] He was in Paris early in May, desperately pulling wires to obtain Jore's freedom and to save himself.

The Abbé Rothelin and M. Rouille did their best for him, but the ecclesiastic and civil authorities were now seriously enraged against a book which struck so sharply, in spite of its air of lightness, against their authority. Maupertuis counselled flight ; Voltaire still lingered in Paris, but on the 6th of May he received an urgent note from d'Argental " to fly at once " and left that day for Lorraine. On the 8th of May a lettre de cachet was issued against Voltaire, with orders for him to be confined in the Château of Auxerre ; the Parlement condemned the book to be burned in public as " scandalous, contrary to religion, to good morals and respect for the powers that be ", and ordered diligent search to be made for the author. This sentence was kept suspended over Voltaire's head for ten years. Of course the emissary of the police with the lettre de cachet failed to find him ; for Voltaire was safe in Lorraine.

He was now, at forty, once more a fugitive, his papers seized, some (not all, as he lamented) of his money gone, and the enmity against him more bitter than ever. Hardly two months before, he had been at Court under Richelieu's patronage, producing his plays, fraternizing with dukes and princes of the blood, in the hope no doubt of making unto himself friends of the Mammon of unrighteousness. All was now destroyed, and the sneers of Desfontaines and J. B. Rousseau, the little scoffs of Piron and a hundred other enemies, did not make the misfortune any easier

---

[1] The case against Voltaire will be found in Le Duc's *Voltaire et la Police* ; the case for Voltaire in Desnoiresterres.

PARIS TO CIREY

to bear. Voltaire thought of returning to London, but the despair of Mme du Châtelet and his passion for her kept him on the continent. After wandering for some time in Lorraine and a visit to Richelieu with the army at the front (which, for some reason, gave great offence to Versailles) Voltaire went secretly to Cirey where, with sundry interruptions and excursions, he remained for the next ten or twelve years, sharing his time between Mme du Châtelet and work, and replenishing his arsenal for the next campaign in the Philosopher's War.

V

CIREY

1734-1744

These "epochs" of Voltaire's life are never anything but a convention, a convenient frame to the biographer ; for it is quite impossible to pin him down to any one place or manner of life for long ; he darted about Europe like a nervous fish in a tank. Each epoch again tempts one to assert that this is the most fertile, the most important period of his life ; but the truth is he was unceasingly producing and preparing new works and his fertility rather increased than diminished as he grew older. Nevertheless, the period 1734-1744 is always associated with Cirey and the Marquise du Châtelet, and it was there that Voltaire, while continuing his work in poetry and the drama, carried on his extensive studies of history and worked at mathematics and science under the influence of his learned mistress. To name the multitude of works he composed or began at Cirey would show his surprising industry but would be tedious ; it is enough to say that the reader must imagine behind the events of these years a background of intense study and incessant production. The marvel with Voltaire is how he found time for it all ; one would imagine that science, literature, and the fair Émilie, would fill any man's existence, but somehow, somewhere, he found time for friendships and enmities, intrigues and pamphlets, a large correspondence, private theatricals, chess and piquet, excursions and travels,

CIREY

visitors, business speculations, alterations to the Château de Cirey and to Frederick's poems. However much he may boast of his love for philosophic solitude, we may surmise that he would have enjoyed hugely the complexity and hurry of modern life ; and if in the next world they have motors, aeroplanes, mechanical pianos, and listening-in sets, M. de Voltaire possesses them all and of the best. Voltaire was not one of those austere philosophers who despise the good and convenient things of this life ; in his poem *Le Mondain*—the publication of which, by the way, involved him in one of his uncountable scrapes—he says :

> " J'aime le luxe, et même la mollesse,
> Tous les plaisirs, les arts de toute espèce,
> La propreté, le goût, les ornements. . . .
> O le bon temps que ce siècle de fer ! "

Voltaire indeed held—and this is only one of his many differences from the Sage of Craigenputtock—that universal frugality would result in much unemployment and that luxury is on the whole favourable to the arts. He was a some pains and expense to fit up handsomely the apartments of Mme du Châtelet and himself at Cirey. These and the life there have been described by more than one visitor to this singular and agreeable ménage and the subject is one too characteristic to be passed over.

The usual party at Cirey consisted of Voltaire, Mme du Châtelet, her husband, her son and his tutor, some mathematical expert, and occasional visitors. M. le Marquis du Châtelet appears to have possessed a talent for self-effacement ; but, even with this knowledge, the enquirer cannot help wondering how they managed, how

VOLTAIRE

the mathematical Mme du Châtelet applied her trigonometry so as to provide a solution of her eternal triangle. These are questions which, unfortunately, no one seems to have investigated, and information is sadly lacking; one can only point out that Mme du Châtelet was an eighteenth century *grande dame*[1] and that she apparently managed very well indeed, except for a few awkward and explosive scenes.

The repairs and embellishments to Cirey caused Voltaire some trouble and inconvenience. His letters frequently refer to them ; at one time he and Mme du Châtelet are reduced to the " entre-sols " ; he boasts to M. de la Faye of being the " architect " of Cirey ; he complains to Thiériot that Émilie's time is wasted by terraces fifty feet wide, " des cours en balustrade ", porcelain baths, yellow and silver appartments and " des niches en magots de Chine ".[2] Different visitors to Cirey have left different accounts of this splendour and the life which went on there. Voltaire's niece, Mme Denis, came to Cirey with her husband in March, 1738 ; she did not greatly approve of the liaison with Mme du Châtelet ; she was " in despair " ; she thought Voltaire was " lost to his friends " and that he would never succeed in " breaking his chains "; moreover, " they are in a solitude terrifying to human beings. Cirey is four leagues from any house, in a district where nothing can be seen but mountains and untilled land ; abandoned by all their friends and hardly ever having anyone from Paris."[3] This eighteenth

---

[1] The reader may consult with profit in this connection Longchamp et Wagnière's *Mémoires sur Voltaire*, vol. 2, pp. 119-120 (edition of 1826).

[2] *Œuvres*, vol. 29, Letters 457, 468, 488.

[3] Mme Denis to Thiériot, 10th of March, 1738.

CIREY

century horror of " deserts " is sensational ; M. Lanson, who took the trouble to visit Cirey, assures us that it is a pleasant place in an agreeable situation. Perhaps Mme Denis feared that Voltaire would leave his money to the Marquise and this made her notice the less smiling aspects of Cirey ; in any case, she was compelled to admit Mme du Châtelet's attentions to Voltaire and described her as a woman of wit, very pretty, " who employs all the art imaginable to seduce him ". It is pleasant to learn this, for Voltaire in turn was most attentive to her ; at table, for example, he never lost sight of her for a moment and every order to the servants was accompanied by " et qu'on ait bien soin de Madame " or some other compliment, while his conversation in her presence was witty, charming, and graceful in the extreme.

The Abbé Le Blanc, who was at Cirey in September, 1736, has left an amusing and satirical account of life there. According to him, Mme du Châtelet wore too many diamonds, everything in the Château was regulated by the sound of the bell, and the day began at four a.m. with " l'exercice de poésie et de littérature ". Mme de Grafigny paid a long visit to Cirey in 1739 and gratifies our curiosity with more complaisance and at greater length. She was a poor aristocrat,[1] invited to Cirey half out of charity, and, though her earlier letters are full of enthusiasm about Cirey and its inhabitants, she eventually found her dependent position there extremely painful. She arrived in December, 1738, at two o'clock in the morning and was received by Mme du Châtelet ; then Voltaire suddenly appeared with a candlestick and kissed the lady's hand a dozen times in his exuberant manner

---

[1] Through the influence of Voltaire she obtained a post in the entourage of the Duchesse de Richelieu.

VOLTAIRE

Two days later Mme de Grafigny wrote to a friend a long description of the apartments at Cirey; though Mme du Châtelet's was the more gorgeous and impressive, our interest goes to Voltaire's apartment, where he lived and wrote for so many years. He had a small wing in the house to himself, containing among others an ante-room, a reception-room, and a "gallery" with a door to the garden. The ante-room was very small; the room was low and hung with crimson velvet; there were "charming" pictures, mirrors, lacquer corner-pieces, porcelain, "marabouts", a clock and an "infinite number of rare and expensive things," silver services, rings, diamonds; all exquisitely clean. (Like Swift, Voltaire was almost fanatical in his insistence on cleanliness.) The gallery was about thirty or forty feet long; between the windows were statues of the Farnese Venus and Hercules. The other wall was occupied by two cupboards, one containing Voltaire's books and the other "machines de physique". Between these stood a stove which "made the air as warm as spring" and there was a statue of Amour on a large pedestal apparently meant to hide the stove. The gallery was panelled and stained a light yellow. It contained numerous clocks, writing-desks, and tables, but only one sofa and no comfortable armchairs. The "chambre obscure" and the room for the physics machines were not then ready. This gallery is the famous rococo gallery of Voltaire so often referred to; it still exists with the private stairway to Mme du Châtelet's room and the little theatre where so many of Voltaire's plays were interpreted by the marionettes in which he delighted.

The order of life at Cirey was studious and laborious. The inhabitants were divided into two sects or classes;

the " cochers ", who were of no importance, and the rest. The cochers consisted of M. du Châtelet, his son, and Mme de Champbonin. Guests were rigidly disciplined; they had to remain in their rooms until the servants announced coffee, which was consumed in Voltaire's gallery between 10.30 and 11.30. At noon, the cochers dined; those who were not cochers remained in conversation with Voltaire until he rose and made a low bow — the signal for everyone to go. Sometimes there was a light repast about four, but generally Voltaire did not appear again until supper, served at nine, and then he was nearly always late. Mme du Châtelet spent the night reading or writing, did not go to bed until some time between five and seven, and rose again at nine, or ten at the latest ; except for meals and occasional recreations, she and Voltaire spent the whole of their time at their writing-desks. For exercise Mme du Châtelet rode her horse and Voltaire tried to shoot wild deer, which he almost invariably missed. One of the principal recreations was the theatre, where these tireless philosophers gave tragedies, comedies, operas, magic-lantern shows, in rapid succession ; on one occasion thirty-three acts were performed in twenty-four hours ; at another time Mme du Châtelet, who was an excellent musician, sang a whole opera after supper.[1] And this went on for years. What gusto, what an appetite for life, what truly admirable love of knowledge and the arts, what amazing concentration and industry !

The usual serenity of Cirey was sometimes disturbed by little tempests which generally arose from the vivacity

[1] For the details, see *Vie privée de Voltaire et Madame du Châtelet* by Mme de Grafigny (1820) and Longchamp and Wagnière's *Mémoires*.

VOLTAIRE

of Voltaire's impressions and his total inability to control them. He and his divine Émilie usually quarrelled in English, and the disturbances often had some trivial or non-existent cause. On one occasion Voltaire sulked and declined to read a new canto of *La Pucelle*, because Mme du Châtelet had refused to let him have a glass of Rhine-wine which he wanted. Later there was a positively frightful clamour, the air filled with accusations, laments, denunciations, reproaches, because poor Mme de Grafigny was suspected of having made public several cantos of *La Pucelle*, a piece of perfidy of which she was entirely guiltless.

But what are we to say of the philosophers of Cirey, when we learn that the evidence for this accusation was the misinterpretation of a phrase in Mme de Grafigny's correspondence, which they were in the habit of reading before it reached her ?

The most amusing of these squabbles took place in Paris much later than the events just related, but is so characteristic of Voltaire's relations with Émilie that it is given here as typical of many other little affairs of the kind. The Marquise was revising her book on Newton with Clairaut, and, to avoid interruptions, they worked behind locked doors. Ordinarily they supped with Voltaire who, at this time, was dieting. One evening he came home with a good appetite, ordered supper for an earlier hour than usual, and sent Longchamp to call the two savants ; but Mme du Châtelet was immersed in calculations and asked for a quarter of an hour's grace, which became half an hour with still no sign of Clairaut and the Marquise. Longchamp was sent up again, knocked, and received the answer, " nous descendons ", whereupon Voltaire ordered supper to be served and sat down to wait for them—in vain, and the food was growing cold. Suddenly he rose in fury, rushed up stairs, and, finding the door locked, kicked it down and burst madly in upon the amazed mathematicians who followed him humbly down to supper amid exclamations of "vous êtes donc de concert pour me faire mourir ? "[1]

One important effect of the life with Mme du Châtelet was to confirm Voltaire in his philosophical studies and to stimulate his interest in physics and mathematics. It is true that Voltaire still regarded himself primarily as a poet and was even a little annoyed when, on returning to Paris in 1735 (thanks to the influence of Mme du Châtelet), he found that there was a fashion for physics and geometry, due no doubt to the vogue of Maupertuis and perhaps his own *Lettres Philosophiques*. In a letter to Cideville[2] he laments that sentiment, imagination, and grace are banished, that " les belles-lettres périssent à vue d'oeil "; and announces that for his part he intends to go from an experiment in physics to a comedy or an opera and not to allow his taste to be blunted by study. Nevertheless, only a month later (May, 1735), having fled from Paris once more because of " strange rumours " of *La Pucelle*, he spent his days at Lunéville with three philosophers in a " riche cabinet de physique."

In his *Mémoires*[3] Voltaire dwells with affectionate regret on the days at Cirey (which he calls " une délicieuse retraite "), exaggerates Mme du Châtelet's talents, relates how he taught her English and Italian, and admires her researches in the philosophy of Leibnitz and Newton.

[1] Longchamp's *Mémoires*, pp. 175, 176.
[2] *Œuvres*, vol. 29, Letter 338.
[3] Written in 1759 ; not published until 1784. *Œuvres*, vol. 23, p. 304 *et seq*.

VOLTAIRE

"There are two marvels", says Voltaire,[1] "one that Newton should have written this work, the other that this lady should have translated and elucidated it". The most permanent results of all this philosophising in Voltaire's case during the Cirey period were his *Universal History*, which he began at Émilie's request, his *Eléments de la Philosophie de Newton* and his *Essai sur la Nature du Feu*. He took the copy of his Newton book to Holland in 1737, when for various reasons (which included the protests of certain puritanical relatives of Émilie) Voltaire thought it wise to absent himself from felicity a while; but the urgent letters of his mistress brought him back from Holland before the book was half through the press. Meanwhile, the usual "approbation" was applied for in France and, to Voltaire's intense indignation, refused; the French government was determined to suppress free thought and enquiry, particularly when it came from an author so dangerously popular as Voltaire. "Apparently", he exclaims,[2] "a poor Frenchman is not allowed to say that attraction is possible and proved, that the earth must be flattened at the poles, that void is demonstrated, etc". Unluckily, a pirated edition, completed by someone else, was issued by the Dutch printers early in 1738; a sub-title *mise à la portée de tout le monde* gave an opportunity to some wag to say the book was "mise à la porte de tout le monde". Voltaire smiled at this, but was rendered speechless and frantic with rage by a perfidious review from Desfontaines, which congratulated him on abandoning poetry for

[1] *Eloge Historique de la Marquise du Châtelet* (1752), *Œuvres*, vol. 23, p. 196.
[2] Letter 616, to Maupertuis.

philosophy at his " already advanced age ", with a malicious reference to the " turpe vates senex ".

Voltaire was absurdly sensitive to this kind of raillery and, in his furious answers to such literary small fry as Desfontaines, made himself completely and publicly ridiculous ; but that is an essential part of Voltaire, to whose alert and restless intelligence such a squib assumed an almost tragic importance. The years at Cirey were by no means free from annoyances of this kind ; and the characteristic of Voltaire was that at such moments all his " philosophy " abruptly deserted him and he stamped, raved, protested, and counter-libelled like an indignant child. As his successes (the *Eléments* was a most popular book) and reputation continued to grow, his little swarm of gadflies increased. The Jore affair dragged on until 1738 ; and J. B. Rousseau, Saint-Hyacinthe, Desfontaines plagued him with lampoons, which he could not forbear answering. The *Préservatif* which he directed at Desfontaines was answered by the atrocious *Voltairomanie* in December 1738. When a copy reached Mme du Châtelet she was in consternation ; she wrote to all his friends to conceal it from him, and later discovered—which is quite charming—that he was concealing it from her. Legal action was taken against Desfontaines and he was compelled to disavow his libel. What is most striking in these squabbles is first Voltaire's extreme susceptibility, then his pettiness in prolonging them beyond measure, and then the paradoxical bursts of magnanimity during which he forgave and even aided his tormentors. It is like his long-suffering kindness to the poor authors he protected—Thiériot, Linant, d'Arnaud, Lamarre, Mouhy—and the calm way he endured considerable losses of money ; he is always surprising us by this

VOLTAIRE

unexpected mixture of pettiness and indulgence ; it can be seen in his relations with Mme du Châtelet. He could quarrel violently with her over a glass of wine, a broken tea-cup or a suit of clothes, and then forgive her for taking another lover when she explained (with the frankness of an eighteenth century *grande dame*) that he was getting a little old and that she needed the embraces of a younger man.

There was one notable occasion when the names of Voltaire and gammon " came into contract." As early as 1730 he had received verses from a Mlle Malcrais de la Vigne, to which he gallantly responded, and a correspondance in verse and prose sprang up between Voltaire and the lady. Mlle de la Vigne addressed poems to other eminent writers and received in return quantities of epistles and amorous madrigals. Some years later Mlle de la Vigne came to Paris and, to the joy of everyone but Voltaire and her other dupes, turned out to be a great lubberly boy named Desforges-Maillard. Voltaire pretended to be amiable about it, though he twice took a sharp little vengeance in those cunningly worded " notes " at which he was so apt ; he would have liked the incident forgotten, but, unluckily for him, Piron took hold of it and made the jest immortal by his brilliant comedy, *La Métromanie*.

The *Essai sur la Nature du Feu*, mentioned above, was also a source of disappointment. The Academy of Science offered a prize for the best essay on this subject ; Voltaire and Mme du Châtelet both competed and both failed. When the authorship of the two essays was revealed, M. de Réaumur wrote " une lettre très galante " and a doctor of the Sorbonne likened the two philosophers to Theseus and Ariadne, to the disadvantage of the

CIREY

latter. This must have been an immense consolation, but hardly atoned for Voltaire's failure to enter either the Académie Française or the Académie des Sciences.

Science by no means diminished Voltaire's unquenchable flow of verse, tragic, epic, and occasional. Writing *La Pucelle*, already referred to, formed one of his chief diversions during this epoch and was also a source of great anxiety to him. This innocuous burlesque, now only shocking to the primitive or depraved mind, is supposed to have given deep offence to the Chancellor Maurepas ; such rumours and fragments as reached the devout of course aroused their worst passions, and Voltaire is said to have been threatened with perpetual imprisonment if he allowed it to be printed. The poem is supposed to have been started as early as 1730, in consequence of a conversation at one of Richelieu's supper-parties. Voltaire worked over it at leisure moments for years and was continually altering and improving it. Private readings of *La Pucelle* to small gatherings of friends were popular and eagerly attended ; one of the first things Frederick begged of Voltaire was a canto or more of "Jeanne". Among Voltaire's other work of this epoch must be mentioned the tragedies of *Alzire*, an enormous financial success ; *Mérope*, where an enthusiastic audience called for the author to appear on the stage (the first time this happened, it is said) ; and *Mahomet*, which had a success of scandal owing to its denunciations of religious bigotry and fanaticism which, needless to say, were applied by the audience to other than Mahommedans. Voltaire skilfully parried the malice of his enemies and prepared his way to the Académie Française by dedicating *Mahomet* to Pope Benedict XIV, who accepted the dedication ; the letters which passed between these two

VOLTAIRE

artful personages are agreeable examples of eighteenth century polite irony.[1] It is charming to read Voltaire's little hypocrisies about "la vera religione", ending with a "bacio" on the "sacri piedi" of his "beatissimo Padre"; and it is even more delightful to read of the "sommo piacere" with which his Holiness eagerly devoured the "bellissima tragedia" he had doubtless never looked at. Thus history is written; and thus a Roman Pontiff secured the election to the Académie Française of an author whose complete works are now on the Index Expurgatorius.

[1] *Œuvres*, vol. 3, pp. 189-192.

VI

MADAME DU CHÂTELET AND THE KING OF PRUSSIA

Madame du Châtelet was in many respects a remarkable woman and an ideal mistress for a man of letters. Her knowledge and accomplishments, though less extensive than Voltaire fondly believed, were considerable and prevented her from boring others or herself. She was a reasonable and intelligent person, quite free from sentimentality and cant ; energetic, witty, and vivacious. She was rather vain and quick to take offence, but she was capable of strong affections ; and, unlike romantic and devout women, she succeeded in making her old lovers into friends. If she was eventually unfaithful to Voltaire, she managed to keep on friendly terms with him even when he found it out. Her greatest trouble with him was the necessity of watching his correspondance with Frederick the Great who had made up his mind to bring Voltaire to Germany permanently. Frederick used any means that came to hand, and not the least remarkable thing about Mme du Châtelet is that she remained victorious in this Homeric duel for the body of Voltaire ; that, in spite of everything Frederick could do, he was never able to keep Voltaire for more than a short visit as long as she was alive. To appreciate her diplomatic skill and force of character we must glance at her opponent.

VOLTAIRE

Frederick the Great was an unusual King, very different from the shining abstractions of later epochs. His father, old Frederick William, was a lunatic with a mania for huge grenadiers and for tormenting his family. Prince Frederick experienced a very unpleasant youth, but on the death of his father he inherited liberty and the best trained army in Europe. Frederick's military abilities were not confined to falling off his horse on the lines of communication, he was one of the ablest generals of his age ; nor did his political abilities exhaust themselves in a few inane platitudes, on the contrary he was capable of planning vast schemes of aggrandisement and possessed the unscrupulous resolution and skill to carry them out successfully. In his recreations and private life he again differed from many of his class. Instead of numbing his faculties in the company of aristocratic dullards or drifting into the hebetude induced by field sports when practised in excess, Frederick the Great surrounded himself with philosophers and men of letters and gave up his leisure to music, literature, the arts, and philosophy. Disparaging remarks to the contrary, he was an excellent flute-player. But his great passion was French literature, his cherished ambition was to be a French poet, and his model, his literary hero, his " cher maître ", was Voltaire. No one will ever know whether Frederick most wanted Silesia or Voltaire.[1]

The reader's familiarity with this situation must not blind him to its unique aspects. Here, on the one hand, was the greatest man-of-letters of the age, held in the remote Château de Cirey by the charms of a she-

---

[1] This is an exaggeration, but Frederick's admiration for Voltaire as a writer can scarcely be exaggerated. See Sainte-Beuve for an admirable passage on this theme.

philosopher who was quite determined not to give him up to anyone—Heaven knows how many times she saved her imprudent lover from lettres de cachet and exile—and, on the other hand, there was Frederick, at first, merely one of the crowd of kings, but rapidly proving that he was fit to associate with philosophers and poets ; and, remarkably enough, he was a King who wished to make his capital a centre of culture by attracting great foreigners to his Court. The uneasiness of Mme du Châtelet is comprehensible. But consider the effect of this royal flattery and attention upon Voltaire. He would scarcely have been human had he not been pleased and flattered ; but to a man of Voltaire's vanity the advances and incense of Frederick were delicious. With what exultation he informs his friends that he has received yet another letter from His Royal Highness, the Crown Prince of Prussia, and how careful he is to circulate copies of the correspondence. Yet there was more in this than mere vanity. Voltaire, it will be remembered, had a lettre de cachet impending over him after the condemnation of his *Lettres Philosophiques,* since he was continually giving new offence by his attitude to religion and privilege ; he was really not safe in France. In the event of some more colossal disturbance following, let us say, the pirating of the unpublished *La Pucelle*—a refuge at Potsdam would be more than welcome. Again, it was very agreeable to have a Crown Prince and then a King to play off against the indifference or hostility of Versailles ; it was a sort of triumph over the not forgotten Rohan-Chabots. Voltaire, too, still caressed political chimæras and seems to have hoped that his friendship with Frederick might lead to " something turning up "—for his aspirations were vague.

VOLTAIRE

All this induced modifications in Voltaire's conduct, thought and writing. Between 1736, when Frederick's first letter arrived, and 1753, when they finally quarrelled[1] in Berlin, Voltaire considerably modified the austere republican virtues he had acquired in exile and had expressed in *Brutus*. He did not wholly abandon the ideas of the *Lettres Philosophiques* and occasionally continued his alarums and excursions against the ancien régime; but he doubtless felt that the salvation of mankind was perhaps best attained by philosopher rulers; say, Frederick as King of Prussia, and M. de Voltaire as chief minister of France. And really it was not such a foolish idea; none of Louis XV's Ministers was as able as Voltaire with his immense energy and clear common sense. In any event, he and Frederick would certainly have changed the face of Europe and there might have been no French Revolution. This is nothing but a fancy; but it is worth observing that Voltaire did not finally appear as the avowed reformer and enemy of Kings until after 1753.

Frederick was twenty-two when, in his first rapturous enthusiasm, he wrote to Voltaire and received in reply a letter which is a masterpiece of flattery, while it is full of generous exhortations and contains an excellent portrait of what a philosopher-king ought to be. The exchange of letters was followed by presents; the first was a little bust of Socrates sent to Voltaire by Frederick, with no intention of irony.[2] Frederick offered his house in London, sent his portrait, despatched (March 1737) Von Kaiserling as "ambassador" to Cirey with more

---

[1] And yet not finally; after a lapse of years the correspondence was renewed, not with the old enthusiasm, but in obedience to an irresistible and mutual attraction.

[2] So we are assured, but it certainly implied that Mme du Châtelet was a Xantippe.

MADAME DU CHATELET

presents, in exchange for which he received manuscript copies of the early portions of *Louis XIV*,[1] quantities of verses, fragments of "philosophy", but no *Pucelle*. Voltaire was at Brussels, owing to the interminable law-suit of the Châtelets, when Frederick became King in 1740 ; he at once wrote enthusiastically to "your humanity". Later he was in Holland, vainly attempting to suppress Frederick's *Anti-Machiavel*. The same year a meeting was arranged (and cancelled) at Brussels ; but in spite of Mme du Châtelet's jealousy the King and the philosopher met in October at Cleves. They met again in Berlin during November of the same year. As her correspondence shows, Mme du Châtelet became more and more anxious about this friendship, knowing as she did Frederick's determination to keep Voltaire permanently settled in Germany. Frederick's own letters and Machiavellian tricks to harm Voltaire in France in order that he might have no refuge but Berlin are equally entertaining. If some of the incoherence of Voltaire's conduct was due to his own heedlessness and petulance, much of it was the result of the machinations and influence of the lady and the king as they fought for their poet ; obviously, Voltaire could not enjoy his Émilie if he were away from France, and therefore he temporised with the French authorities, no doubt at her command. Mme du Châtelet laboured to make France as attractive to him as possible, while Frederick missed no opportunity of compromising him with the authorities.

---

[1] The recital of Voltaire's troubles with authority over his publications becomes monotonous, but it must be noted that when the apparently harmless first chapter of *Louis XIV* was published in a Miscellany, the police intervened and suppressed the publication. It is one more proof of the continual hostility of a powerful party.

VOLTAIRE

She kept her poet successfully to herself (except for a few days' visit to Aix-la-Chapelle) until the middle of 1743, when Voltaire made a long and important visit to Germany, to the despair of Mme du Châtelet who was still further afflicted by the infrequency of her lover's letters.

There were several reasons for this journey. To everyone's relief, but especially Voltaire's, old Cardinal Fleury[1] died in January, 1743, thereby renewing Voltaire's political ambitions, to which end he hoped to exploit his friendship with the King of Prussia. At the same time a number of literary disappointments disgusted him with Paris; two of his tragedies were suppressed by the police, and the intrigues of his enemies prevented him from attaining a seat in either the Académie Française or the Académie des Sciences. He went off to Frederick; but this time he was charged with a secret diplomatic mission by the French government (always so ready to exploit the literary prestige of its citizens) and, by a characteristic arrangement, all the correspondence passed through Émilie's hands. Voltaire was delighted with his reception and yet, when he and Frederick parted, discovery of their mutual treachery had destroyed their first full confidence—for ever. On the return journey, Voltaire stayed a fortnight at Bayreuth, flirting poetically with the Margravine; he also spent a few days at the Court of Brunswick—minor infidelities which distressed the Marquise even more than the triumphs at Potsdam and Berlin. But when in November Voltaire rejoined his Émilie in Brussels, all was forgotten and forgiven, and

[1] He was virtual ruler of France for seventeen years, and mistrusted Voltaire completely.

they proceeded amicably together to Paris, where Voltaire did not at first receive any reward for his diplomatic labours.[1]

[1] Voltaire has left an amusing account of all this in his *Mémoires*. It is possible that his diplomatic errand was not quite unsuccessful, though most authorities think it a failure. In any case, the visit was an immense personal success.

VII

VOLTAIRE AT COURT—DEATH OF MADAME DU CHÂTELET

(1744-1749)

It appears that this latest expedition into Germany caused Mme du Châtelet so much alarm that she used all her influence over Voltaire and her undoubted powers of intrigue to counteract the attractions of Frederick and to retain her poet in France. Fortunately for her plans, Richelieu was in favour at Court, Voltaire's old friend d'Argenson foreign minister, and a little later another friend, Madame de Pompadour, became the ruling mistress. Consciously or unconsciously Voltaire fell in with Mme du Châtelet's plans and allowed himself to be metamorphosed for a third time into a courtier. He had several reasons for this temporary abandonment of his intransigeance towards authority. He was now fifty years old and felt that France owed some reparation and homage to its greatest living author, who hitherto had been chiefly honoured officially by disapproval, persecution, and exile. He was not sorry to play off Louis XV against Frederick and to show the world that he could tame his own as well as foreign potentates. He had the pleasure, which he valued highly, of annoying enemies by his success. The protection of the Court, like the approval of the Pope, was some defence against the malignity of those who disapproved of him—certainly at this date a larger number than his partisans. It enabled him to remain near Mme du Châtelet, to gratify his extreme

AT COURT

vanity, to secure election to the Académie Française, and possibly to indulge again in his dreams of political power.

At first, with all his powerful interest at Court, matters went well for Voltaire. He was commissioned by Richelieu to write the *Princesse de Navarre* for the marriage of the Dauphin, a task he took most seriously. In writing an Opera for the Court, he endured with admirable patience the caprices of his collaborator, Rameau. During the *fêtes* after the recovery of Louis XV, Voltaire was in Paris and wrote his poem *On the Events of* 1744 as a piece of Court flattery. Early in 1745 we find him at Versailles, delighted with himself, pretending to despise his favour with phrases such as, " I am become the King's jester at fifty " or " At Versailles, I am like an atheist in a Church "[1] ; but of course he was charmed to be there. Fortune showered gifts upon him. In February his Jansenist brother died, leaving him a life interest in half his estate. After the fête at Versailles, Voltaire was made a gentleman of the bedchamber, historiographer royal of France, and received another pension of 2,000 livres. On this occasion he wrote the following characteristic epigram which aptly enough described the situation and had the additional merit of forestalling a certain amount of the inevitable satire which followed all Voltaire's actions :

" Mon *Henri Quatre,* et ma *Zaïre,*
   Et mon Américaine *Alzire,*
Ne m'ont valu jamais un seul regard du roi ;
J'avais mille ennemis avec très peu de gloire.
Les honneurs et les biens pleuvent enfin sur moi
   Pour une farce de la Foire." [2]

[1] *Lettres Inédites,* p. 149.   [2] *Œuvres,* vol. 7, p. 337. The ' Farce de la Foire " is the *Princesse de Navarre.*

VOLTAIRE

Nearly three years were spent in these delightful intrigues and successes, but not only were they the least fertile period of Voltaire's life—in spite of his industry—they were so embittered by a series of petty wars with detractors that much of the enjoyment of success must have been lost. Not very much could be said against Royal patronage, but Voltaire's manoeuvres to get into the Académie produced a whole swarm of malevolent pamphlets. If his older enemies desisted from their attacks from weariness, new aggressors were continually appearing—Fréron, Roi, La Beaumelle, Clément. As usual they provoked Voltaire to absurd resentment, and, in the case of a musician named Travenol, he allowed himself to become involved in a law-suit which lasted sixteen months and would have brought anyone but Voltaire to the verge of a nervous breakdown. This interminable and foolish quarrel undoubtedly harmed Voltaire's contemporary reputation—just at the moment he had become so respectable. Mme du Châtelet must have felt like slapping him sometimes; he behaved so exactly like a petulant child.

His election to the Académie occurred in April, 1746, when Voltaire was fifty-two; a disgracefully late age, considering how many youthful mediocrities were then members of that body. Even so, prodigious and elaborate intrigues were necessary to secure election—declarations of religious orthodoxy, correspondence with the Pope, and a thousand démarches—and Voltaire almost had the honour of joining Molière as the second great French writer excluded from the Académie by jealousy and prejudice. Voltaire's reception discourse was a good one; he threw over none of his ideals and friends and went out of his way to praise the then obscure Vauvenar-

AT COURT

gues. Probably for the first time in its history the roof above the immortal forty rang with the name "Shakespeare"; in fact, the indignant echo could only be stilled by the hasty addition " quoique barbare "; but the occasion is an important one in literary history. One hundred and thirty years after his death Shakespeare was officially noticed by a daring rebel in the bosom of the greatest literary academy in the world; nothing could better illustrate the rapid spread of literary fame and the open-mindedness of orthodox defenders of literary faith.

This event was followed by a fresh outburst of enemy pamphlets. The new Academician was almost physically incapacitated with rage; his letters to d'Argental alternately scream and cajole; police aid was invoked, poets and book-sellers and book-smugglers were raided and dragged off to prison. Meanwhile Voltaire was serenading Louis XV with the implacable energy he put into everything. The battle of Fontenoy (May, 1745) was celebrated by a patriotic poem, whose chief merit seems to be that sixty persons present at the battle were mentioned by name in verse, whereas in Boileau's ode to Louis XIV the poet had only succeeded in naming fifteen. One recognises the progress. Voltaire and Rameau collaborated in producing an Opera, *Le Temple de la Gloire*, to celebrate the virtues and heroism of Louis XV. But this was not enough. When Voltaire accepted the post of historiographer, he had negligently sent out word that of course he would not write anything in that capacity; a few months later we find him daily at the War Office, industriously chronicling the heroism of Louis XV[1] and declaring to d'Argenson; " J'y travaille, comme j'ai toujours travaillé, avec

[1] *Histoire de la Guerre de* 1741.

VOLTAIRE

passion ". (That, by the way, might be put as a motto to the collected edition of Voltaire.) He was also employed to write one or two government declarations, including the French proclamation on behalf of Prince Charles Edward in the rebellion of '45 ; this is one of the oddities of history, the classical Voltaire touching so closely an event many of us see through the romantic prism of Scott's novels.[1]

A characteristic imprudence brought this Court life temporarily to an end ; and, amusingly enough, Mme du Châtelet was the immediate cause of the philosopher's disgrace. She gambled furiously at Fontainebleau for several days, in spite of Voltaire's timid protests, lost all her ready money, some of his, and ended up with a debt of honour of 80,000 francs. Voltaire had watched this disaster with growing agitation and could not prevent himself from telling her in English that she had been playing with cheats. Unfortunately the remark was overheard and understood ; the company began to whisper and Mme du Châtelet realised that Voltaire had committed one more of his perpetual indiscretions. To call the greatest nobles in France a set of cheats was a serious matter, involving the possibility of another holiday in the Bastille ; the fact that the observation was probably true only made it the more dangerous. The learned lovers decided that immediate flight was imperative and they left Fontainebleau with such precipitation that they forgot to take any money with them ; and this plunged them into comic and embarrassing adventures from which they were only released by the fortunate arrival of a friend.[2]

[1] The news of the arrest of Prince Charles in 1748 was received by Voltaire with indignation ; but there is no serious proof of the story that he broke off his *Louis XV* as a protest.
[2] Longchamp, p. 139. This happened in October, 1747.

AT COURT

Voltaire took refuge with the Duchesse du Maine, while Mme du Châtelet returned to face her creditors. Voltaire observed the strictest incognito at Sceaux. The philosopher was hidden in a room whose shutters were always kept closed, so that he was forced to live by candle-light ; no one in the Château knew of his presence except the Duchess, Longchamp, a footman and a "petit Savoyard" who was sent upon errands. The day was spent in writing and, at two o'clock in the morning, Voltaire would go secretly to the Duchess's bedroom, eat his supper while they conversed, and then read to her the manuscript he had composed during the day for her amusement. To this captivity, we owe the brilliant little pieces *Babouc, Memnon, Scarmentado, Micromégas,* and *Zadig,* all written in about six weeks.[1] Who but Voltaire could so turn a disgrace to immortal advantage? And what a curious glimpse of eighteenth century royalty to find the Duchesse du Maine taking delight in these subversive pamphlets, these raids in the philosopher's war.

The confinement, the life in artificial light, the monotony, were beginning to irritate Voltaire and even to harm his health when fortunately Mme du Châtelet arrived at Sceaux, having settled her debt and calmed the indignation aroused by Voltaire's remark. Voltaire appeared openly at Sceaux and was entertained, or rather helped to provide entertainment, with a succession of comedies, operas, balls, and concerts [2] ; he remained at

[1] Longchamp says two months, but probably overestimates. Voltaire wrote no letters—at least none are preserved—during this period. I am not quite convinced that these pieces were written at Sceaux, but such is the tradition.

[2] See Longchamp ; Mme du Châtelet and Voltaire both played parts in comedies.

VOLTAIRE

Sceaux until the early part of December, 1747. Hardly was he back in Paris when he gave fresh offence at Court ; this time it was a flattering madrigal to Mme de Pompadour, interpreted by his enemies as an insult to the Queen ; it is said that Louis's daughters were prompted by the religious party to beg for Voltaire's exile. It is certain that Louis XV always disliked Voltaire—they were two such different personalities !—and it is also certain that the philosophic couple soon left for Cirey. Indeed, though Voltaire still kept in touch with the French Court, there was a growing sense of incompatibility on either side. It is true that *L'Enfant Prodigue* was performed at Court by aristocratic actors, including Mme de Pompadour and the Duc de Chartres ; and it is also true that the King gave 5,000 francs for the staging of *Sémiramis* ; but in the dramatic contest between Voltaire and Crébillon, the King's dislike of Voltaire made him a warm if unintelligent partisan of Crébillon and compelled Mme de Pompadour to extreme caution in her favours to the greater man. This withdrawal from the French Court was gradual but obvious ; Voltaire spent more and more time at Lunéville, the residence of the King of Poland, though the motive for this was principally the interests of Mme du Châtelet, whose fortunes Voltaire followed like a faithful satellite. In 1749 he sold his Court post for 60,000 livres and, by a special grace, was allowed to retain the title and privileges ; a typical example of Voltairean prudence. All this time Frederick was persistently corresponding and renewing his invitations, but Mme du Châtelet kept her poet too well in hand to allow even a short visit to her rival. For her sake Voltaire suffered many things with extraordinary tolerance ; he might, and did, erupt occasionally into nervous protests,

AT COURT

but always acquiesced eventually ; her domination over him was complete. We have seen how her gambling involved him in an unpleasant adventure : an eccentricity of hers involved him in another which though brief might have been fatal. Mme du Châtelet insisted upon travelling by night on one of their journeys to Cirey ; the roads were heavy with snow, the night was freezing cold and starry, the carriage was old ; half way between two posting-stations there came a lurch, a crash, and the coach fell over on its side with M. de Voltaire " qui poussait des cris aigues " underneath Madame and the maid and the parcels and the boxes. The lackeys removed the boxes first, then the ladies, and finally M. de Voltaire, dragging them up through the side of the coach by whatever limbs—legs or arms—they could grasp in the darkness, and sliding the victims down to other lackeys on the ground. But great is the power of philosophy ; when it was found that no one was seriously hurt, messengers were sent for help ; our two philosophers seated themselves on cushions in the snow and discoursed of the nature and movements of the heavenly bodies, while their teeth chattered and their limbs quaked in the January frost.[1]

The long association between Voltaire and his divine Émilie was now drawing to a close. Voltaire was twelve years the elder and had never been an ardent lover ; Mme du Châtelet was his dearest friend rather than his mistress, though, as Frederick remarked, they did not live ten years together merely to talk of philosophy. In these later years their intimate relations had grown rare, if they had not entirely ceased, a state of affairs quite acceptable to the now elderly and always frigid Voltaire but very

[1] Longchamp's *Mémoires*.

VOLTAIRE

unsatisfactory to his ardent and impulsive partner. She fell in love, deeply and uncontrollably, with a handsome young officer and poet, named Saint-Lambert. For some considerable time the philosopher was as blind as the husband, but one day at Lunéville he surprised Saint-Lambert and Émilie in a situation which left him no room for doubt. The philosopher did not retire discreetly ; on the contrary, advancing with precipitation, he denounced them with all the furious eloquence he could so well display, but not command. Saint-Lambert grew angry (the only thing to do in such circumstances) and challenged Voltaire to a duel—a duel between an invalid of fifty-four and a soldier of thirty-one ! Voltaire rushed back to his apartment, and ordered Longchamp to prepare for an immediate departure early next morning : Longchamp secretly warned Mme du Châtelet who, having pacified Saint-Lambert, went to deal with Voltaire. We have already seen that his common sense and indulgence came to the rescue and enabled him to accept an almost inevitable event for which in a sense he was indirectly responsible. The next day Saint-Lambert was sent to make excuses for his behaviour and the response is typically Voltairean. "Scarcely was his phrase finished", says Longchamp, "when M. de Voltaire grasped both his hands, embraced him, and said, ' Mon enfant, I have forgotten everything, it is I am in the wrong. You are at the happy age when people love and are loved ; enjoy these too brief moments ; an old man, a sick man, like myself is no longer fit for such pleasures ! ' "

The next day all three dined amicably together with Mme de Boufflers. Voltaire's behaviour after the first outburst of indignation showed a tolerance, an absence of jealous vanity, and a sense of human values which are extremely rare. In this affair we can indeed say that nothing became him like the leaving it.

Unhappily Mme du Châtelet became pregnant. A feverish council between Voltaire, Saint-Lambert, and Mme du Châtelet was held, at which Voltaire suggested that the child should be attributed to the *Œuvres Mêlées de Mme du Châtelet* ; it was finally decided that M. du Châtelet should be imposed upon, and this deceit was accordingly carried out with the connivance of Voltaire and Saint-Lambert. During her pregnancy Mme du Châtelet was afflicted with dismal presentiments and believed she would die ; she was safely delivered, but died a few days later at Lunéville. Saint-Lambert and Voltaire were stricken with consternation at this unexpected event ; as the latter stumbled in blind grief from the room he fell at the foot of the stairway and in his despair beat his head upon the ground. A lackey and Saint-Lambert ran to lift him up. Sobbing, and in "the most pathetic accents", Voltaire said : "Ah ! mon ami, c'est vous qui me l'avez tuée !" Then suddenly, as if starting from a profound sleep, he exclaimed in a tone of reproach and despair: " Eh, mon Dieu ! Monsieur ! de quoi vous avisiez-vous de lui faire un enfant ! "

The next day Voltaire learned that in a ring with a movable stone which he had given to Mme du Châtelet, the portrait of Saint-Lambert had been substituted by her for his own. " O ciel ", cried the philosopher, clasping his hands and lifting them to heaven, " voilà bien les femmes ! "[1]

[1] Longchamp's *Mémoires.*

VIII

FREDERICK

(1749-1753)

The death of Madame du Châtelet, following close upon her infidelities, was as important in its effect upon Voltaire as her entry into his life. At the time when the *Lettres Philosophiques* were published and so brutally condemned (it will be remembered), Voltaire in disgust had intended to go into voluntary exile ; he was restrained by his passion for Mme du Châtelet. Then began a new period of his life, fruitful indeed in study, in preparation, but during which he was always subject to her influence, always compromising with authority. His amour-propre was gratified by his court success in France ; but it was largely owing to Mme du Châtelet's advice and influence that he flattered Madame de Pompadour—which is excusable, for she was accomplished and charming—and that he likened Louis XV to Trajan. Voltaire, of all men, should have felt the difference between a Louis XIV and a Louis XV ; and he must have realized how greatly Louis XV disliked him. But the idea of " philosophers and kings " working together for the good of humanity possibly disguised to Voltaire his own undefined political ambitions and justified to him a flattery that approached ignominy. Yet we must not judge Voltaire fanatically, nor suppose that it is worse to flatter a king than a mob. Voltaire was a well-bred man of the world ; hence his long tergiversation, which so irritates the fanatic, whose pride it is never to render to Caesar the things that are Caesar's.

Mme du Châtelet's death left a void in Voltaire's life ; and Frederick smiled, for he saw that he would now get his poet. At first, Voltaire was sincerely and deeply afflicted[1] ; but the rapidity and vivacity of his sentiments were such that their very sharpness made them brief. Longchamp relates that he found Voltaire wandering at night through Mme du Châtelet's apartments,[2] calling lamentably upon her name and then—for comedy is never far absent from Voltaire's most tragic moments— tumbling in a half-swoon over a pile of books.[3] Marmontel found him in mournful solitude. " Come ", said Voltaire, " share my grief. I have lost my illustrious friend ; I am in despair ; I am inconsolable". Marmontel, to " make him see some reason for consolation in the death itself ", asked him what caused her death. " What ! " exclaimed the philosopher sharply, " You don't know ? Ah ! my friend, that brute killed her. He got her with child ". And, redoubling his tears and sobs, Voltaire praised his incomparable Émilie. At that moment Chauvelin came in and told some amusing story, at which Voltaire laughed heartily, perhaps hysterically ; the mobility of such a temperament must always cause surprise to our more phlegmatic minds.

Characteristically, Voltaire was distracted from his gloom, not by Frederick, but by love of the theatre and

[1] See *Œuvres*, Letters 1647-1650 inclusive. He tells Mme du Deffand that this event " will poison the remainder of his miserable life."
[2] Voltaire took over her house in Paris, and brought there all his possessions at Cirey ; his niece, Mme Denis, kept house for him.
[3] Longchamp, vol. 2, p. 264.
[4] Marmontel, *Œuvres*, cited by Desnoiresterres.

VOLTAIRE

rivalry with Crébillon. He wrote his *Catalina* and his *Oreste* with amazing rapidity—the first draft of *Catalina* was written in a week—to prove that he could handle these themes better than Mme de Pompadour's dramatist. The Comédie Française refused one or two of his tragedies and this, of course, stimulated him immensely; something had to be done and Voltaire did it. First of all he discovered Le Kain[1]—the greatest tragic actor of his time—and with his usual impetuous generosity embraced him, wept, lifted up his voice in thanksgiving for such a discovery, and placed his purse and influence at the young man's disposal. Then, he gave private performances of his tragedies, with Le Kain in leading parts; these were so successful, brought such distinguished audiences, that the Comédie Française actors grew frightened, re-opened negotiations, and took back the rejected tragedies.

Meanwhile, the curtain had rung up on the second act of the immortal comedy of Frederick the Great and Voltaire; for if Voltaire could not write comedies, he could live them. He had promised Frederick a visit as soon as Mme du Châtelet had recovered from her illness; her death upset that project, but it opened up possibilities of a permanent residence at Potsdam, instead of a mere visit. In November, 1749, Voltaire promised a summer visit only, which was to include several days at the Court of Stanislas, but Frederick wanted his poet-philosopher " for ever ", and played his game accordingly. One difficulty was money. Voltaire did not mean to come at his own expense, and invented a

---

[1] Le Kain's *Mémoires* are eloquent in praise of Voltaire and with gratitude for his early encouragement and help.

FREDERICK

splendid little ruse for drawing money from the King; Frederick grimaced at the letter, struggled with his avarice for several days, and finally gave way with royal grace. But, fearing that Voltaire might yet escape him, he played a devilish trick which he knew would pique the poet and make his visit certain. Baculard d'Arnaud a protégé of Voltaire's, had just been secured for the Potsdam menagerie; Frederick greeted him with poetic epistle which contained the lines :

> " Voltaire est à son couchant
> Vous êtes à votre aurore."

Two kind friends in Paris showed this poem to Voltaire, who was in bed; he leaped up in his night-shirt and danced on the bed with fury; the visit to Potsdam was irrevocably decided. Cunning Frederick!

Money matters settled and amour-propre artfully piqued, there was left to obtain only the consent of Louis XV. It is said the King told Voltaire " he could go when he liked " and turned his back on him; but, however brusque and tactless, Louis XV was a gentleman, and such rudeness seems unlikely. What does surprise is the carelessness of the French government in allowing Voltaire to slip out of its clutches; their politic course, with a man of his immense gifts, popularity, and persuasiveness, was to flatter him with honours, retain him in France, and check his attacks on authority by alternate threats of the Bastille and blandishments. But, in the first place, officials and the official mind always underestimate the force of ideas and the intangible power of a great writer; and then in this case they thought the visit to Frederick was temporary and that it would be a

VOLTAIRE

failure—as it was, but they did not foresee Ferney.[1] If the exile to England marks the first stage of the Philosopher's War, the residence at Potsdam began a new phase after the semi-truce of nearly twenty years. Under the stimulus of Frederick's free thought, Voltaire became more daring in his expression of ideas and in his criticism ; a result Chesterfield foresaw. Two more such emancipations may be mentioned ; the retreat from Berlin, which left Voltaire free from Courts and free to develop his attacks on despotism[2] ; and the publication of Rousseau's

Confession de foi d'un Vicaire Savoyard" in *Emile*, which piqued Voltaire to much sharper and more open attacks on Christianity.

Voltaire left Compiègne in June, 1750, was at Cleves on the 2nd of July, and, after passing through the desolate landscape of Westphalia,[3] reached Potsdam on the 10th. Everything delighted him and he received adulation and honours enough to content the most ambitious poet, enough to delight even his vanity. He was made chamberlain and was given a Prussian order ; he received a pension of 20,000 francs a year and the promise of a life-pension of 4,000 francs to his niece if she came to keep house for him.[4] At the visit of his sister, the Margravine of Beyreuth, Frederick departed momentarily from his economy and gave a magnificent fête, "worthy of Louis XIV", with costume quadrilles illuminated by

---

[1] They ought to have realised too that it was impossible to suppress wholly the clandestine editions of Voltaire's works, that Amsterdam, the Hague, Berlin, London, Geneva, even Lyons and Rouen would pour them out and that prohibition, as always, would stimulate interest and encourage disobedience.
[2] The pamphlet, *La Voix du Sage et du Peuple* (1750), is an example.
[3] We shall find it again in *Candide*.
[4] Letter 1625.

FREDERICK

thousands of lights. The Queen of Prussia, the Queen-mother, the princes of the blood, flattered the King's new acquisition, and Frederick himself abounded in philosophic and poetic caresses. For once, all was for the best in this best of possible worlds. In the earlier correspondence (about money) Frederick had likened himself to Jupiter and Voltaire to Danäe—a singular and grotesque comparison ; now, Voltaire likened Frederick to the Emperor Julian, Lucullus, and to Marcus Aurelius.[1] All Voltaire's letters at this period abound with eulogies of the philosopher-king and references to ill-treatment in France; if he had concealed his resentment, he had not forgotten the Chevalier de Rohan, the Bastilles, the condemnation and suppression of so many of his books. At Potsdam, at least in these early days, he was more than flattered ; he felt free ; the police would never come knocking at his door because of a jest or a sally against the clergy or an opinion contrary to Descartes or a suggestion that certain reforms of government were in accordance with justice and common sense. And there is no reason to doubt the two men's friendship. There were selfishness, self-interest, and vanity on both sides, doubtless ; but Frederick and Voltaire were the two most interesting minds of that age ; they would never lack conversation. Under Voltaire's rhetorical language we can discover a core of friendship, and there can be no doubt of Frederick's feelings for Voltaire. In a letter,[2] written in answer to objections and warnings from Mme Denis, Frederick says :

"No, my dear Voltaire, if I could foresee that your transplantation might in the least turn to your disadvantage, I should be the first to dissuade you

[1] Letter 1633.   [2] *Œuvres*, Letter 1628.

from it. Yes, I should prefer your happiness to the extreme pleasure of seeing you. But you are a philosopher ; I am the same ; what is more natural, more simple, more in the order of things, than that philosophers, made to live together, united by the same studies, the same taste, by a similar way of thought, should enjoy this satisfaction ? I respect you as my master in eloquence and knowledge ; I love you as a virtuous friend. What slavery, what misfortune, what change, what inconstancy of fortune, is there to fear in a land where you are as much esteemed as in your own country, at the house of a friend who has a warm heart ! "

Comedy ? Perhaps ; but who could resist such words from a King and that King, Frederick the Great ? Voltaire did not resist But in France his " permanent establishment " with the King of Prussia was not well received. He was deprived of his post as historiographer, but allowed to keep his pension ; Argental and Mme Denis tried hard to dissuade him from remaining in Prussia ; Mme de Pompadour and the King were deeply offended ; Voltaire's literary rivals said he had sold himself for a pension, and in the streets of Paris his portrait was hawked for six sous to the cry of " Portrait of Voltaire, the famous Prussian, in his fur cap ! " There was a storm of disapproval and argument ; but, after all, that was only another advertisement for the works of M. de Voltaire.

Life at Sans-Souci in these first months was tranquil, studious, and agreeable. Voltaire spent an hour each morning with Frederick, polishing the King's prose and verse ; the rest of the day was his own, except that Frederick expected him to be present at the philosophical supper-parties where the conversation was both free and brilliant. The philosophers of Frederick's intimacy included Maupertuis, a distinguished scientist and head of the Berlin Academy; Lord Tyrconnel, an Irish Jacobite, ambassador of France; La Mettrie, an irresponsible but clever sceptic, known as the "homme machine" from the title of his best book; Algarotti, the Italian Fontenelle; Chasot, who saved Frederick's life in battle; the Marquis d'Argens, Pollnitz, and the Jacobite Keith brothers, the elder of whom was Earl Marishal of Scotland. The conversation of Voltaire, Algarotti, and d'Argens at these suppers is said to have been remarkable for wit and brilliance; naturally, these dependents of the great king exerted all their faculties in his presence. We possess one permanent result of these discussions—the *Dictionnaire Philosophique*, first proposed as a joint work but carried out in fact by Voltaire alone. His leisure was largely devoted to the study and writing of history. *Le Siècle de Louis XIV*, begun so long before, was completed at Potsdam and published in 1751; about the same time he was studying the history of the Crusades, while several fragments of this period found their final place in the *Essai sur les Moeurs et l'Esprit des Nations*, published in 1769. These works were the fruit of more than twenty years of researches and labour.

One would like to dwell on these more smiling aspects of the Prussian Court, above all on the friendly relations of Frederick the Great and Voltaire the Great; it seem a luckless and unhappy thing for the world that the friendship of two such men should so soon be poisoned by suspicion and treachery, that the whole situation should become a comedy-farce acted for the mirth of all Europe.

VOLTAIRE

The details of the two and a half years in Prussia would easily fill this book ; yet the fundamental reasons for the discord can be shown in a few words. Though neither of the two men trusted the other, each miscalculated ; Voltaire had not foreseen that Frederick, the philosopher friend and poetic pupil, could unexpectedly give place to the cold, hard monarch who would suffer no liberties and no disobedience ; and Frederick had not realised what an incorrigible *frondeur* he had in Voltaire, that the Frenchman thought himself entitled to every freedom, recognised no authority, would in his impetuosity, in his love of gain, in his malice and vanity, stop short of nothing. If Frederick made the mistake of thinking that Voltaire would be docile and reasonable in his conduct under such flattering patronage, Voltaire was equally mistaken in supposing that his friendship with the king would enable him to do everything he liked. Voltaire would endure no rival and no master ; Frederick would not excuse Voltaire's vanity and financial speculations, and above all was enraged by his mocking Maupertuis and indirectly himself.

Do not trust the expressions of delight and boasts of happiness in Voltaire's ordinary letters to Paris ; he expressed himself freely only to Mme Denis, and already in October, 1750—less than four months after his arrival—he had sent her a letter enumerating his privileges and honours, with a significant " but " after each. Already he had discovered that his philosophic paradise bore some of the aspects of a prison ; but to everyone except Mme Denis he pretended a delicious enchantment. He could not admit so soon that he had been wrong in going to Berlin ; for vanity's sake he would not leave abruptly, and he did not mean to depart in open disgrace. Yet six months after he reached Potsdam he was bored with life there ; apart from his work, the society of Frederick and of the small circle of intimates, there was no " monde " in Prussia, there was no social and literary life like that of Paris and London. It is significant that Voltaire did not trouble to learn German as he had learned English ; for the good reason that Germany then possessed no living culture worth the trouble. Intellectually it was a French province ; and Lessing, afterwards so important in the great German literary movement, only came in contact with Voltaire in the rôle of an impudent young man who borrowed a copy of *Louis XIV* without the author's knowledge.

Once we perceive the fundamental differences between Frederick and Voltaire and feel how inevitable it was that they should quarrel, the details of the gradual estrangement become less important. So many of them are trifling matters of paltry gossip. La Mettrie told Voltaire that Frederick had said of him : "We squeeze the orange and then throw away the peel " ; and this little wound to his vanity kept the poet awake at nights. His enmity to Maupertuis, who had been formerly a warm friend to Voltaire and Mme du Châtelet, was partly the result of uncompromising vanity which would endure no rival, partly due to Voltaire's belief that Maupertuis had repeated to Frederick some of his own malicious remarks about the king, and had invented others. It is all petty, on the scale of village gossip ; we expect such things from the curate's wife and the solicitor's wife, but not from the greatest minds of the eighteenth century. If one can see the comic side of the situation, so much the better ; life can show few such comedies ; but the dignity of man is not enhanced by these antics.

VOLTAIRE

The first serious breach occurred early in 1751, through an unlucky speculation in exchanges of Voltaire's which came to light through his imprudence in taking legal action against a Jewish go-between, named Hirschell. This was indeed "une ténébreuse affaire" and no attempt will be made here to unthread its mazes.[1] Voltaire indeed won his case, but he emerged with a damaged reputation ; relying obviously upon Frederick's infatuation, he had attempted an illegal speculation and was under suspicion of falsifying a receipt. When Frederick heard of this affair he was fiercely angry ; the order for Voltaire to leave Prussia in twenty-four hours was actually given and only on second thoughts altered to a command not to appear in Frederick's presence until the case was over. Had Voltaire lost it, he would have been dismissed with ignominy. The following extracts from two letters written by Frederick to Voltaire will show the King's state of mind and some of the reasons he had to complain of Voltaire.

" . . . . you exacted that I should not take Fréron to write me news. I had the weakness or complaisance to grant it you, although it was not for you to decide whom I should take into my service. D'Arnaud did you some wrong ; a generous man would have forgiven him ; a vindictive man pursues those he hates. . . . You went to the Russian ambassador and talked of things which did not concern you and it was thought I ordered you to do so.

---

[1] See Desnoiresterres, *Voltaire et Frédéric*. Mr Lytton Strachey has written a brilliantly clever essay on Voltaire and Frederick ; everyone with the least interest in Voltaire should read it.

FREDERICK

You interfered in Mme de Bentinck's affairs, which were assuredly not in your department. Now you have the basest affair imaginable with a Jew. . . . The affair of the Saxony notes[1] is so well-known in Dresden that I have received serious complaints. . . . For my part, I maintained order in my house until your arrival ; and I warn you that if you have a passion for intrigue and cabal, you have come to the wrong place. I like quiet and peaceable people who do not put into their conduct the violent passions of a tragedy. If you can make up your mind to live as a philosopher I shall be glad to see you ; but if you yield to all the fury of your passions and bear malice against everyone, you will do me no pleasure in coming here and you may as well stay in Berlin."[2]

" . . . . I hope you will have no more quarrels with the old or the new Testament ; such compromises are damaging and the talents of the finest mind in France will not hide the stains which your conduct will finally imprint on your reputation. A bookseller Gosse [Jore], a violin-player at the Opera, a Jew goldsmith are indeed people whose names should never be found beside yours in any affair."

The rebuke is stinging and not wholly undeserved ; but was Frederick the man to make it, Frederick whose financial transactions are quite as deplorable as Voltaire's? And if Frederick thought a poet's standard of morals should be higher than a king's, Voltaire might have retorted that even a poet may prefer unscrupulous opulence to righteous penury. After such very frank speaking, cordial relations between the two men could only be superficial.

[1] Refers to Voltaire's exchange speculations.
[2] *Œuvres*, vol. 31, Letter 1701.

VOLTAIRE

The puzzle is to know why Voltaire bowed to these insults and remained another two years at Potsdam. Was it servility or dissimulation? Did he accept from a king a condemnation he would never have endured from another writer or philosopher; or did he feel that to leave Prussia then would appear so much a public disgrace that he determined to dissimulate? Or finally, did he truly think that he had behaved unworthily and honestly acknowledged it? And if the last is the true explanation, would he have admitted it to anyone but King Frederick?

The final breach occurred through Maupertuis. Neither Voltaire nor Maupertuis was the sort of man to admit a rival; both were distinguished by their talents, both were highly prized by Frederick, both were possessed of immense vanity, each was determined to oust the other, and both had few scruples about the means of doing so. The services rendered by Maupertuis to science and the Berlin Academy made him second only to Voltaire in Frederick's esteem. But the scientist's vanity was inordinate (as great as his enemy's), and involved him in ceaseless polemics; he was a man who resented the mildest criticism of himself and censured others with unreserved freedom and severity. One cannot know for certain that he spoke of Voltaire to Frederick in the terms the poet attributed to him, but it is obvious that by 1752 Voltaire and Maupertuis were completely estranged. Maupertuis's conduct in what was known as the Koenig affair was insolent and grossly domineering; Voltaire secretly supported Koenig against Maupertuis, and Maupertuis supported La Beaumelle in his libels of Voltaire. Frederick published a silly pamphlet in support of Maupertuis, justifying a scientific blunder by the mere " ipse dico " of royal authority. And then Maupertuis made his second mistake ; the first, of course, was making an enemy of the great master of ridicule ; the second was publishing his *Letters*, which contained several wild and rather foolish proposals such as digging a hole to the centre of the earth, founding a community where nothing but Latin would be spoken, and the like. Voltaire fell gleefully upon his prey and in a few weeks produced the famous *Diatribe du Dr Akakia*, a pitiless, unquenchable, unanswerable piece of raillery,which rendered the unhappy Maupertuis the laughing-stock of Europe and extinguished his reputation for life. *Dr Akakia* is such complete and witty ridicule that even Maupertuis's best friends could not help laughing at it.

Frederick himself was seized with uncontrollable laughter when Voltaire read *Akakia* to him ; he only insisted that the pamphlet should not be published and this Voltaire readily granted, of course with no intention of carrying it out. What was the use of writing the wittiest pamphlet in the world if the world was not to know and to enjoy it? Voltaire had already taken measures for the circulation of *Akakia* through Europe before he went through the solemn farce of burning it in Frederick's presence. A day or two later the King was enraged to learn that copies of *Akakia* had been smuggled into Prussia and were secretly passing from hand to hand. The insult was flagrant ; not only was Frederick derided through the president of his Academy which he valued so highly, the president he had himself defended with his royal pen ; he had been duped and derided in his own person by his irrepressible chamberlain. Frederick the Great duped and laughed at ! Yet he could take no startling revenge ; he could not dismiss Voltaire ignominiously for an offence which the culprit attributed

VOLTAIRE

to accident and the deplorable conduct of enemies ; and he was restrained from acting openly as an arbitrary monarch after so much posing as a philosophic friend. Moreover, what if Frederick himself became the hero of another *Akakia*? In the intervals of his fears at violent reprisals, the malicious old satirist must have worn his most provoking smile.

Once again the common hangman was invoked to express enraged authority's disapproval of Voltaire ; but this time it was not at despotic Paris, but at the " Athens of the North " and by command of the northern Solomon, Julian, Lucullus, and Marcus Aurelius. *Dr Akakia* was publicly and solemnly burned in the streets of Berlin on Christmas Eve, 1752. Someone informed Voltaire that a crowd had gathered about a large fire in the street outside his lodgings : " Je parie," exclaimed the pamphleteer, " que c'est mon docteur ! "[1]

Voltaire, who for months had been longing to get away from Prussia, now found his pretext. On New Year's Day, 1753, he sent Frederick his decoration, his chamberlain's key, and the order for his pension ; yet he was induced to take them again and did not leave Potsdam until March. Even then, he was too artful to admit that he had no intention of returning ; he pretended that ill-health forced him to take a temporary cure at Plombières ; but this time he did not dupe Frederick. Their last meeting was brief and frigid ; on the parade-ground. Having obtained there the King's permission to go, Voltaire did not waste a moment. He took leave of no one, and did not pause until he was safely over the Prussian frontier. What a breath of relief must he have sighed when the spires of Leipsic came into view and he

[1] Only a legend I fear, but an amusing one.

FREDERICK

could feel at last that he had escaped the prison of royal philosophy. Such were his delight and mansuetude that he spent several days at Leipsic in adding more and yet more stinging witticisms to *Akakia* and in arranging the widest possible circulation for his pamphlet.

The most remarkable scene of this Prussian adventure is yet to come. What is known as the "Frankfort incident" was a blunder on Frederick's part, aggravated by the truly Prussian behaviour of his subordinates who exceeded their orders in servile anxiety to please the Hohenzollern; it was an odious and arbitrary violation of international law and a still more odious violation of his friendship with Voltaire, of his reiterated protestations and promises. Here Frederick obviously placed himself in the wrong and by this absurd exercise of tyranny secured for his victim the sympathy of contemporaries and of posterity. Even though Voltaire did not meet this outrage with the firmness and dignity one would wish, though in more than one scene he played a comic or even deplorable part, he came out of it on the whole with enhanced prestige. We may regret for his sake that he was compelled to endure this singular brutality, but we are the gainers by it. After Frankfort, Voltaire could have few illusions about despots, philosophic or otherwise; at last he learned his lesson and, at an age when most men have finished their work, he began a new career—perhaps the most important to posterity—that of the patriarch of Ferney, the reformer of abuses, the enemy of arbitrary power, the defender of the weak and unfortunate. Naturally, most of the old weaknesses remained; and we must admit that he did not take this course until every court in Europe seemed closed to him; but it is important for us and the world that he did take

VOLTAIRE

it, that Frederick's violence at length removed the only restraint to the full and vigorous prosecution of the Philosopher's War, for which he found able auxiliaries in the contributors to the *Encyclopédie*.

Voltaire has related the events at Frankfort with his customary verve and exaggerations[1] ; but there is no necessity to rely on his account alone. The Prussian archives have yielded up original documents which give the other side of the story ; between them we have an edifying tale.

In the eighteenth century Frankfort was a free city ; de jure owning no authority but its own and the suzerainty of the Emperor, de facto compelled to subservience to the greater powers near it and in particular to the majesty of Prussia. Voltaire probably believed he was safe from Frederick's resentment as long as he remained outside Prussian territory ; and we may well surmise that he had fully determined never to pass its frontier again. But Frederick in his anger or his interest cared little for frontiers and international law.[2] After Voltaire's departure Frederick, who had hitherto controlled his anger tolerably well, must have reflected on Voltaire's real and supposed offences until he had worked himself into a state of resentful indignation, increased no doubt by the Leipsic additions to *Akakia*. It will be remembered that Voltaire had taken back his insignia of office and his pension-warrant after resigning them in January; he had not returned them when leaving Potsdam in March, probably because he felt compelled to pretend

[1] *Œuvres*, vol. 23, pp. 331, 332. There exists another account of the affair by Voltaire, probably written for the Austrian envoy at Frankfort.
[2] Witness the kidnapping of Baron Trenck in the free city of Danzig by Prussian myrmidons under orders from Frederick the Great.

FREDERICK

that his departure was only temporary. In addition to these properties of the Prussian King, Voltaire took with him a presentation volume of Frederick's privately-printed poems and some of his letters and manuscripts. This volume of poems contained a burlesque macaronic work entitled the *Palladion* which Frederick was strongly desirous of keeping for intimate perusal only, its nature being such that he judged publicity inadvisable ; and, in reflecting upon the matter, he must have seen that his own conduct in the past, when he betrayed Voltaire's confidence by sending a private poem to the French ministry, gave Voltaire every excuse for retaliating upon him in a like way. To prevent any use of these documents and, no doubt, as an intentional insult, orders were sent to one Freytag, the Prussian Minister at Frankfort, to intercept Voltaire and to request him to hand over the insignia of office, the documents, and above all the famous book of "*poëshies* du roi mon gracieux maître". If Voltaire refused he was to be threatened with arrest and, if needful, arrested and not released until he complied.

This Freytag was not an ex-convict, as Voltaire asserted ; he was a Prussian Dogberry of a stiff, efficient sort, servile to superiors, domineering to others. He took his ambiguous orders from Potsdam with the greatest seriousness and made elaborate plans to waylay this enemy of the Fatherland. Voltaire arrived at Frankfort on the 31st of May, 1753. The next morning he received a visit, as unexpected as it was disagreeable, from his excellency Freytag, accompanied by Councillor Schmid, Ratsherr Rucker, and a recruiting officer named Brettwitz. Imagine the gaze of the astonished poet as these four worthies entered his appartment in rigid order, clicked heels and saluted in unison, according to the gospel

VOLTAIRE

of Prussian "Infantry Training". After the "usual greetings of politeness"—these are Freytag's own words—Freytag "informed Voltaire of his gracious Majesty's will", which was that the objects specified should be handed over at once, and if not, that M. de Voltaire would be placed under arrest until such time as he should comply with his Majesty's pleasure—placed under arrest, if you please, by the Prussian envoy to a "free city" outside the jurisdiction of Prussia. Voltaire's reply was to feign a swoon ; no doubt to gain time to arrange his thoughts. On recovery, Voltaire called for his secretary, opened his baggage, and swooned again. For eight hours that day he was afflicted with the presence of these creatures All the required effects were handed over and all Voltaire's own papers were taken from him, carefully sealed, and sent to Potsdam. Unfortunately, the "*poêshies* du roi mon gracieux maître" were in a box at Leipsic—no great proof of Voltaire's regard for them—and he was forced to consent to remain in captivity at the Lion d'Or until the box could be obtained. He signed a paper to that effect and gave it to Freytag.

Except for the artificial swoons, Voltaire endured this day with firmness and dignity. There is something almost sublime in his sitting down calmly to work at his *Annales de l'Empire* as soon as the door closed on his tormentors. That, as Desnoiresterres says, is Voltaire's strength ; the storms, the griefs, the persecutions in his life, the vanities and furibund rages, never darkened that clear mind ; the weak humanity in Voltaire was dismissed with a gesture, and the great master sat down at his writing-table. Miserably enough, this calm dignity did not endure. Dorn, a bookseller Voltaire believed had cheated him, suddenly came upon him in

FREDERICK

the garden of the Lion d'Or; Voltaire darted forward in a rage and slapped the man's face, a foolish piece of humour which cost him some score of ducats. Then, he had reflected no doubt on the arbitrary nature of these Prussian proceedings, and, relying on the dubious aid of the Burgomaster of Frankfort, felt himself able to make some resistance. " Comment ! " said he to Freytag[1], " Votre roi me veut arrêter ici, dans une ville impériale ? Pourquoi ne l'a-t-il pas fait dans ses États ? " Why not, indeed? And Voltaire's restlessness and apprehensions were still further increased by his impatience and by Freytag's firm refusal to allow him to leave the inn. That evening he sent a long and pathetic letter of protest to the Emperor, relating his plight and requesting the protection of the Austrian minister at Frankfort. He repeated these requests later, but the Imperial Majesty of the Holy Roman Empire could not be moved to action in so slight an affair.

On the 9th of June, Mme Denis arrived from Strasbourg and wrote immediately in her own name, but plainly at Voltaire's dictation, to d'Argenson, Frederick, and Keith, the Prussian ambassador in Paris. She was indirectly involved in the affair, for Frederick had demanded the return of his pension-grant to her ; and this could not be found. She promised on her Uncle's behalf the immediate return of the " poëshies " and the pension, and respectfully and rightly reminded Frederick of the many flattering promises[2] he had formerly made to Voltaire.

At last the box from Leipsic arrived on the 18th.[3] Once

[1] Freytag's letter to Frederick of 5th June, 1753.
[2] See, for example, Frederick's letter (*Œuvres*, Letter 1628) quoted above, p. 84.
[3] Voltaire says the 17th.

VOLTAIRE

the " poëshies " were handed over Voltaire believed he would be free to go—what else could be wanted of him when he had complied with all the King's demands? And had he not Freytag's written promise to this effect? But subsequent orders from Potsdam had confused Freytag's mind, and he informed Voltaire that he must continue a prisoner until the mail came in from Prussia on Thursday, the 21st, with fresh orders from Frederick. This note filled Voltaire with anger and consternation ; not unjustifiably, considering Freytag was violating his agreement and that this adjournment for " further orders " appeared to promise a sinister future. " A year's imprisonment at Spandau " were words commonly in Frederick's mouth and were easily spoken ; so, although Voltaire's fears were in fact groundless and due only to the imbecility of an underling, a more phlegmatic man might reasonably have felt the same apprehensions.

When Voltaire was in this mood of mingled resentment and terror, he invariably made mistake after mistake. He began by insulting Freytag's servant and then apologised abjectly and excessively ; worse than this, he planned an escape, leaving all his baggage behind. On the 29th he and his secretary Coligni slipped out of the Lion d'Or, hired a chaise, and were almost out of the territory of Frankfort when Freytag and his soldiers caught them. The Frankfort non-commissioned officer took the grave responsibility of arresting a French subject at the mere request of a foreign envoy ; the fugitives were taken back to Frankfort in a carriage surrounded with soldiers and were placed in the house of Councillor Schmid. Meanwhile, the intelligent Freytag had decided that Mme Denis was not Voltaire's niece, but his " Weibsmensch "—a shameless baggage ! Meeting her

FREDERICK

at the Burgomaster's house where she had gone to protest, Freytag so worked on this magistrate that Mme Denis was arrested, taken through the town, and imprisoned at the Lion d'Or.

At Schmid's house Voltaire and Coligni were subjected to further insults and outrage. Their money was taken from them and Voltaire was even deprived of his watch, snuff-box, and rings. When Voltaire asked for a receipt, Schmid said to his clerk, "Count the money, these rogues[1] are capable of claiming twice as much as there is." Then, Voltaire twice rushed out to the garden (while Frau Schmid and the clerks and Coligni tore after him) and tried to make himself sick in order to be pathetic. "Fingo ! Fingo !"[2] he whispered in reply to Coligni's anxious enquiries. Schmid then raged at Voltaire—"Wretch ! you shall be treated without pity and without consideration !" Growing calmer but thirsty from these noble efforts, Schmid called for wine and drank to the health of "His Excellency Monseigneur Freytag". Could Desfontaines or Maupertuis or the Grand Inquisitor himself have imagined a more ingenious and grotesque humiliation ? To add the final touch "His Excellency Monseigneur Freytag" informed Voltaire that "if he had dared to set foot in the territory of Mayence he would have put a pistol-bullet in his head !"

After two hours spent in these amenities, Voltaire's effects were placed in an empty valise and sealed. The prisoners were then taken, under armed escort, to the Corne de Bouc, since the proprietor of the Lion d'Or now refused to receive them. Voltaire and Coligni were placed in separate rooms and guarded by soldiers

---
[1] "Drôles", in the French account.
[2] Italian: "I'm pretending."

with fixed bayonets. While this was going on, a certain Dorn (an accomplice of Freytag's) went to the Lion d'Or and offered to escort Mme Denis to her uncle at the other inn. At the door she was seized by three soldiers and dragged through the streets in the midst of a crowd; at the Corne de Bouc Dorn had her placed in a garret, guarded by soldiers, and ate his supper there. According to Voltaire, Dorn got drunk, spent the night in Mme Denis's room and tried to ravish her; an enterprise from which he desisted at the shrill cries of his victim.

Altogether, the events of this day were a great triumph for Prussian arms and the glory of Frederick the Great. An old man of sixty, who happened to be the greatest living French author, his niece and secretary, were deprived of liberty, dragged violently through the streets of Frankfort, robbed, insulted, and placed under the restraint of a guard-room. Such were the inconveniences suffered by "Apollo" when "Marcus Aurelius" lost his temper.

The captivity lasted another seventeen days. The sufferings of the prisoners compelled Voltaire to wretched humiliations—a letter from Mme Denis to Frederick, a letter from himself to Freytag, even concessions to Dorn. On the 25th of June, Freytag received orders from Potsdam to release Voltaire at once; but, unluckily, this letter was not in answer to Freytag's indignant report on Voltaire's effort to escape. The stupid official had now taken it into his head that some "punishment" would certainly be meted out to this insolent defier of the majesty of Prussia; and so he determined not to release the party until the answer came to this report. Meanwhile, the town council and Burgomaster of Frankfort at last grew uneasy about this succession of

FREDERICK

illegal violences. The Burgomaster paid a visit to Voltaire who immediately handed him a written protest to the Emperor. Voltaire now regained courage; he refused to receive Freytag and Schmid, refused to take back a portion of his plundered property which they sent him and swore an affidavit before a notary against them. On the 26th of June and again on the 2nd of July, Frederick sent peremptory orders for Voltaire's release; and at length Freytag began to feel that he had blundered, at any rate in his methods.

On the morning of the 7th of July, Voltaire committed his last indiscretion in this affair. Dorn was sent to him with the balance of his money, after deducting 122 *talers* a day for the expenses of a hospitality which had assuredly not been requested. The sight of this Dorn and the memory of his insolence to Mme Denis roused Voltaire to such a fury that he rushed at the man with a pistol; fortunately Coligni ran forward and prevented a homicide, but of course Dorn and Freytag made the most of this incident. Finally, Voltaire and Coligni got out of the town and directed their way towards Mainz.

His Excellency Freytag, Councillor Schmid, Ratsherr Rucker, Herr Leutnant Brettwitz, and the amiable Dorn, received only the slightest of rebukes from His Prussian Majesty and continued on their respective paths of inoffensive virtue, unconscious that they had rendered their names immortal and infamous.[1]

[1] By an odd coincidence one of the noblest minds of Germany and indeed of Europe was present at Frankfort during these extraordinary scenes; Goethe, then a child of four, was living in Frankfort with his family in 1753.

IX

THE PATRIARCH OF FERNEY

(1753-1778)

After these events, Voltaire, disgusted with despotism, withdrew to an austere seclusion and devoted the remaining years of his life to a stern war whose object was to overthrow the monarchy, to humiliate the noblesse, to abolish " Jesuitry and the powers of darkness ", and to establish Liberty, Equality, and Fraternity? To make such a statement would be to misunderstand completely both Voltaire and the society of his time. Voltaire had a profound dislike for martyrdom and he was not a fanatic, even in the matter of Shakespeare, the Bible, and l'infâme. He had serious purposes, but he was a mocker and a "malin" ; he had none of the solemn pedantry which marked the generation of 1790, none of the facile declamations and chimerical projects of the Rousseauites. As a reformer he was an opportunist ; he took society as it was and pressed only for those reforms which were immediately realizable. If he thought democracy the most reasonable form of government, he held that it was only suitable for small countries and that the interest of order and peace demanded that the Frenchman should be a royalist.[1] He had so many friends among the nobility and was himself so proud of his droits de seigneur that we can be certain he wished only to reform and not to abolish that privileged part of the nation. When

[1] Lanson, pp. 180-181.

the Jesuits were suppressed, Voltaire was one of the first to regret a step which strengthened the more austere and fanatical Jansenists[1]; and he was far more delighted by Maupeou's exile of the Jansenist Parlement de Paris. It was no part of Voltaire's programme to make men virtuous in spite of themselves or to enroll them forcibly in a ready-made system for attaining the perfect life. Tolerance is the virtue he most commended, though he did not always practise it; he wanted people to be just and reasonable, and thought they would more likely become so by living comfortably and enjoying life than by paying too many taxes, listening to gloomy sermons, and despising the good things of this life. His resentment was swift but not rancourous; he was too successful and too wealthy to feel envy for success and wealth. Rousseau's "back to nature" struck Voltaire as being merely silly[2]; the only work of Rousseau's he admired was the *Vicaire Savoyard*. We must be careful, therefore, not to exaggerate the heroism of Voltaire's Philosopher's War. He had the honour of beginning it and endured discomfort and persecution, but he never intended to carry matters "à outrance" and to compromise himself completely with the ruling classes; Voltaire's adherents numbered many royal and noble personages.

The ovation Voltaire received on arriving at Mainz (7th of July, 1753) may have been a sop to his damaged vanity, but it was impossible for him not to realize that events and his own indiscretions had placed him in a very awkward position. He naturally felt insecure in Germany, yet did not know where to go; his object was to return

---

[1] "Jansenist" is used here as a sort of French equivalent to "puritan."
[2] See letter to Rousseau, *Œuvres*, vol. 32, Letter 2245.

VOLTAIRE

to Paris, but he had so offended Louis XV that permission to do so was refused him.[1] To attain this object, which became almost an idée fixe with him, he stopped short of no humiliation. Despairing letters to his "angels" (the d'Argentals), flattery to the minister, to Mme de Pompadour, to Louis XV, were the least of his subterfuges ; when a pirated edition of his *Abrégé de l' Histoire Universelle* gave offence to authority, he disclaimed it on oath before a notary, and he went to the length of taking the Sacrament at Easter, 1754, to give "proof" of his orthodoxy. This was not the only time he went through this sacrilegious farce with some ulterior object. But all was in vain, and he was compelled to accept the situation and to organize his life at a distance from the delights of Paris, for which he pined so impatiently. We owe the patriarch of Ferney to the prejudice of Louis XV.

The negotiations for a return to Paris occupied some time, and Voltaire did not abandon them until he was forced to recognize their hopelessness. His ever-growing wealth, his age, the necessity for a hole to hide in, a bourgeois joy in property, all urged him to set up an establishment of his own ; but the sense of insecurity kept him hesitant. Part of 1753 and most of 1754 were spent in Alsace, at Strasbourg, and Colmar, but any thoughts of a permanent settlement there were quenched by an agitation against him worked up by the Jesuits. In June, 1754, he spent a month at a Benedictine monastery, with the learned Dom Calmet, and from

[1] The general impression in France was that a lettre de cachet had been issued against Voltaire. When he returned to Paris at the end of his life, Louis XVI was so certain of this that he ordered the registers to be searched for it, but no lettre de cachet was found. Possibly Voltaire was threatened with one by Louis XV if he returned to Paris.

there proceeded to Plombières where he met Mme Denis and his "angels". The result of discussions with the d'Argentals was to destroy any lingering hope of a return to Paris and, on separating from them, Voltaire and Mme Denis went back to Colmar. He spent three months there in cruel uncertainty. At one time he thought seriously of transferring himself to Pennsylvania, where he would assuredly have cut an odd figure among Penn's Quakers. Finally, after a visit to Lyons and a sharp encounter with Cardinal Tencin, he fixed upon Switzerland. He rented a winter house at Monrion between Lausanne and Lake Leman and he spent 87,000 livres on a summer residence (which he called "Les Délices") near Geneva.

Voltaire plunged with his usual enthusiasm into the joys and responsibilities of proprietorship. "Mme Denis and I", he writes to Thiériot, "are engaged in building rooms for our guests and our chickens. We are getting carriages and wheelbarrows; we are planting oranges and onions, tulips and carrots."[1] He even became interested in "Nature" and discoursed rapturously of his views across the Lake and the Rhone, to Geneva, the open country, and the Alps. He liked to boast that the Rhone ran past the end of his garden and, in his new enthusiasm for a rustic life, he trimmed vines, cut trees, knocked down walls. His household at Les Délices consisted of Mme Denis, a secretary, a French cook, a scullion, a valet de chambre, a valet de campagne, two lackeys, a coachman, and a postillion. He had four carriages and six mares. It occurred to him later that he might found a stud with these mares, and he set energetically about horse-breeding; unfortunately, the stallion

[1] *Œuvres*, vol. 32, Letter 2171.

VOLTAIRE

he procured was too old and to the philosopher's surprise and chagrin his seraglio produced no offspring, which gave rise to almost as many risky jests as the adventures of La Pucelle.

With an income approaching 100,000 livres, he could afford to live in luxury, to give dinners, to entertain the ever increasing hordes of distinguished pilgrims to his shrine, to build a private theatre where Le Kain acted for him. His doctor was Tronchin, the famous physician of Geneva, so renowned for his defence of "inoculation" for small-pox against ignorant opposition. His lavish expenditure persuaded the authorities of Geneva to wink at his religious views, but the scandal of his private theatricals called down the wrath of the godly and he was compelled to abandon them in Geneva, though they were allowed in Lausanne. In 1756, he gave money to help fit out a punitive expedition against the Jesuits of Paraguay.[1]

At Les Délices and Lausanne he re-wrote his *Histoire Universelle* and took prodigious, unveracious, and useless pains to deny his authorship of *La Pucelle*. The earthquake of Lisbon strengthened his doubts concerning the beneficence of Providence and the optimism of Leibnitz. His poem, *Le Désastre de Lisbon*, expressing these doubts, was disapproved of by Jean Jacques, who criticised it in a pamphlet and maintained that " tout est bien ". Voltaire grimaced at this, made no direct answer, but meditated a counter-blast ; when it appeared it was called *Candide*. He tried to save Byng's life, chicaned with Grasset, lost his secretary Coligni, quarrelled courteously with Haller,

---

[1] This was one of Voltaire's worst sins. The Jesuit state of Paraguay was a sort of earthly paradise under their enlightened rule.

THE PATRIARCH OF FERNEY

acted as intermediary between the desperate[1] Frederick and the French Government. The miracle of Rossbach saved Frederick from the suicide he had announced and their correspondence languished once more, not to be renewed until 1765. If we feel surprised at any renewal of correspondence after the events of Frankfort, it is because we fail to realize the extraordinary attraction of each of these two minds for the other.

The disturbances and anger at Geneva which followed d'Alembert's article on Genève in the *Encyclopaedia*—in the writing of which he had been abetted and encouraged by the philosophical brother at Les Délices—and a renewal of underground rumblings about theatres, decided Voltaire in the opinion that his virtuous Swiss were not as obsequious to genius as could be wished. He formed and carried out a strategical plan which was as artful as only Voltaire could devise. He bought the estates of Ferney and Tournay (which carried with it the inappreciable advantage of the title, Comte de Tournay, so useful to put after "gentilhomme ordinaire du roi" on letters and legal documents) and these estates were situated in the district of Gex in France, just over the Swiss frontier, and close to his Geneva and Lausanne properties. Thus, as he said, he had his front legs in Switzerland and his hind legs in France. Did the King of France appear at the point of openly resenting *Candides* and *Encyclopédies* and *Pucelles*, it was only necessary to harness the six mares to the coach and a short drive brought the erring philosopher to safety and Switzerland; and, similarly, another short drive would leave the Magnificent Council helpless. The only point to observe was not to be at war with both authorities at once. What

[1] After the disaster of the Seven Years War.

VOLTAIRE

could be more neat and desirable? The seigneurial privileges of Ferney were confirmed to Voltaire through the influence of Choiseul who had his reasons for conciliating the friend of Frederick the Great and the correspondent of Catherine of Russia. After 1760, Voltaire resided principally in the Château de Ferney, which he had re-built.

There is one incident worth repeating because of its light on Voltaire's character. His busy and happy life at Ferney was only seriously disturbed once. In 1765, the Chevalier de la Barre was executed for mutilating a crucifix; among the victim's possessions were many Voltaire pamphlets, and the *Dictionnaire Philosophique* was burned with the body. Certain ecclesiastical resentments threatened Voltaire, but he was in no real danger. An extraordinary panic seized him; Ferney must be abandoned, life was intolerable and too dangerous in France; d'Alembert, Diderot, and the rest must fly immediately and they would form a colony of "philosophes" at Cleves. The poor old man was in such a state that Tronchin came out from Geneva to console him, pointed out how ridiculous these fears were, and asked him point-blank why he gave way to them. Voltaire gazed at him, acknowledged his arguments were just, and then exclaimed, " Je suis fou ", and burst into tears. Might we not justifiably see a sort of Bastille-complex here, an unreasoning apprehension of imprisonment which harried him into these vain terrors?

Apart from this momentary failure, the patriarch of Ferney lived in the enjoyment of his immense fame and even more immense activities. With his superb sense of advertisement and his capacity for amusing people, he performed the extraordinary feat of keeping all Europe interested

THE PATRIARCH OF FERNEY

in him for over twenty years. A rumour of his death had to be contradicted officially to allay the public excitement. The colics, the communions, the gardening, the philanthropy, the manufactures, the guests, the pamphlets, the bons-mots, the private theatricals, of M. de Voltaire, each and all of his thousand and one activities, excited the interest, applause, laughter, disapprobation, enthusiasm of Europe. He attained a prestige and influence which has perhaps never been the lot of any other man whose power was the intangible one of words. Les Délices and Ferney were a rendezvous for tourists of all nations, who refused to go away until they had caught a glimpse of the active old man, with his thin face, glittering eyes, and indescribable smile, dressed either in his " robe de chambre de perse " or in his " noble habit mordoré ", with the large wig and the long lace ruffles at the wrist. Favoured visitors might be admitted to his bedroom, where he read and wrote indefatigably, or be allowed to take part in the incessant private theatricals. It seemed as if his wit grew sharper, his prose more masterly, his conversation more sparkling, as he drew nearer to eighty. The new generation of French writers were his disciples; who but Voltaire himself cared what Clément or Fréron said when d'Alembert, Diderot, Marmontel, Grimm, and Holbach were at his feet? Beautiful and accomplished young women trembled before meeting him, as if they were going to meet a lover, fell on their knees before him and kissed his withered hand with tears in their eyes.

His distinguished visitors were innumerable—d'Alembert, Mme d'Épinay, Mme du Bocage, Gibbon, Sherlock, Moore, Bertinelli, Palissot, Le Kain, Turgot, Marmontel, Chauvelin, le Duc de Villars, le Duc de Richelieu, l'abbé Morellet, Laborde, le Président de Brosses, le

VOLTAIRE

Chevalier de Boufflers, Florian, Chabanon, Grétry, La Harpe, Dr Burney, Casanova, Séguier, Condorcet, Mme Suard, Denon, Mme de Genlis, the Margrave of Hesse, the prince of Brunswick, the prince de Ligne. All that was most distinguished in Europe came to pay homage to the alert, sober, witty, mocking old man, who seduced even the hostile who came prepared to resist his charm.

In these latter years Voltaire gave the support of his fame, his pen, and his energy to the party of reform which he had himself created. The project of the *Encyclopaedia* stimulated his enthusiasm and he rained articles upon d'Alembert, treating every subject from Force to Fornication, from Gazette to Grace.[1] He even acquired a little of the fanaticism of the Encyclopaedists and laboured intolerantly for the cause of toleration ; "écrasez l'infâme" occurs and recurs in his letters with monotonous malice. As he felt the support of followers and public opinion, he grew bolder in his expressions of hatred for Christianity and priests, for lawyers and tax-farmers. The Philosopher's War he had begun so long ago with his *Lettres Philosophiques* was now in full swing, supported by the very society it was attacking and eventually destroyed. Do not ask for consistency and tolerance from these "philosophes" ; any weapon was good to "écraser l'infâme". If the presence of fossil shells on mountain-tops give the "infâme" an argument in favour of the deluge, let us deny that there are shells there or say they were dropped on the Alps by pilgrims. If the devout party satirize us in a comedy, *Les Philosophes*, with what dignity do we and M d'Alembert express our

[1] Many of these articles re-appeared in the *Dictionnaire Philosophique*.

contempt for this ignoble practice of bringing on to the stage the persons of our greatest writers ; but with what gleeful chuckles of malice we set about libelling the obscure Fréron in the character of " Frélon " in the comedy L'Écossaise. No matter, écrasez l'infâme !

One must try to be just. While the Church had control over men's minds, toleration was impossible ; for the Catholic Church will only endure toleration when it is a minority power. As long as the Church held immense wealth and paid taxes only as a voluntary gift, the fearful injustices in the distribution of wealth could not be obliterated. Ferocious sentences of death would be passed on innocent Protestants like Calas and Sirven, on foolish youths like the Chevalier de la Barre, as long as ignorant judges and fanatical mobs could be worked upon by Catholic prejudices. Even Voltaire, prepared for any infamy from l'infâme, stood aghast at discovering that the canons of Saint-Claude in his district still owned serfs, and his discouragement was black when he found he could not alter the situation. Serfs in the eighteenth century, serfs within a few miles of Ferney ! It was not surprising that intolerance and abuse bred intolerance and abuse in the reformers.

There were two methods—two weapons—employed by Voltaire as he became more and more absorbed in this contest ; precept and example. He soon saw that an expensive book like the *Encyclopaedia* (it cost 1,200 livres), even when not suppressed or censored, could only reach a small audience. To reach the great mass of men, cheap, readable, convincing pamphlets, " costing no more than the gospels ", were needed. Voltaire was exactly the man for this sort of journalism. He was interested in everything, he had very wide if not profound learning,

VOLTAIRE

and an exact knowledge of men; he knew precisely the tastes and prejudices of his audience; he possessed unbounded fertility, unflagging energy, and wit; he could serve up any serious idea or piece of propaganda in the sparkling champagne style which intoxicated his readers. Pamphlets, letters, speeches, sermons, pleadings, edicts, dialogues, biographies, anecdotes, poured from the unquenchable sources of Ferney; few or none were signed except by that unmistakable style of witty malice. It was useless for the authorities to condemn and to try to suppress these "rogatons" (odds and ends), as Voltaire called them; they were too popular, too profitable to booksellers. They sprang up everywhere, appeared at coffee-houses, on dressing-tables, wrapped round parcels of books, under doors. The innumerable visitors to Ferney unconsciously became part of the system of distribution, for how could they resist the flattery of a handful or a box-full of pamphlets from the Patriarch and how resist showing them to friends? And the devil of it was, the old man wrote with such verve and sparkle that once a reader started he was compelled to finish the pamphlet and as like as not was convinced by it. The results of this twenty years' bombardment of pamphlets are inestimable; they had a far wider and deeper effect than the Encyclopaedia. Satirical little masterpieces like *Candide* and the *Princesse de Babylon*, personal satires on people like le Franc Pompignon, *Les Quand, Les Ah! Ah!* the *Relation du Voyage*—crushing, annihilating to the victim—pamphlets against "l'infâme", *Extrait des Sentiments de Jean Meslier, Sermon des Cinquante, Lettre d'un Quaker*, political and miscellaneous tracts, *L'Homme aux quarante écus, Lettres d'Amabed, Sermon prêché à Bâle, Pyrrhonisme de l'Histoire, Canonisation*

THE PATRIARCH OF FERNEY

de Saint Cucufin, Profession de foi d'un théiste; these and innumerable others found their way everywhere and exerted an incalculable influence on public opinion.

Voltaire laboured also by example. He found Ferney a wretched hamlet of huts; he left it a flourishing and prosperous village. Expert watch- and clock-makers were allowed to settle at Ferney; houses were built for them; religious toleration was enforced; so that Protestant and Catholic worked harmoniously together: while Voltaire advertised his watches all over Europe, praised them in letters to kings, empresses, and grand dukes, and ambassadors, who hastened obediently to buy them. He founded a silk manufactory and sent the first pair of stockings, made with his own hands, to the Duchesse de Choiseul; of course, all the other Court ladies had to wear Ferney stockings. He started lace-making; turned himself into a first-rate farmer; cultivated his land scientifically; made experiments in agriculture; struggled with the climate to preserve his young trees, failed four times and persisted to success; advocated scientific afforestation. He negotiated and carried out successfully a scheme for ridding the district of Gex of the tax-farmers by a fixed annual payment. Having made the announcement to the "trois états" of Gex and received their consent, he poked his head out of window and shouted "Vive la liberté!" to the crowd of tenants, who responded with, "Vive le Roi! Vive M. de Voltaire!"[1] They cheered and escorted him home to Ferney. And then what a stream of letters to illustrious correspondents, so that all Europe should know it! What an example and reproof to Versailles, what an encouragement to the "enlightened" and the "philosophic"! Ah, ce bonhomme de Voltaire!

[1] Probably apocryphal, but a pleasant story.

VOLTAIRE

C'est un philosophe, c'est un dieu ! Vive Voltaire !

But the enthusiasm for ameliorations and wise government waned before the enthusiasm for Voltaire the protector of the weak, the defender of the innocent. Perhaps there was more ironic malice than true charity in giving alms to ex-Jesuits who knocked at the doors of Ferney to ask for employment ; and it was surely cruel to send a message to know if they had come for the post of lackey. The same gleeful malice suggested to Voltaire that another ex-Jesuit, Père Adam, should be taken into his house as chess-player and audience for anti-Christian pleasantries. Although it was annoying to find Père Adam's chess-playing too good for him, Voltaire was compensated by being able to write to the Bishop of Annecy about " my almoner, Father Adam ", by teasing the phlegmatic priest with impieties, and by calling, " Adam, where art thou ? " when the Jesuit's services were required. A more genuine spirit of compassion inspired him to send a large sum of money to the French prisoners taken by Frederick at Rossbach.

As we have noticed, Voltaire's first impulses were often generous. Immediately he heard that the last of the Corneille family was in distress, he dashed off an impulsive letter—" Send her to me ". And, although he was disappointed to find Mlle Corneille was not a direct descendant of the poet, he carried out his obligations loyally and generously and wrote a huge commentary to an edition of Corneille in order to provide her with a dowry. The cynical may object that Voltaire was rich enough to gratify such impulses with no particular sacrifice and that the whole affair was a most successful advertisement for himself. The same mixed motives may be detected in his plunge into ecclesiastical architecture ; his church cost him money but it enabled him to annoy the clergy, to improve his view, to put up the inscription " Deo erexit Voltaire," and to say " ôtez-moi cette potence " when the crucifix outside the old church was removed. Such pleasures were surely worth a few thousand livres. And then he could play his farce of taking the sacrament at Easter, to the confusion of both friends and enemies ; while as seigneur and church benefactor he even dared to preach during Mass a little sermon against theft.

By intervention in cases of judicial error and oppression, like the Calas and Sirven affairs, Voltaire best displayed his generosity and love of justice and wrung approval even from his enemies. There is no need to enlarge upon the defective and mediaeval machinery of justice in eighteenth century France. Reverence for precedent, attachment to the letter of the law, the effort to bend changed ways of life to obsolete statutes, habits of chop-logic, pedantry and cynicism masquerading as austerity, habitual distrust of human nature and of generous impulses, professional vanity, all these render members of the legal profession liable to fanatical reaction, to frigid cruelty, to oppressive injustice, in an often honest passion for social order. The worst traits of the legal mind were embodied in some of the eighteenth century French judicial tribunals ; they not only exercised the usual privilege of being the most reactionary part of society, they armed themselves with bigotry and fanaticism, they wielded torture, they involved the simplest affair in a huge tangle of procedure, they hampered common sense with a long heritage of old laws made by other ages for other conditions. In attacking them Voltaire attacked abuses almost as venerable and even more oppressive than the rapacity and intolerance of the clergy, the absurd and unjust fiscal system, the inequalities

VOLTAIRE

of privilege, the extravagance of the Court, the corruptions of favouritism. The cases of Calas and Sirven were peculiarly important because they showed how the judiciary might be influenced by religious intolerance to condemn Protestants to torture and death, when the evidence was not only insufficient to secure conviction, but plainly pointed to the innocence of the accused persons.

There was a great similarity in these cases ; both the Calas and Sirven families were accused of murdering one of their children for becoming a Catholic, when the victim had, in fact, committed suicide. An ambiguous but fanatical precept of Calvin's about parental authority gave colour to the popular Catholic belief that such murders were enjoined on Protestants by their religion. Calas was broken alive on the wheel, his sons exiled, his wife ruined, his daughters imprisoned in convents ; the Sirven family, warned by the fate of the Calas, fled to Geneva and were condemned in their absence. On the first rumours of the Calas case, Voltaire, like every one else, believed that a dreadful crime had been committed ; reflection and several interviews with survivors of the Calas family convinced him that bigotry and judicial intolerance had condemned innocent persons to a dreadful fate. He devoted himself to securing a reversal of the verdict against Calas, the rehabilitation of the family, and the release of the daughters. It was a prodigious task, for against the immense allied forces of the judiciary and the clergy, he had only his pen, his power over public opinion, and his influence with eminent persons. The matter was not one to be settled by writing a few letters and pamphlets and spending a little money ; it needed intense and persistent energy, uncommon ability in negociation, considerable expenditure, an artful but irrefutable

THE PATRIARCH OF FERNEY

and untiring appeal to public opinion. The contest lasted for years (it was nine years before the Sirven case was finally settled) and Voltaire had nothing to urge him on but his sense of justice and his pity for the victims.

It is always hard to visualize these occurrences of another age ; let us try to imagine an analagous case in our own time. Let us suppose that a church has been robbed, that no culprit is discovered, that it is proved that an atheistic Communist had visited the building with two members of his family on the day of the crime. Now, it is not impossible that the unconscious prejudices of judge and jury would allow them to accept as evidence what was really only suspicion founded on the fact that the prisoner was admittedly an atheist and a Communist, for whom sacrilege was no crime and private property not sacred. And let us suppose that Mr. Bernard Shaw came to the conclusion that the man had been unjustly sentenced, and with characteristic generosity determined to get the sentence revoked. The difficulties he would have to overcome, the prejudices, and opposition he would have to face, the dangers he would run, would not be one tenth of those confronted by Voltaire in the cases of Calas and Sirven. This at least enables us to understand the prestige and admiration Voltaire acquired by his finally successful championship of these unfortunates. Add to this that his action and pamphlets convinced innumerable people of the existence of religious intolerance and judicial partiality, such as would be unlikely in our time, and it will be seen how great a service he performed for France, for justice, and for tolerance. Allowing for all differences of time and circumstance, the "affaire Calas", if less important than the "affaire Dreyfus", made nearly as much noise. The affairs of Monbailli, Lally, Morangies,

VOLTAIRE

d'Étallonde—the companion of the unfortunate de la Barre—were subsidiary to those of Calas and Sirven, and only served to show the frequency of these judicial errors.

It is pleasant to think of the old man in this halo of adoration, reconciled with Frederick, reconciled with Buffon, sculptured by Pigalle, admired by innumerable readers, rich, successful, beneficent. Little reproductions of his features were circulated throughout Europe. In 1772, Mlle Clairon crowned his bust with laurel before a circle of admirers and recited an ode in his praise. The only sign of age was that he became rather more obstinate. He wrote a tragedy when he was over eighty, worked in his garden until he was seventy-six, was as " malin " and witty and charming at eighty-three as he had been at twenty-three. Perhaps he felt sometimes distressed by the prolongation of his quarrel with Jean Jacques—he certainly was piqued when Jean Jacques subscribed two louis towards Pigalle's statue—but he assuredly enjoyed skirmishing by pamphlet with his hordes of minor enemies; for by this time battle was the very breath of his nostrils and you could have done M. de Voltaire no worse service than to reconcile him with all the world.

One wish remained to be gratified. Paris, that Paris he adored and had not seen for a quarter of a century, had still to pay its homage to the Patriarch. The visitors who came to Ferney were only a fraction of his innumerable admirers, and again, he longed to see his city once more before he died. Louis XV was dead ; the ministry, if not enthusiastic, was at least tolerant ; a pretext was found for a visit to Paris, and on the 4th of February, 1778, Voltaire, aged eighty-four, left his weeping vassals and set out on the last but the most remarkable of his journeys, a triumphal progress such as no other man of letters, who was nothing but a man of letters, has ever known.

X

THE LAST JOURNEY
1778

Although we have hitherto investigated chiefly the "natural man" in Voltaire, his human husk, in order to consider his permanent self at leisure in an analysis of his writings, it is not possible to contemplate this last journey, this final apotheosis, without emotion. There is always a moving irony in the honour paid to illustrious old age ; what is noisy praise to an old man who would give all his glory for a year of ignorant but exuberant youth ? How strange, how curiously ironic, this wild enthusiasm of young men and women for an aged author who looked like an intensely animated corpse. But how characteristic of that splendid Voltairean energy which is one of his most attractive traits ! At eighty-four he abandons the gruel and night-caps of eld and plunges vigorously into the whirlpool of Paris. Had he remained at Ferney, the doctors promised at least another ten years of life ; Voltaire preferred to let his life burn out in a brief but unique flame of glory.

No ominous thoughts afflicted Voltaire as his heavy carriage lumbered away from Ferney. He was in good health and excellent spirits, read and slept in the carriage, jested with Wagnière, and even found energy to play practical jokes ; the anticipation of Paris stimulated and delighted him. The journey itself was a triumphal

VOLTAIRE

progress, a foretaste of what was to come in Paris, a demonstration of the reverence and affection of France for the little old man who had given, however imperfectly, lessons of justice, tolerance, and enlightenment. At Bourg-en-Bresse Voltaire was recognised by an enthusiastic crowd whose attentions forced him to hide in a locked room ; at another posting-station the postillion was cursed by the host for bringing a poor horse to Voltaire's carriage—" Va bon train, crève mes chevaux, je m'en fous, tu mènes M. de Voltaire ! " His apartment at the Croix d'Or, Dijon, was crowded with visitors ; enthusiastic young men bribed the servants to obtain a glimpse of his room, disguised themselves as waiters to procure the glory of looking at the Patriarch. At the gates of Paris his carriage was stopped for the octroi examination. One of the guards recognised him—" C'est, nom de Dieu, M. de Voltaire ! " Pass, M. de Voltaire ; pass, fifty years of glory ; pass, Revolution !

To feel the emotion of Paris at this visit we must read the enthusiastic accounts of Grimm and Wagnière. All other topics of news were forgotten and Paris threw itself at the Patriarch's feet with a mobile excitement and eager homage known only to that city. This unexpected return after an absence of twenty-seven years was in itself sufficient to excite curiosity, but it became the occasion of remarkable social, political, and literary demonstrations. To the educated classes generally Voltaire was the greatest author and intelligence in Europe ; to the party of reform, he was the prophet of a new, regenerated France ; to the philosophes he was the triumphant crusher of the infâme, to the people he was the saviour of the Calas. True, the Church party held aloof and attempted a few excursions of disapproval ; Versailles officially frowned ;

THE LAST JOURNEY

but even the princes of the blood went to witness the spectacle of this strange spontaneous enthusiasm. Visitors besieged his room, and a crowd seemed gathered permanently outside the Hôtel de Beaune where Voltaire lodged. The Academy sent deputations; Franklin brought his grandson to receive the Patriarch's blessing; d'Argental and Richelieu, Glück and Mme du Barry, d'Alembert, Mme Necker, the British ambassador—"all Paris" came to see him. Whenever he drove out, enthusiastic crowds followed his carriage.

The great day of apotheosis was the 30th of March, 1778. At four o'clock, Voltaire drove to the Academy through cheering crowds; at the Cour du Louvre upwards of 2,000 persons had gathered, and greeted his arrival with shouts of "Vive Voltaire!" The Academy—minus the Church members—advanced to meet him in a body, an honour not paid even to foreign monarchs. Voltaire was ordered to take the president's seat, while d'Alembert read an *Eloge de Despréaux*, containing such delicate and flattering compliments to the poet of *La Henriade* that the old man's eyes were filled with tears. From the Academy he drove to the Comédie Française to see a performance of his latest tragedy *Irène*. By this time the crowd outside the Academy had grown to a vast size and, as Voltaire entered his carriage, there went up a continuous roar of "Vive Voltaire!" accompanied by the clapping of hands and the waving of handkerchiefs. Outside the theatre, men climbed on to his carriage and leaned through the window to kiss his hand; many wept as the old man walked slowly into the theatre supported on a friend's arm. Every seat in the theatre was occupied, every corridor crowded. As Voltaire entered his box, every man and woman rose

VOLTAIRE

spontaneously and another cry of "Voltaire! Voltaire!" swept up to him. He tried to conceal himself behind Mme Denis and Mme de Villette, but the unending cries from the whole theatre forced him to come forward. "The wreath!" shouted the crowd; and, at that moment, the actor Brizard entered the box and placed a crown of laurel on Voltaire's head. "Ah! Dieu! vous voulez donc me faire mourir à force de gloire!" exclaimed Voltaire in a voice broken by emotion, and put off the wreath. But the crowd would not suffer this and the Prince de Beauvau, taking up the wreath, forced Voltaire to wear it. This extraordinary scene lasted over twenty minutes, during which the whole theatre was an uproar of cheering and "Vive Voltaire". It was with difficulty that the actors were able to begin the play.

The emotions of this strange day were not exhausted. The enthusiasm of the audience, who applauded every trace of the old fire in the weak tragedy of *Irène*, infected the actors; they grasped the fact that there was something unique, almost epic, in this crescendo of demonstration, and prepared a surprise homage of their own. The curtain fell upon *Irène* amid tremendous applause. It rose again on a remarkable scene. The centre of the stage was occupied by the statue of Voltaire (brought from the foyer) and round it in a half-circle stood the performers in their costumes with palms and garlands in their hands; the guards of *Irène* were mingled with the French sentinels, and spectators from the lobbies and foyer occupied the wings. The effect on the emotional French audience was instantaneous; it seemed that the theatre had become one vast voice—"Voltaire! Voltaire!" The old man had retired to the back of his box, half exhausted by these continual ovations; but as the volume

THE LAST JOURNEY

of sound increased rather than diminished, he rose, tottered forward to the front of the box and stood for a moment with his head bowed on the rail; then raised his face, his eyes streaming with tears, a prey to an inexpressible emotion. Mlle Vestris then advanced and recited a poem in Voltaire's honour; his bust was crowned with a laurel-wreath and, in her ardour, Mlle Fanier aroused immense applause by kissing the Patriarch's statue. When order was at length restored, *Nanine* was performed with the crowned statue still on the stage.

At last it was time for Voltaire to leave, but the excited audience could not bear to let him go; they could not do enough to show their affection and admiration. From his box to the door of the Comédie Française, the old man walked between two rows of the prettiest women in Paris. At the door they delayed him again. Some called for torches to escort him home in triumph, others talked of taking out the horses and dragging his carriage in triumph through Paris. Even when he had taken his seat, the crowd swirled round the slowly advancing coach, climbed on the wheels and the step to catch a glimpse of him, to kiss his hands. "Who is that?" said one poor woman to another; "Voltaire, qui a sauvé les Calas", was the reply.

When Voltaire reached the Hôtel de Beaune, he sat down and "wept like a child"[1]; assuredly, few men have ever received so spontaneous a homage from a nation. Whatever one may think of this frenzy of adoration, it was the legitimate reward for a life-time "consacrée à charmer, à instruire, à éclairer ce siècle, dont il fut bien le guide et l'instituteur."

After this apotheosis the remaining weeks of Voltaire'

[1] Wagnière's *Mémoires*.

VOLTAIRE

life seem almost an anti-climax, though he continued to receive extraordinary honours. He died, as he had lived, from over-work. He had persuaded the Academy to adopt a scheme for the reform of the dictionary and, in preparing his plan, sat up late, drank too much coffee, then took opium, fell into delirium, and recovered his senses only to die. Is it necessary to touch upon the priestly intrigues about his death-bed, the attempts to wring recantations from the dying man, the controversies about his last moments? He signed a recantation indeed, but some months earlier he had placed in Wagnière's hands his true declaration of faith :

> "Je meurs en adorant Dieu, en aidant mes amis, en ne haïssant pas mes ennemis, et en détestant la superstition."
>
> 28 février, 1778.
VOLTAIRE.

This document is now preserved in the Bibliothèque Nationale.

The reason for Voltaire's temporizing with the Church was not dread of hell-fire but a legitimate desire to protect his remains from the indignity of being cast into the public sewer—the usual fate of those who differed from the Church. The memory of poor Adrienne Lecouvreur haunted him. Yet, in spite of these manoeuvres, it is doubtful if Voltaire communicated; and when the priest tormented him with questions, "Do you recognise the divinity of Jesus Christ?" a last flash of the old Voltaire showed itself and he exclaimed: "For God's sake, let me die in peace."

Even as he lay dying he did not forget those whose

THE LAST JOURNEY

cause he had defended. On the 26th of May, he received a letter from the Comte de Lally informing him that the sentence of death against his father had been reversed by the parlement. Voltaire roused himself from the death-stupor and wrote these lines :

> " Le mourant réssuscite en apprenant cette grande nouvelle ; il embrasse bien tendrement M. de Lally ; il voit que le roi est le défenseur de la justice : il mourra content."

His last words, spoken to an attendant, were : " Adieu, mon cher Morand, je me meurs." Ten minutes later he was dead ; he expired at 11 p.m. on the 30th of May, 1778, aged 84.

Voltaire had expressed a desire to be buried at Ferney, but it was found impossible to comply with this. Indeed, the Archbishop of Paris forbade Christian burial, but Voltaire's family acted with celerity and secured his inhumation in the priory at Scellières, where the prior was one of his relatives. The burial was carried out so quickly that all was over and the vault sealed before the Archbishop's commands were delivered.

The news of Voltaire's death caused universal interest and regret throughout Europe. Among innumerable instances of regard for his memory may be mentioned the *Eloge de Voltaire* by Frederick the Great, the purchase of Voltaire's library and MSS by the Empress Catherine of Russia (they are still at the Leningrad Library), and the proposal by the French Academy to make the *Eloge de Voltaire* the subject of that year's contest for the poetry prize.

The body of Voltaire was not destined to remain peacefully in the vaults at Scellières and became a victim of that

VOLTAIRE

ghoulish curiosity which has ravished so many graves of the great men of France. In 1791, two years after the outbreak of the Revolution and two years before that odious profanation of the sepulchres of the Kings at St Denis, it was decreed that the remains of Voltaire should be interred with honour in the Panthéon. The shrunken corpse, crowned with oak-leaves, was actually exposed to the people after the exhumation in May. On the 10th of July, a few days after the flight to Varennes and the ignominious return of the royal family, Voltaire's body was brought in procession to the Panthéon with extraordinary pomp and civic ceremonies which lasted all day. The details of this strange episode of Revolutionary history deserve more space than can be given here ; all that can be mentioned is the inscription on the enormous catafalque :

"Il vengea Calas, La Barre, Sirven et Monbailly.
Poète, philosophe, historien, il a fait prendre un grand essor à l'esprit humain ; il nous a préparés à devenir libres."

Time passed on. The forces of Revolution were organized by Napoleon, flooded over Europe, and were gradually driven back to France ; a Bourbon King was once more settled precariously on the throne of Louis XVI. It was once believed that, after the Restoration, the bodies of Voltaire and Rousseau were secretly removed from the Panthéon (once more consecrated as a church) and the universal belief was that the remains of these two great men were cast into the sewers of Paris.

The investigations of the 1890's proved that the bodies were still there. In any case, it would have been a vain and foolish insult to dead bones ! The immortal part of Voltaire, that vivid, brilliant mind which still lives

THE LAST JOURNEY

in his books, could not be destroyed ; in spite of proscription and government repression, the circulation of the works of Voltaire during the whole period of the Restauration was intense. Between 1778 and 1835 it is calculated that thirty-four complete editions of Voltaire's works were issued, besides innumerable reprints of separate books. M. Lanson estimates that in the period 1817-24 alone, 31,600 complete sets of Voltaire's works were published, making the extraordinary total of 1,598,000 volumes.

We now turn from the life of Voltaire to consider the records of his mind.

VOLTAIRE
PART II

Voltaire is a poet in the manner of Marot, Voiture, La Fontaine, Chaulieu, Hamilton. . . .
G. LANSON

. . . the Henriade is all sense from the beginning to the end, often adorned by the justest and liveliest reflections, the most beautiful descriptions, the noblest images, and the sublimest sentiments. . . .
CHESTERFIELD

Alzire et Mahomet sont des monuments immortels. . . .
CONDORCET

The whole modern conception of history comes from Voltaire's Essai.
HETTNER

Lord Bolingbroke has just taught me how history should be read Voltaire shows me how it should be written.
CHESTERFIELD

Pensez et laissez penser.
VOLTAIRE

M. de Voltaire est le premier homme au monde pour écrire ce que les autres ont pensé.
ANON

Il charme et fatigue par sa mobilité ; il vous enchante et vous dégoûte ; on ne sait quelle est la forme qui lui est propre : il serait insensé s'il n'était si sage, et méchant si sa vie n'était remplie de traits de bienfaisance.
CHATEAUBRIAND

> *Son enseigne est à l'Encyclopédie.*
> *Que vous plaît-il ? de l'anglais, du toscan ?*
> *Vers, prose, algèbre, opéra, comédie ?*
> *Poëme épique, histoire, ode ou roman ?*
> *Parlez ! C'est fait. . . .*
PIRON

. . . Arouet fut mis à la Bastille pour avoir fait des vers très-effrontés. . . . Il étoit fils du notaire de mon père. . . .
DUC DE SAINT-SIMON

VOLTAIRE

PART II: VOLTAIRE'S WORKS

XI

The reduction of the vast and often contradictory information about Voltaire's life to a reasonably concise narrative is a task whose difficulties can only be appreciated by those who have attempted it. To deal adequately with his works is an even more complicated and formidable undertaking. In the one case we are wrestling only with flesh and blood; in the other we have to attack more gigantic and shadowy powers. The mind of Voltaire overwhelms us with its energy and mobility. How are we to bind this Proteus and force him to tell us his secrets? There are twenty aspects of Voltaire, any one of which would provide a specialist with material for a volume. His fertility alone is a problem of great interest. Other writers grow exhausted, need repose, degenerate into mediocrity or imbecility; Voltaire was apparently inexhaustible and unable to rest, urged on by some mysterious force; much of his best work was composed between fifty and eighty. The study of science and philosophy did not cramp his creative force; even more remarkably, his devotion to a narrow standard of taste could not quench his powers of production. He derived from the Jesuits an exaggerated respect for the

VOLTAIRE

medium of verse, but, though he wrote thousands of lines of verse, his prose remained unaffected—pure, sober, clear, sparkling. Respect for a factitious ideal of tragedy did not prevent him from writing delicious occasional verse and an amusing burlesque epic. Indeed, his mind was so mobile that, as we have already seen, he worked simultaneously upon five or six different books in as many different genres. Few writers, therefore, have attained to Voltaire's self-discipline ; few can have possessed so exact a knowledge of their powers ; few have directed their talents with such precision and mastery.

Consider for a moment Voltaire as a writer of tragedies, an aspect we think of minor importance, but one we cannot neglect, if only from the esteem in which they were held by himself and his contemporaries. How many problems are raised by this topic alone. How did Voltaire arrive at his conception of tragedy ; what were his sources and the influences which affected him ; how did he modify them ; what novelties did he introduce ; why were his plays so admired ; whence did he derive his plots ; how do we explain his attitude to Racine, Shakespeare, and Sophocles ; why did he admire Shakespeare in 1735 and disparage him in 1770 ; how was he affected by the attitude of his actors and his audiences, by opposition and by success ; to what extent did he influence the art of tragedy in France, and was this for good or bad ? These are some of the questions which we naturally ask (quite apart from a consideration of the intrinsic value of the tragedies to a modern reader) and ask about a part of his work which is admittedly of minor importance. But to answer even these questions accurately and fully demands not a brief chapter, but a carefully documented volume by someone with an expert knowledge of the development of tragedy in Europe and particularly in seventeenth and eighteenth century France.

These merely literary problems fade into insignificance when compared with the far more complex and elusive problems of Voltaire's influence as a social, political, and intellectual force. Ask but this question: How far was Voltaire responsible for the French Revolution and to what extent did it carry out, fall short of, or exceed his conceptions? There is a theme for long and leisurely investigation by a widely-informed historian. Napoleon read Voltaire carefully—there is another subject which might be investigated. Ask again: What was the influence of Voltaire upon French free thought and French prose literature? An immense topic. One thinks in an instant of the generations of Frenchmen who were Voltaireans in outlook and sympathy. There was till recently living a great French author, Anatole France, who in some respects seems a more mellow and poetic re-incarnation of Voltaire. Even those French writers of the last century who are apparently most hostile to Voltaire came under his influence. Flaubert frankly admired him and, paradoxical as it may sound, the Voltairean hatred of the "infâme" is not without some relation to Flaubert's hatred of the bourgeois; moreover, the prose of Voltaire did to some extent modify the prose of Flaubert. Take down the *Génie du Christianisme* and observe how profoundly the creator of the Romantic movement in France is influenced by Voltaire, how Chateaubriand struggles between admiration and hatred for Voltaire. For Chateaubriand Voltaire is in a different class from Diderot and d'Alembert, he is almost worthy to rank with the writers of the age of Louis XIV, he

VOLTAIRE

lacked only religious sentiment to make him a writer of surpassing genius. Look at Baudelaire's journals and note how he wrestles with the Voltairean ideal.

These questions concerning Voltaire's influence might be indefinitely prolonged. But there are at least two questions which cannot be avoided : What was the influence of Voltaire on the religious thought of Europe and to what extent is he responsible for the present tyranny of commercialism ? Renan has condemned in a famous passage the Voltairean attitude to religion. Again, though we cannot make Voltaire responsible for the industrial revolution, we cannot acquit him of doing harm by his championship of a " terre-à-terre " ideal of commercial felicity. If the world is now the prey of the successful tradesman, must we not in part blame Voltaire ?

I cannot hope to treat adequately these and a hundred other aspects of Voltaire's writings and thought ; I can but pilot the reader round the archipelago of his books and indicate some of their qualities, beauties, defects, and significance.

XII

VOLTAIRE AS POET

The simplest method of disposing of Voltaire's verse is to say that he was not a poet at all and then to proceed to consider some other part of his immense production. This is an impossible attitude except for a critic who is confident he knows precisely what is poetry and what is not poetry and who does not hesitate to apply his formula with rigid precision. It is a position one cannot but consider untenable ; it implies a mind too omniscient and a priori in its judgments. Standards and ideals of poetry have changed so much in the past (and will continue to change so long as poetry is a living art) that no abstract definition can possibly enclose all the excellent kinds of poetry that have been written. A person whose taste is founded upon the mock simplicity and quaintness of a section of modern English poetry might easily assert that Voltaire was not a poet ; but if we look at the matter from slightly higher ground we shall note that all through the eighteenth and early nineteenth centuries Voltaire was universally esteemed as a poet ; that even Matthew Arnold thought him a poet, a great poet. Any work that Matthew Arnold has praised might be treated seriously and with respect. Voltaire wrote verse over a period of something more than seventy years and he touched nearly every genre allowed by the taste of his age. That taste was in some respects false and narrow, but it was suited

VOLTAIRE

to Voltaire's temperament ; indeed, it is not always easy to say how much Voltaire created eighteenth century taste in poetry and how much it created him as a poet. The virtues of Voltaire's verse are in the main the virtues of good prose ; facility, smoothness, clarity, evenness of tone, epigrammatic felicity, good sense, invention. It is deficient in imagination, passion, vivid metaphors and images, a plastic sense.

The passage beginning,

"Ibant obscuri sola sub nocte per umbram,"

contains several of the poetic qualities which Voltaire never possessed and represents a height of poetry he never attained. In fact, several of the qualities which in poetry give us the greatest pleasure appeared to Voltaire as defects and extravagancies. Homer made him uneasy ; Sophocles distressed him ; Dante appeared to him a bizarre though brilliant fanatic and Shakespeare a drunken savage of genius ; for, in their works, where was the politeness, the elegance, the good sense, the "vraisemblance?" But though Voltaire lacked precisely the qualities which are needed for the more profound and imaginative kinds of poetry, he was eminently endowed with those which achieve success in the minor forms of intellectual and occasional poetry. He was wonderfully skilful in expressing ideas in verse ; he was a master of verse persiflage, compliment, and persuasion. The less elevated and noble the genre, the greater Voltaire's success. He is the master of French light verse, a genre in which he remains indisputably supreme. For more than half a century Voltaire dominated French poetry and even those who threw off his tyranny were influenced by him, even André Chénier and Hugo, and especially

THE POET

Lamartine. Leaving the enormous mass of Voltaire's dramatic verse for discussion later, let us examine his poetic works more particularly. At the head must come *La Henriade*, the delight and admiration of Voltaire's contemporaries, the solid block which founded his reputation and secured him wealth, that epic of good sense which ravished Lord Chesterfield and interested him far more than Homer, Virgil, and Milton ; *La Henriade*, which to us is a frigid and colourless failure, an " Ersatz " epic, a synthetic production which lacks the mysterious gift of life, a Galatea never warmed by the embrace of a Pygmalion. Fable, action, characters, machinery, heroisms, personifications, episodes, descriptions, elevated and sustained language ; all are there, all are skilfully arranged according to the rules—and yet we yawn. Is it our fault or Voltaire's ?

> " Il le faut avouer, parmi ces courtisans
> Que moissonna le fer en la fleur de leurs ans,
> Aucun ne fut percé que de coups honorables ;
> Tous fermes dans leur poste, et tous inébranlables,
> Ils voyaient devant eux avancer le trépas,
> Sans détourner les yeux, sans reculer d'un pas.
> Des courtisans français tel est le caractère :
> La paix n'amollit point leur valeur ordinaire ;
> De l'ombre du repos ils volent aux hasards ;
> Vils flatteurs à la cour, héros aux champs de Mars."

These lines are from the admired description of the battle of Coutras in Book III. Why do they, like the rest of *La Henriade*, leave us cold ? The death of these young Renaissance noblemen ought to rouse some emotion in us ; the contrast between their worthless lives in peace and their gallantry in war should be stirring. Does not

VOLTAIRE

the failure come from the frigid imagination of the poet? He describes where he should present and, instead of striking us with some image of pity or admiration or terror, he presents us with a piece of good sense, a reflection on a social fact—the character of the French courtier. Not thus does Roland die. The mere fact that the poet can halt to utter so prosaic a reflection at such a moment is a damning indictment of his imagination and sincerity. Plainly Voltaire does not feel his subject with any intensity. He pitches his voice too high for his compass and it rings false. This " harvest " of the sword, this " trépas " seen advancing, these courtiers who " volent aux hasards ", the trifling antithesis of " flatteurs à la cour " and " héros aux champs de Mars "—how commonplace, how flat, how unimaginative, how unconvincingly rhetorical!

Yet there is a kind of energy in *La Henriade* which renders it just readable; it is not a frightful relic of misdirected zeal like Glover's *Leonidas*. The story is interesting as a narrative; human nature peers through the sounding verbiage; Walter Scott would have made a first-rate prose tale out of it. Behind *La Henriade* there is a mind at work; unfortunately it is a mind devoid of high poetic passion and imagination. The work manages to secure a place, the lowest, among the minor artificial epics. The two great *original* epic poems of Europe are those of Homer and Dante; far below their poems, but respectable for its primitive, rough-hewn originality, comes the *Chanson de Roland*; first among the artificial or literary epics come the *Æneid* and *Paradise Lost*. These are all great and noble poems, in a class far superior to *La Henriade*. The Italian epics of Tasso and Boiardo are not truly epics but long, fanciful narrative poems; Ariosto is already in the regions of burlesque.

Still, they are greater works than the *Henriade*, and so, no doubt, are the minor narrative epics of antiquity, the *Pharsalia* and the *Argonauts*. Again, the fire and passion of Agrippa d'Aubigné's extraordinary *Tragiques* put it far above *La Henriade*. On the whole, then, we must rank the *La Henriade* rather low, a little beneath the abortive epics of Ronsard and Tennyson, beneath *La Franciade* and the *Idylls of the King*, because the authors of those poems possessed gifts which Fate denied to Voltaire. But if *La Henriade* is inferior to the two last-named poems in incidental beauties and charm of versification, it is perhaps superior in energy and "ordonnance." Tennyson would have had every right to smile at the much vaunted description of the Temple of Love (Book IX); never would he have committed such a commonplace as :

"Partout on voit mûrir, partout on voit éclore
Et les fruits de Pomone et les présents de Flore ; "

but Tennyson could not compose on the grand scale like Voltaire, nor did he possess that restless energy which rolls all these commonplaces along in a narrative which does actually move. *La Henriade* is frigid but active ; like its author.

La Pucelle is a very different affair and is generally rated far too low. It is not much inferior to those two excellent poems, *Orlando Furioso* and *Don Juan*. One reason for the failure of *La Henriade* is that Voltaire did not truly believe in heroism or in strong passions ; the personalities of the artist-Kings, the Valois, were as complete an enigma to him as the heroism of Jeanne d'Arc. He saw only the vices of the one and the ridiculousness of the other. *La Pucelle* is the poem of

VOLTAIRE

wit and mockery, the sneering titters of an eighteenth century Sancho Panza at the exploits of a fifteenth century Don Quixote. But Voltaire was eminently witty and skilful in mockery; his sense of the ridiculous was acute and his powers of expressing it inexhaustible. The comic traits of character always escaped Voltaire, which is why his comedies are so feeble; but he could seize and render in quick stinging phrases the absurdities of opinions and customs. For all of us there is something ridiculous and shocking in the virtues and qualities to which we have no claim; for example, as " l'amour passion " is almost unknown to the English it is necessary in public to speak of Raphael's beautiful and charming mistress as his " fiancée." M. de Voltaire had the same capacity for being shocked by those opinions and customs which were not his; but as he was intelligent, gay, and witty (and a Frenchman), he translated the shock into mockery, not into moral indignation. Chivalry, mysticism religious emotion, a mail-clad virgin leading an army, were all completely foreign ideas to M. de Voltaire and hence extremely entertaining to him.

" Je ne suis né pour célébrer les saints : "

is the first line of *La Pucelle*, and it is exactly true; Voltaire was quite incapable of understanding the force wielded by a Francis of Assisi or a Jeanne d'Arc. Incontestably these saints had exercised a power over men and women, and the Voltairean explanation is that the saints were impostors and their followers superstitious dupes and fools. He could not see that, in an ignorant age, genius must work through superstition.

Let us not complain. If Voltaire had understood the Middle Ages and Jeanne d'Arc, we should be the poorer,

THE POET

for *La Pucelle* is a masterpiece of burlesque. The confused and mystic aspirations of the middle ages, its curious mixture of chivalrous idealism and ferocious militarism, have never been criticized with more acumen or laughed at with more pitiless wit than in the pages of *La Pucelle*. The disparity between human idealism and the crass realities of daily life is for us a sad and humiliating spectacle; it filled Voltaire with chuckling delight. We sigh to think that the hero must eat twice a day, that the ascetic sooner or later succumbs to temptation, that the poet must turn an honest penny, that the girl must learn to wash babies; Voltaire's mocking temperament was sardonically amused by these humiliating and abrupt descents from the ideal. He is the mouth-piece of those reasonable people who believe in solid comfort and no fantastic notions; but, unlike them, he was never bored and seldom boring.

Nothing illustrates better than this poem the limits to Voltaire's imagination and his peculiar sense of humour. To a person of vivid imagination the ravishing of a convent of nuns by soldiery is an intolerable and distressing thought. But there is something comic in the idea of a company of persons who, having piqued themselves on a useless virtue they may at times be not unwilling to lose, are suddenly and forcibly deprived of their illusory superiority. The spectacle would be heart-rending, the mere idea is amusing; Voltaire saw only the idea, not the spectacle. His ravished nuns are the merest intellectual counters, lay-figures, Aunt Sallies, to be knocked down triumphantly in the interest of Reason and Common-sense.

Freedom from the restraint of the grand manner allowed Voltaire to write passages of *La Pucelle* which

VOLTAIRE

to us are more poetic and charming than anything in *La Henriade*. Take these lines from Chant XIX:

" Dans un vallon qu'arrose une onde pure,
　Au fond d'un bois de cyprès toujours verts,
　Qu'en pyramide a formés la nature,
　Et dont le faîte a bravé cent hivers,
　Il est un antre où souvent les Naïades
　Et les Sylvains viennent prendre le frais.
　Un clair ruisseau, par des conduits secrets,
　Y tombe en nappe, et forme vingt cascades.
　Un tapis vert est tendu tout auprès ;
　Le serpolet, la mélisse naissante,
　Le blanc jasmin, la jonquille odorante,
　Y semblent dire aux bergers d'alentour :
　' Reposez-vous sur ce lit de l'Amour.' "

Voltaire always preferred *La Pucelle* to *La Henriade* and he was right to do so ; the genre was far better suited to his genius and he wrote the poem with much more vigour and interest. *La Henriade* was for contemporaries, *La Pucelle* for posterity. And how amusing its genial cynicism is :

" Heureux cent fois qui trouve un pucelage !
　C'est un grand bien ; mais de toucher un coeur
　Est, à mon sens, un plus cher avantage."

And :

" Voyez-vous pas le pauvre Galilée
　Qui tout contrit leur demande pardon,
　Bien condamné pour avoir eu raison ? "

And :

" Comme il lui plait Dieu fait justice ou grâce ;
　Quesnel l'a dit, nul ne peut en douter."

THE POET

And:

"Soyez au moins des pécheurs fortunés ;
Et puisqu'il faut que vouz soyez damnés,
Damnez-vous donc pour des fautes aimables."

And:

" Parfait Anglais, voyageant sans dessin,
Achetant cher des modernes antiques,
Regardant tout avec un air hautain,
Et méprisant les saints et les reliques."

La Pucelle is Voltaire's one real poetic success outside the realms of occasional verse. There is good didactic verse in the *Discours en Vers sur l'Homme* and the *Poème sur la Loi naturelle*, but these are in essence semi-philosophical tracts, put into rhyme by an able virtuoso. The reader can safely neglect them, but he should by no means neglect *La Pucelle*, even if he is liable to be shocked by its improprieties. Nobody need take Voltaire's pleasantries as matters of faith. The merits of the poem are Voltaire's own, but he certainly owed a good deal to the Italians, Pulci, Berni, and Ariosto. We know he read Italian poetry industriously with Mme du Châtelet, and to our taste his verse gains immensely when modelled on Ariosto rather than on Racine ; Voltaire wrote too rapidly and impatiently to achieve that perfection of elegance and sober beauty attained by Racine at the expense of infinite care.

In *La Pucelle* Voltaire gave triumphant expression to the " libertinisme " he acquired in youth from his friends of the Temple. Doubtless the tale of Châteauneuf's teaching the infant Voltaire to lisp the impieties of *Moïsade* is a " pious chanson " invented after the publication of *La Pucelle* to show the dangers of early influence ;

VOLTAIRE

but we can pick a critical truth from it. A considerable portion of Voltaire's successful light verse is a masterly development of the "libertin" tradition of verse which he acquired by contact from Chaulieu, and by reading from Hamilton and La Fontaine, the La Fontaine of *Poésies diverses*, not of the *Fables*. In reading Chaulieu[1] one is greatly struck by the resemblance of his manner to Voltaire's; his poems are Voltairean, but with less liveliness, wit, charm, and verve. To a less extent the same remark applies to Hamilton's verse.[2]

This kind of poetry has been cultivated with more success by the French than by the English and Italians, for psychological reasons which may be sought in the pages of Stendhal. Of course, the English definers of poetry will not allow us to call this "poetry", ma non ragioniam di lor. It is the poetry of gay, worldly, and refined people, pitched in a low key and written in a familiar tone. It abandons the declamatory clichés of the false noble style and uses a speech which is more direct and natural; no doubt it falls into clichés of situation and expression, but they are less offensive, because less pretentious, than those of the false noble style. None of these French poets was sufficiently earnest, none possessed the passion and imagination, to breathe vigour and truth into the flabby bladders of the false noble style; the best they can compass there is a dignified rumble of alexandrines. But in their own style and on their own ground they are delightful and inimitable. "Joli comme un madrigal de Voltaire" is almost a proverb. A reader who knows no French can obtain an approximate impression of their

---

[1] *Poésies de Chaulieu*, An VII de la République, Paris.
[2] Chaulieu was a pupil of Hamilton; see, for example, Hamilton's charming "*Lettres et Épitres*".

THE POET

charm and manner from the best pieces of Prior and Chesterfield's inimitable "Whenever, Chloe, I begin". But the Frenchmen are far more accomplished, more fertile, and more elegant.

The type of poetry I am endeavouring to describe is eminently a production of French court-life and politeness. It can be traced back as far as Marot, perhaps even to Charles d'Orléans, and, with Musset, into the nineteenth century; its most flourishing epoch was the seventeenth and eighteenth centuries from, let us say, the youth of Saint-Evremond[1] to the death of Voltaire. After the Revolution, with its miseries and heroisms, its storms of passion and violence, its vast changes in society, this sort of poetry dwindled rapidly and has now practically disappeared. French charm and elegance are now exploited by the French commercial classes and therefore the poets have entirely abandoned qualities which mark the work of so many of their predecessors. When the old spirit of badinage moves a modern French poet he is almost certain to give his verse a touch of violence or vulgarity. For example, this couplet of P. J. Toulet:

> "Tiens ! . . . Isadora Duncan
> Va danser . . . foutons le camp !"[2]

Never would an eighteenth century poet have been guilty of such a breach of manners. Gallantry to the ladies was one of the strictest conventions of Voltairean light verse, gallantry entirely devoid of any deeper feeling and especially of the metaphysic of love. It was exactly the poetry to suit an elegant society which had few illusions,

---

[1] Why did Voltaire disparage the verse of Saint-Evremond? Mystery.
[2] Quoted in *Les Marges*, a monthly French periodical.

VOLTAIRE

except those necessary to support the idea of its superiority to all other societies. The noble subjects for a poet, says Dante, are God, War, and Love. These Frenchmen did not believe in God and only approached the idea in a spirit of incredulous levity ; they retained the French ability to die unflinchingly and carelessly, but they generally refused to admit heroism or salf-sacrifice or patriotism as a subject for verse ; as to Love, which was their principal topic, it was treated in a spirit of light gallantry or smiling sensuality ; they died, they flamed, they were pierced with Love—for Doris yesterday, for Chloë to-day, for Madame la Marquise de . . . to-morrow.

This is not wholly fair to Voltaire's poetry, which in several respects is greatly superior to that of his rivals in the genre ; but if the reader has acquired the impression that it is seldom more than half-serious and never profound, that is very nearly correct. Voltaire attempted several kinds of shorter poems, not all with the same success. His *Odes* are disastrous exercises in rhetoric, completely unreadable, and certainly inferior to those of J. B. Rousseau, his master in this very difficult form. There is something unluckily comic in declamations of this sort :

" O vérité sublime ! O céleste Uranie !
   Esprit né de l'esprit qui forma l'univers,
   Qui mesures des cieux la carrière infinie,
      Et qui pèses les airs :

Tandis que tu conduis sur les gouffres de l'onde
Ces voyageurs savants, ministres de tes lois,
De l'ardent équateur ou du pôle du monde,
      Entends ma faible voix."

THE POET

Can it be, we ask anxiously, that these are meant to be Sapphics? What is all this hubbub about? What an odd resemblance it bears to the least successful declamations of Hugo and how strange it seems that this capering on stilts should have been thought sublime and noble. To an English taste, and indeed to the taste of most modern Frenchmen, there is little or no pleasure to be found in Voltaire's *Odes*.

With all his satirical gifts, Voltaire is not so successful in formal satire as one would expect. The object of satire is to render odious to honest men some person or institution or social absurdity or fashionable vice; its emotional energy is hatred, its chief weapon is wit. Voltaire possessed hatred and wit, and both his satires and occasional poems abound with successful traits of satire; but his verse is too loose, too little concentrated, to achieve a complete satire. In the great satiric poems line after line come whistling in like bullets—force concentrated into compact and dangerous missiles. Voltaire censured the *Sporus* of Pope as contrary to "bon goût." So it is, but so is *Hamlet*. In his verse Voltaire aimed at a sort of elegant urbanity which is contrary to the tart vigour so essential to satire; or, when he forgot his urbanity and hit out, he wrote from personal irritation, not from a kind of ideal hatred. Not one of his formal satires equals those of Boileau and Pope, but all of them contain a few excellent couplets and passages, while there are many happy touches of satire throughout his miscellaneous poems. His best pieces in this style are not invective, but familiar and humorous reflections on the absurdities of opinions and habits. *La Vanité* is a good example of Voltairean formal satire; it is witty, it is amusing, it concludes with the famous stinging couplet:

VOLTAIRE

"César n'a point d'asile où son ombre répose,
    Et l'ami Pompignon[1] pense être quelque chose!"

But the easy skill with which Voltaire turns his alexandrines cannot conceal the fact that the poem lacks concentration and energy; perhaps because he was only half in earnest, perhaps because of the fetters of good taste. Far better are the semi-satires *Le Mondain* and *Défense du Mondain*. There Voltaire is attacking an an opinion he detested and defending one he really believed in, and he finds happy expressions for his thought. The praise of elegant sensuality has seldom been sung with more conviction and verve than in these lines:

"Allons souper. Que ces brilliants services,
    Que ces ragoûts ont pour moi des délices!
Qu'un cuisinier est un mortel divin!
Chloris, Églé, me versent de leur main
D'un vin d'Ai dont la mousse pressée,
De la bouteille avec force elancée,
Comme un éclair fait voler le bouchon;
Il part, on rit; il frappe le plafond.
De ce vin frais l'écume pétillante
De nos Français est l'image brillante.
Le lendemain donne d'autres désirs,
D'autres soupers, et de nouveaux plaisirs."

There is indeed a large gulf between that kind of poetry and the grand style, and between those sentiments and the moral improvement which still lurks behind much of our verse and criticism. But take such lines for what they are—light verse. Was ever light verse handled with more skill and charm? They are only "satire" from

---

[1] Le Franc Pompignon, an enemy of Voltaire's, with no particular talent.

THE POET

the contrast to puritan severity and the notion of primitive simplicity of morals which Voltaire is attacking, an attack which he rounds off with an amiable impertinence to orthodoxy :

> " Et vous, jardin de ce premier bon homme,
> Jardin fameux par le diable et la pomme,
> C'est en vain que, par l'orgueil séduits,
> Huet, Calmet, dans leur savante audace,
> Du paradis ont recherché la place ;
> Le paradis terrestre est où je suis."

But the cream of the joke perhaps lies in the fact that during most of his life the state of Voltaire's health absolutely forebade him from taking any share in these sensual gratifications he praises so highly.

The satirical epigram was often well-turned by Voltaire. Take this little shaft at the poet-painter, Coypel :

> " On dit que notre ami Coypel
> Imite Horace et Raphaël :
> A les surpasser il s'efforce ;
> Et nous n'avons point aujourd'hui
> De rimeur peignant de sa force
> Ni peintre rimant comme lui."

Epîtres, Contes en Vers, Stances, miscellaneous epigrams flowed from Voltaire's ready pen and showed him at his best as a poet. The " Epître " was used by Voltaire as a convenient and elastic verse form for the expressing of his innumerable moods and interests. Almost the only rules for the Epître are that it must not be too serious or too long, must not be pompous or in the grand

VOLTAIRE

style, but familiar, graceful, and attractive. It is essentially the form for an accomplished man of the world, for his interests and ideas can be expressed with far more propriety in the guise of a verse letter than in any more elevated and serious sort of verse. Voltaire's Epîtres contain a few formal and stately addresses to monarchs ; and these are almost invariably bad. The remainder of the Epîtres astonish by the variety and charm, by their skill, elegance, and wit. Queens and actresses, Kings and critics, abbés and dukes, poets dead and living, were addressed in these epistles, the first of which is dated 1706 and the last 1778 ; there are 123 of them. The tone varies according to the person addressed and the subject treated. An epistle to an abbé who was mourning the death of his mistress, begins :

" Toi qui fus des plaisirs le délicat arbitre,
   Tu languis, cher abbé ; je vois, malgré tes soins,
  Que ton triple menton, l'honneur de ton chapitre,
    Aura bientôt deux étages de moins."

But the Prince de Conti is at once addressed from the stilts of the eighteenth century grand style :

" Conti, digne héritier des vertus de ton père,
  Toi que l'honneur conduit, que la justice éclaire. . ."

A number are addressed to the King of Prussia. But if one lingers over this charming, familiar light verse one will never be done ; there is concentrated the essence of Voltaire's poetic genius, and in these poems he did indeed marry to immortal verse his gifts of badinage, compliment, and wit. Who can turn a compliment like Voltaire?

THE POET

Take these lines to Madame la Marquise de B——:

" On ne peut faire ton portrait :
Folâtre et sérieuse, agaçante et sévère,
    Prudente avec l'air indiscret,
Vertueuse, coquette, à toi-même contraire,
La ressemblance échappe en rendant chaque trait
Si l'on te peint constante, on t'aperçoit légère :
    Ce n'est jamais toi qu'on a fait.
Fidèle au sentiment avec des goûts volages,
Tous les coeurs à ton char s'enchaînent tour à tour:
Tu plais aux libertins, tu captives les sages,
    Tu domptes les plus fiers courages,
    Tu fais l'office de l'Amour.
On croit voir cet enfant en te voyant paraître ;
    Sa jeunesse, ses traits, son art,
Ses plaisirs, ses erreurs, sa malice peut-être :
    Serais-tu ce dieu par hasard ? "

I would gladly dwell longer on these charming productions of Voltaire's more playful moods, which give us eighteenth century gaiety and politeness at its best ; the more so since the spirit and the art which it embodies have vanished from the world. But I have already far exceeded the space I ought to allot to a part of Voltaire's work which I am afraid most people think unimportant. my excuse must be that I delight in " le Voltaire badin " and that I first became interested in him many years ago from reading the selection of his poems in the *Classiques Garnier*. It is pleasant to hope that others might share this taste.

The influence of Voltaire on French poetry, at least in the eighteenth century, was considerable. All the delicious light poets of the French eighteenth century, the Voisenons, the Bertins, the Gentil-Bernards, were

VOLTAIRE

pupils of Voltaire. One might almost ask if there is any French poet, with the possible exception of André Chénier, writing between 1740 and 1820, who was not deeply influenced by Voltaire ; and even André Chenier shows some traces of a study of Voltaire's poems. Many of the earlier Romantics, especially Lamartine, owe something to Voltaire, if only the fluidity of their alexandrines. With Baudelaire, who hated Voltaire, the influence ceases, yet is it altogether fantastic to hear a last echo of " le Voltaire badin " in some of the lighter and more graceful pieces of Verlaine? Perhaps that is a little fantastic and yet there are more grace and feeling in Voltaire's smaller poems than is generally allowed. As a proof of this statement, take the two following quotations, from the *Stances* this time. The first is from a poem to Mme du Châtelet, written in 1741 :

> " Si vous voulez que j'aime encore,
> Rendez-moi l'âge des amours ;
> Au crépuscule de mes jours
> Rejoignez, s'il se peut, l'aurore.
>
> On meurt deux fois, je le vois bien ;
> Cesser d'aimer et d'être aimable,
> C'est une mort insupportable ;
> Cesser de vivre, ce n'est rien."

And this was written in his eightieth year :

> " Délie elle-même à son tour
> S'en va dans la nuit éternelle,
> En oubliant qu'elle fut belle,
> Et qu'elle a vécu pour l'amour.
>
> Nous naissons, nous vivons, bergère,
> Nous mourons sans savoir comment.
> Chacun est parti du néant :
> Où va-t-il ? . . . Dieu le sait, ma chère."

XIII

VOLTAIRE AS DRAMATIST

Voltaire's dramatic productions number about fifty, mostly tragedies; but though I have held enthusiastic converse about plays with many persons, I have very seldom found anyone who had read Voltaire's and never anyone who liked them. Indeed, it must be admitted that a knowledge of Shakespeare is an almost complete handicap to an admiration for Voltaire's tragedies. There are some tastes which appear to be mutually exclusive and there is some limit to the widest and most tolerant eclecticism. If we are penetrated with the excellence of *Othello* and *Julius Caesar*, how in the name of Apollo and the Nine can we read *Zaire* and *La Mort de César* without langour and contempt?

"But yesterday the word of Caesar might
 Have stood against the world; now lies he there,
 And none so poor to do him reverence."

"Du plus grand des Romains voilà ce qui vous reste;
 Voilà ce dieu vengeur, idolâtré par vous,
 Que ses assassins même adoraient à genoux. . . ."

And yet we cannot dispose of Voltaire's tragedies in a cavalier manner. In the first part of this book frequent reference was made to Voltaire's repeated successes as a tragic dramatist. During his life-time no one but his enemies and Englishmen would have even suggested that Shakespeare was Voltaire's equal, far less his superior. At the pompous burial of Voltaire in the Panthéon in 1791 the façade of the Comédie Française bore this inscription in vast letters : " He wrote *Œdipe* at eighteen"; and the Odéon responded with : " He wrote *Irène* at eighty ". Take any eighteenth century French writer who has discussed these tragedies—La Harpe, Grimm, Condorcet, Prince de Ligne—and you will find only respectful and enthusiastic praise. So much for contemporaries and fellow-countrymen, but who would have thought to find Lord Byron among the admiring throng? The following appears in the notes to " Don Juan " :

"Voltaire has even been termed a 'shallow fellow' by some of the same school who called Dryden's *Ode* ' a drunken song ';—a *school* (as it is called, I presume, from their education being still incomplete) the whole of whose filthy trash of Epics, Excursions, &c, &c, &c, is not worth the two words in *Zaïre*, ' Vous pleurez ', or a single speech of *Tancred*. . . ."

Perhaps that outburst is due more to hatred for Southey and Wordsworth than to admiration for Voltaire, but let us examine this famous scene, this renowned " vous pleurez." Zaïre is a Christian slave of the noblest blood, beloved by and in love with the Sultan Orosmane ; she discovers her father and brother among the Sultan's Christian captives and is moved by family affection and scruples of religion ; the Sultan, who does not know Nérestan is her brother, is jealous after the manner of Othello—for this play was partly composed to show how *Othello* should have been conducted in accordance with

THE DRAMATIST

good taste and the "rules of Aristotle". Here is a fragment of the famous scene :

OROSMANE

... Madame, c'en est fait, une autre va monter
Au rang que mon amour vous daignait présenter ;
Une autre aura des yeux, et va du moins connaître
De quel prix mon amour et ma main devaient être.
Il pourra m'en coûter, mais mon coeur s'y résout.
Apprenez qu' Orosmane est capable de tout ;
Que j'aime mieux vous perdre, et, loin de votre vue,
Mourir désespéré de vous avoir perdue,
Que de vous posséder, s'il faut qu'à votre foi
Il en coûte un soupir qui ne soit pas pour moi.
Allez, mes yeux jamais ne reverront vos charmes.

ZAÏRE

Tu m'as donc tout ravi, Dieu témoin de mes larmes !
Tu veux commander seul à mes sens éperdus. . . .
Eh bien ! puisqu'il est vrai que vous ne m'aimez plus,
Seigneur. . . .

OROSMANE

Il est trop vrai que l'honnour me l'ordonne,
Que je vous adorai, que je vous abandonne,
Que je renonce à vous, que vous le désirez,
Que sous une autre loi. . . Zaïre, vous pleurez ?

It is to be hoped the reader admires. Those stilted sentiments and baggy alexandrines will leave most English readers totally unmoved, while the death of Zaïre, with its stage-directions to preserve decency and the "rules of Aristotle", is more likely to create mirth than compassion.

VOLTAIRE

ACTE V, SCENE IX

OROSMANE, ZAÏRE, et FATIME, *marchant pendant la nuit dans l'enfoncement du théâtre.*

ZAÏRE

Viens, Fatime.

OROSMANE

Qu'entends-je ! Est-ce là cette voix
Dont les sons enchanteurs m'ont séduit tant de fois ?
Cette voix qui trahit un feu si légitime ?
Cette voix infidèle, et l'organe du crime ?
Perfide ! . . . vengeons-nous. . . quoi ! c'est elle ?
ô destin !
(*Il tire son poignard*).
Zaïre ! Ah ! Dieu ! . . . ce fer échappe de ma main.

ZAÏRE à FATIME

C'est ici le chemin ; viens, soutiens mon courage.

FATIME

Il va venir.

OROSMANE

Ce mot me rend toute ma rage.

ZAÏRE

Je marche en frissonnant, mon coeur est éperdu. . . .
Est-ce vous, Nérestan, que j'ai tant attendu ?

OROSMANE, *courant à* ZAÏRE,

C'est moi que tu trahis : Tombe à mes pieds, parjure !

ZAÏRE, *tombant dans la coulisse,*

Je me meurs, O mon Dieu !

OROSMANE

J'ai vengé mon injure. &c.

THE DRAMATIST

With all the good will in the world one can see that only as a schoolboy's exercise in tragedy ; yet it was written when Voltaire was nearly forty, was immensely successful on the stage, was widely read and admired when printed. Where was Voltaire's sense of humour when he added that fatal stage-direction, "tombant dans la coulisse"? It may be objected that it is acting unfairly to tear scenes from their context. The reply might be that this was exactly what Voltaire did to Shakespeare ; but as to the situations of the plays, M. Lanson calls them "clichés" and describes them thus : "sons, fathers, mothers who kill or intend to kill their fathers, mothers or sons, hatreds of brothers, homicidal jealousies, unnatural sentiments and crimes, disguises which lead to misfortunes, fatalities which devastate life."

How then are we to explain the great popularity of Voltaire's tragedies?

It is a commonplace that most cultured audiences do not ask of a dramatist original genius but skilled talent ; they wish for able variations on a style which tradition or their own preference has induced them to believe is the unsurpassable point of excellence. Audiences grow weary of masterpieces when repeated too often ; they are indignant when a new kind of excellence is presented to them ; what they want is the old dish dressed up with new spices. That is what Voltaire did with French tragedy. In his day Racine was accepted in Paris as the ultimate excellence of the art of tragedy ; but in spite of the exigencies of "bon goût" people wearied of repeated performances of *Andromache* and *Britannicus*. Voltaire introduced into post-Racinean tragedy a dash of Shakespearean melodrama, seldom so much as to be censured for "mauvais goût", never any of the pro-

VOLTAIRE

fundity, poetry, and living characterisation of Shakespeare, but some piece of sensationalism (like the production of Caesar's body) to stimulate the jaded palate of the habitual theatre-goer. Voltaire's theatrical verse is nearly always uninspired and mediocre; he can perpetrate horrid inversions of this sort :

" De ses republicains la triste austérité
De son coeur généreux révolte la fierté ; "

His plots and situations are commonplace ; he is unable to draw characters except in vague, general lines—hence, by the way, his complete failure in comedy. But his verses sounded like those of a relaxed and " philosophic " Racine ; his plots were the kind people were accustomed to ; characterization was hardly required in French tragedy, for is tragedy not " the history of a great single *action* " ? And he had the skill to introduce the sensational touches mentioned, to send his puppets on the stage in new, exciting, and exotic costumes—Mediaeval, Roman, Greek, Byzantine, Chinese, Mahommedan. Moreover, the ingredients of Voltairean tragedy are always skilfully varied in different proportions ; if Racine predominates, there are nevertheless artful thefts from Corneille and Shakespeare, Quinault and Sophocles. " Il y a toujours de l'imprévu pour amuser la curiosié, du connu pour rassurer les habitudes."[1]

Voltaire was extremely attentive to popular taste, watching the effect of his lines on the audience, cutting, altering, re-writing, to comply with their whims. He is the type of the skilful manufacture of public amusement. His relation to Racine is rather like the relation of the imitative Harrison Ainsworth to Scott. But let

[1] Lanson, p. 103.

THE DRAMATIST

us give Voltaire his due ; these tragedies contain long tirades, brusque clashes of duty and sentiment, super-noble characters, pathetic situations, tears and bloody daggers, chain-clanking prisoners of high birth, fair damsels in distress, tyrants and heroes, faithful confidantes and faithless friends—all the " tragic " stock-in-trade which people like or used to like. Moreover, there is that Voltairean energy. . . . With his feet held down by conventional plots, his ankles fettered with " tirades ", his arms bound with alexandrines, and his eyes bandaged with bon goût, he yet contrives to push on the action, to advance under these crushing handicaps. Tedious though these long speeches are, they move, they get on with the play ; they stamp, they rave, they utter impossibly noble sentiments, they drown us in floods of conventional verse—but they do not merely mark time. Voltaire's tragedies do embody an action ; and the characters, vague and unreal though they are, do progress towards a climax. One can almost see the restless little man pushing and tugging them about, running from one to the other to suggest what they shall do next, and finally compelling them to murder each other—en tombant dans la coulisse.

Voltaire was a stage dramatist. His text is again unlike Shakespeare's in that the dramatic poetry does not overpower and crush actor, producer, décors, the very theatre itself. Whoever saw a production of Shakespeare which made half the effect which the same play creates when lived in the imagination ? Voltaire's tragedies do not possess any of this overwhelming power. His text is more like an opera libretto, whose purpose is to provide a theme for the ingenious virtuosity of actors and actresses, musicians, painters, stage-directors, costume-

VOLTAIRE

makers, and all the other collaborators towards a grand dramatic spectacle. The Voltairean tragedy is colourless in the study ; set it back in its baroque setting, with elaborate décors, with fiddlers at the right moments, gorgeous costumes, the voice of Mlle Clairon and the tragic energy of Le Kain—then, indeed, one might judge it fairly, one might even find that it was a successfully bizarre entertainment. Add all or any of these decorations to Shakespeare's text and they appear an insult ; Voltaire's text can hardly exist without them.

There is one more reason for Voltaire's contemporary vogue as a dramatist, and that is a very characteristic trait—the skill with which he wove lines capable of a political, social, or anti-Christian interpretation into the texture of an apparently harmless tragedy. (One or two of these have already been quoted in foot-notes to the first part of this book.) If the reader will bear in mind the French delight to " fronder les pouvoirs ", the quickness of a French audience to take a hint, the growing feeling against the monarchy and the Church during the eighteenth century ; he will see how a play might be violently attacked and violently applauded by the two political parties merely because of passages like the following :

" Esclaves de leurs rois, et même de leurs prêtres,
Les Toscans semblent nés pour servir sous des maîtres,
Et, de leur chaine antique adorateurs heureux,
Voudraient que l'univers fût esclave comme eux."

For " Toscans " understand " Français " and it is easy to realise how the philosophes cheered and the abbés hissed.

" Qui naquit dans la pourpre en est rarement digne."
" Soit toujours un héros ; sois plus, sois citoyen."

THE DRAMATIST

Patriotic vanity was not neglected :

> " Vous ne me parlez plus de ces belles contrées
> Où d'un people poli les femmes adorées
> Reçoivent cet encens que l'on doit à vos yeux."

And even the bellicose tendency of the French, which Voltaire really disapproved of, received the passing tribute of a Caesar :

> " L'aigle des légions, que je retiens encore,
> Demande à s'envoler vers les mers du Bosphore."

Égalité and civic virtue also received their homage :

> " Les mortels sont égaux, ce n'est point la naissance,
> C'est la seule vertu qui fait leur différence."

But the most artful shafts are reserved for the " infâme ", who is constantly being crushed in the guise of superstition, fanaticism, or Mahommedanism.

> " O superstition !   tes rigeurs inflexibles
> Privent d'humanité les coeurs les plus sensibles."

And not to multiply citations, let this tirade from *Mahomet* stand in lieu of many such ; Palmire denounces Mahomet:

> " Que le monde, par toi séduit et ravagé,
> Rougisse de ses fers, les brise et soit vengé !
> Que ta religion, qui fonda l'imposture,
> Soit l'éternel mépris de la race future !
> Que l'enfer, dont tes cris menaçaient tant de fo's
> Quiconque osait douter de tes indignes lois ;
> Que l'enfer, que ces lieux de douleur et de rage,
> Pour toi seul préparés, soient ton juste partage. . . ."

VOLTAIRE

These allusions and denunciations have no interest for us, but at a time when they were topical and controversial they brought down the house as effectually as the music-hall comedian now does by some apt political or social allusion. The supposed iniquities of the Church and the monarchy were Voltaire's equivalent to a scrap of paper and the Bolshevists.

The vogue of Voltaire's tragedies continued well into the Revolutionary period, but declined with the growth of Romanticism ; Stendhal, who frequented the Comédie Française assiduously in his youth, shows the increasing tendency to prefer Shakespeare to Voltaire. Strangely enough, the Voltairean tragedy contributed towards the introduction of Shakespeare into France. By his borrowings from Shakespeare, Voltaire opened the way to Ducis and Joseph Chénier, who in turn opened the way for Hugo ; but none of these French adaptations of Shakespeare bears any essential relation to the core of Shakespearean drama. French critics have long since abandoned their old contempt for Shakespeare, but the English poet's effect on French drama has been small and is confined to exteriors. The profundity of Shakespearean tragedy cannot be imitated or imported. The influence of Voltairean tragedy no doubt was exerted over minor French dramatists, but no great work has been produced by his followers.

The operas, comedies, and miscellaneous dramatic pieces of Voltaire are quite unimportant. His comedies are poor because, as Condorcet pointed out, Voltaire saw only the comedy of opinions, not the comedy of character. In fact, inability to create character is a defect inherent in all Voltaire's works ; his best characters are amusingly embodied opinions, a Dr Pangloss, a

THE DRAMATIST

Huron ; or they are even more transparent allegories. One cannot say that Voltaire's comedies are definitely bad—one can hardly say that of any of his work—but they do not rise above the thousand such pieces of the eighteenth century, except from the fact of their authorship. *Nanine* is generally held to be the best.

In fulfilling that ungrateful task of librettist, which consists in furnishing words for a musician to smother with sound, Voltaire's gift for writing light verse served him well. One would gladly believe with the French critics that these are as good as Metastasio, but little resemblance can be found. In all the solemn and noble strains, like the serious parts of *Samson*, Voltaire is extremely feeble ; but in light songs of love, wine and jest, he is excellent. The prologue to *Samson*, is still readable. But where he excels is in light pieces such as *La Fête de Bélébat*,[1] which contains the amusing song of the curé de Courdimanche :

> " Salut au curé de Courdimanche ;
>   Oh ! que c'est un homme divin !
> Sa ménagère est fraîche et blanche,
> Salut au curé de Courdimanche :
>   Sûr d'une soif que rien n'étanche,
>   Il viderait cent brocs de vin ;
> Salut au curé de Courdimanche ;
>   Oh ! que c'est un homme divin ! "

There is little of interest in *Tanis et Zélide* ; *Pandore* is rather better, but most unfortunately challenges comparison with *Prometheus Unbound*. We know what Voltaire himself thought of the Court Operas *La*

[1] Not all this piece is by Voltaire.

VOLTAIRE

Princesse de Navarre and *Le Temple de la Gloire*, he called them "farces de la foire". All have a few touches of graceful light verse.

Generally speaking, Voltaire's earlier tragedies are the best. If the reader is curious to sample Voltaire as a dramatist, he should read *Œdipe*, *Brutus*, *La Mort de César*, *Zaïre*, *Alzire*, *Mahomet*, *l'Orphélin de la Chine*, *Tancrède* and *Mérope*. The comedy of *Nanine* should be added as a tenth.

XIV

VOLTAIRE AS LITERARY CRITIC

It will not be supposed that a writer so energetic and positive, so essentially critical, as Voltaire, could refrain from expounding and defending his literary faith. The amount of Voltaire's literary criticism is large. *The Commentary on Corneille* is an immense and painstaking work. The essay on Epic poetry, the prefaces and notes to Voltaire's own plays and poems, the articles and reviews contributed to the *Gazette Littéraire*,[1] the *Conseils à un Journaliste*, the remarks in the lives of Molière and J. B. Rousseau, the *Lettres* to the Prince of Brunswick-Lunebourg, the *Connaissance de la Poésie et de l'Eloquence* by no means exhaust the list of Voltaire's essays in literary criticism ; while it must be remembered that topics of literary criticism and history are discussed in works like the *Dictionnaire Philosophique* and the *Siècle de Louis XIV*, and, informally, in the *Correspondance*. These pieces are scattered through Voltaire's collected works almost at hazard, and it is not surprising that they are sometimes overlooked among the mass of his other work.

As a literary critic Voltaire distresses us by the narrow, almost finicky standards of good taste which regulated and hampered his judgment. He delights us by the skill and brilliance of his critical faculties within those

[1] The famous and brilliant attack on Marat appeared in *Le Journal de Politique et de Littérature* in 1777. Voltaire contributed a brief but sharp attack on *Tristram Shandy* to the same periodical.

VOLTAIRE

limits and still more by the intellectual curiosity which set him exploring the masterpieces of foreign literature, which at that time in France were almost completely ignored as barbarous. What was the Voltairean " good taste "? In a sentence it was a refinement upon the best writers of the age of Louis XIV with an addition of grace and amiability ; it was the pinnacle of polished good sense and good manners. Who now can fail to see that polished good sense and good manners are nearly as incompatible with the profoundest passions and most towering beauties of literature, especially of poetry, as are moral bigotry and commercial vulgarism? Had Voltaire and his contemporaries been right in their supreme standard of good taste, with its rules and carefully planned limits, then he would have been not only a very great critic, but (as indeed they held him to be), a great epic poet and a great tragic dramatist.

The prime defect of Voltaire's critical standards is not the exaction of compliance to various definitions and "rules from Aristotle", but in the reference of all literature to the touch-stones of good sense and probability, as those qualities were conceived by a refined Frenchman of the eighteenth century. The unities are no serious handicap to the workings of a sublime imagination ; " good sense " and " probability " are. The wonderful Hebrew image, " the mountains skipped like young lambs ",[1] revolted Voltaire ; " nothing could justify it ", for it " passes all the limits of license ". Similarly the images in the *Song of Solomon*, " thy breasts are like two young roes which feed among the lilies " are objectionable because of a " je ne sais quoi de gigantesque " which

---

[1] In the violent glare of midday sunlight the distant mountains of Palestine do appear to leap and bound.

THE LITERARY CRITIC

destroys the grace and the effect. It is not hard, then, to see why Voltaire found Shakespeare " monstrous " and " without the least spark of taste ". That is quite true ; Shakespeare and Isaiah missed the advantages of a Jesuit education and had never read Racine ; it is impossible that they, any more than Homer, should possess Voltairean " good taste " ; and since the Frenchmen of the eighteenth century were convinced that their taste was the supreme test of merit, obviously Shakespeare, Isaiah, and Homer were defective poets when compared with Voltaire. Unluckily for Voltaire, taste changed, as it had changed before and will change again ; but somehow *Romeo and Juliet* and the *Iliad* have survived these changes and *Zaïre* and *La Henriade* have not.

Nevertheless, modern critics are too severe in judging Voltaire's critical attitude. Because he said Shakespeare was a drunken savage, they conclude he was an imbecile. Even M. Lanson misses one point and is, perhaps, wrong when he says Voltaire had no notion of the relativity of taste. Now, in the *Essai sur la Poésie Epique* Voltaire recognizes the relativity of national taste and he only applies his " bon goût " with extreme rigour when judging French works or when defending French literature from contamination by foreign models. I do not say that Voltaire always observed this broad-minded attitude, but I do say that he sometimes did and that he recognized it as a general principle. When writing of English literature in the *Lettres Philosophiques* he praised Shakespeare on the whole ; he only attacked Shakespeare outrageously when French dramatists began to imitate the Englishman and (which was much worse) to contrast Voltaire unfavourably with him. The following lines from the *Essai sur la Poésie* seem to me a certain

VOLTAIRE

indication that Voltaire recognized the mutability and relativity of taste :

> " Il faut dans tous les arts se donner bien de garde de ces définitions trompeuses par lesquelles nous osons exclure toutes les beautés qui nous sont inconnues, ou que la coûtume ne nous a point encore rendues familières. . . . Dans les arts qui dépendent purement de l'imagination, il y a autant de révolutions que dans les États ; ils changent en mille manières, tandis qu'on cherche à les fixer."

And again, even more clearly, he says in the same essay :

> " Ces ténèbres visibles de Milton[1] ne sont point condamnées en Angleterre, et les Espagnols ne reprennent point cette même pensée dans Solis. Il est très-certain que les Français ne souffriraient point de pareilles libertés. Ce n'est pas assez que l'on puisse excuser la license de ces expressions ; l'exactitude française n'admet rien qui ait besoin d'excuse."

And once more :

> " Si donc nous voulons avoir une connaissance un peu étendue de ces arts, il faut nous informer de quelle manière on les cultive chez toutes les nations."

No one, surely, will contend that such ideas show a narrow chauvinism of taste? Voltaire held that it is a good thing to be acquainted with as many foreign literatures as possible, but that in writing a man should conform to the taste of his own country. What could be more sensible?

---

[1] Referring to:
" . . . . yet from those flames
No Light, but rather darkness visible . . ."

THE LITERARY CRITIC

Add to this that Voltaire introduced a whole mass of foreign literature to his countrymen and adapted frequently from foreign sources in his own writing, both prose and verse ; and it is plain that to call Voltaire a " chauvin en goût " is an over-statement.[1] Would *La Pucelle* ever have existed without Pulci, the *Mort de César* without *Julius Caesar*? True, Voltaire altered his imitations to suit French taste, but not entirely, not slavishly ; witness the undeniable fact that French audiences would not endure *La Mort de César* because it did not conform to French standards.

The *Essai sur la Poésie Épique* was an early work ; let us look at a critical essay of another period. In September, 1764, Voltaire wrote a long review of Professor Lowth's (of Oxford) Latin lectures on Hebrew poetry. This was at the moment when the crushing of the " infâme " was in full swing and the campaign against Shakespearean influence in France very severe. One might expect questionable jokes at the Bible and denunciations of Hebrew poetry ; on the contrary, the essay is temperate and, generally speaking, a very just appreciation of the Bible as literature. It is true Voltaire points out, what no one can deny, that the Hebrews lacked " ce que nous appelons goût, délicatesse, convenance." He also says that the metaphors of the Hebrew poets are " outrées ", but immediately adds that this was not necessarily a defect to the Jews. He says too " leurs moeurs étaient simples et encore barbares ". But he points out that the metaphors of the Hebrews are striking because they are taken from familiar objects ; he contrasts

[1] The difficulty is that Voltaire's work is so bulky and his statements at different periods of his life so contradictory that even the most qualified generalisation can be disproved by quotation.

VOLTAIRE

Isaiah's images favourably with Horace's ; he praises the Hebrews for the energy with which they paint the grandeur and majesty of God ; he points out the dramatic qualities of their poetry and says of the book of Job that it is " entirely dramatic " and " truly poetic in style ". " The multitude of grand and powerful things to be met with in the prophets ", says Voltaire, " is truly astonishing. Only the Greeks can be compared with them in this respect ; for the Romans are rather pure, elegant, and correct, than sublime." He compares Isaiah with Homer ; Jeremiah with Simonides ; Ezechiel with Aeschylus. And he winds up by reproaching Lowth for omitting any mention of Hebrew pastoral poetry and adds that the book of Ruth is " precious because of the multitude of pastoral images scattered through it."

In this rapid précis I do less than justice to the acuteness and truth of Voltaire's remarks on Hebrew poetry, but enough remains to show that his judgment here is not warped by any fanaticism of " bon goût " or of irreligion. I do not suppose he invented these appreciations and comparisons ; probably he got them from Lowth. But in any case they show that Voltaire did recognize relativity of taste and could admire poetry the most remote from that of eighteenth century France. An enlightened modern professor, lecturing on the Bible as literature, would echo several of these judgments and probably make the same comparisons. It is true that Voltaire has pitilessly railed at the Bible in a hundred other places, but he is not attacking it there as poetry, but as history, as morals, as a record of divinely inspired truth. That is only what Renan did with more restraint, knowledge, and suavity.

The full fury of Voltairean good taste was displayed

THE LITERARY CRITIC

in his dramatic criticism. His admiration for Racine was unbounded, for Corneille great, but with reserves; he believed that Racine, Corneille, and Molière had created the finest and noblest drama in the world. From their plays he deduced a theory of drama by which he tested the drama of all other languages—the theory in which vraisemblance plays so large a part. His youthful philippics against Sophocles, the ferocious attack upon Shakespeare made from Ferney, were impertinent misunderstandings.[1] But if he judged Shakespeare harshly he was severe in his criticism of Corneille. He is not in the least afraid to call Corneille's style "barbarous". Let that be some consolation to wounded Shakespeareans.

I cannot leave this subject without one more remark. If Voltaire's standards of taste are repugnant to those of imaginative poetry at its most intense sweeps of passion and thought, they are eminently the standards of the best formal prose. Good sense, vraisemblance, sobriety, precision, elegance, clarity, are the qualities Voltaire admired and possessed. The greatest poetry demands in addition profound passion, a towering imagination, an eloquence which rushes from the depths to the heights and back again; those qualities Voltaire did not possess and underestimated. His most ambitious efforts in poetry and the drama are therefore failures and only the minor sorts of poetry were cultivated by him with success; for in them his literary virtues could adequately and acceptably find expression. But Voltaire's true medium is prose, though he may not have thought so himself; and

---

[1] Worse, they lacked candour. Voltaire twice treats Falstaff as a character in a tragedy; to score a point he makes Falstaff the "general of an army" in one place and "Lord Chief Justice" in another.

VOLTAIRE

though he affected to scorn his " romans ", we consider them one of his chief glories. Much elegant and charming and witty verse was written in eighteenth century France, but at its best it was a period of prose-writers, and the fine flower of that prose was Voltaire's. In Voltaire's hands French prose became one of the most supple, elegant, and precise instruments of expression ever framed by civilized men. He inherited a noble tradition of prose and carried that tradition a step nearer perfection ; it may be that he over-perfected it, that he left it nothing but decadence. Yet the best modern French prose, the prose of Renan and France, the clear, precise, sober prose of a hundred other French writers, is still the prose of Voltaire. That tradition is crumbling rapidly before the assaul s of a new age, but until the French language passes into a new dialect, as remote from the speech of the eighteenth century as that is from the language of the fifteenth century, its best prose will bear the mark of Voltaire.

XV

VOLTAIRE AS HISTORIAN AND BIOGRAPHER

Voltaire's principal historical works are : *Essai sur les Moeurs et l'Esprit des Nations* ; *Le Siècle de Louis XIV*; *Le Siècle de Louis XV*; *Histoire du Parlement de Paris* ; *Annales de l'Empire* ; *Charles XII*; *Histoire de l'Empire de Russie sous Pierre le Grand*. The preparation and composition of these works were in progress during nearly half a century—the materials for the *Siècle de Louis XIV* were being gathered before the exile to England and the *Histoire du Parlement* was not published until 1769. The histories run into several thousand closely printed pages and represent one of the most comprehensive surveys of human affairs ever attempted by one man. The history of France naturally is the chief theme, but always in relation to the history of Europe, while the great *Essai* treats the history of Europe in relation to that of the world as it was then known. *Charles XII* traces the extraordinary career of that monarch, and the last incursion of Sweden into Europe as a formidable military power. *Pierre le Grand* again describes a remarkable life history at the period when Russia entered the comity of civilized European powers. Taking Voltaire's histories in bulk, we can assert that he covered a vast tract of the historical ground open to an eighteenth century writer, that he explored regions of history few had entered

VOLTAIRE

before, that he left at least three original contributions to the history of the seventeenth and eighteenth centuries in Europe. But that is not all; his ideals as a historian broke with old traditions, and he bequeathed a conception of history which modern writers have developed and perfected without wholly superseding. Voltaire is one of the creators of modern history; he comes after Clarendon and Bossuet; he precedes Hume and Gibbon. He is one of the first rational historians, one of the first to liberate history from fable and miracle, to reject imitation of classical models, to write something more than chronicles or expanded memoirs.

It is not true, as is sometimes asserted, that Voltaire's histories are dull, biassed, inaccurate, and out-of-date. A more easy and entertaining style than that of Voltaire's histories would be difficult to find. Where will a better be found? In Gibbon? In Carlyle? In Michelet? In the disciples of the École des Chartes? Gibbon is a pupil of Voltaire and so more distantly is Sorel, whose *Europe et la Révolution Française* represents the Voltairean idea of history brought near to perfection. Voltaire is indeed biassed—against the Church of Rome and against "barbarous" absolutism; but think of the prejudices of Carlyle, of the republicanism of Michelet! History is partly a science, but must also be partly an art or it is lifeless; an absolutely impartial history would probably be absolutely dull; the historian must have a point of view, a conception of human development. Moreover, the partiality of Voltaire has been exaggerated; few even among the best historians are more scrupulous, more devoid of fantastic and fine-spun theories. The inaccuracies of fact in Voltaire's histories may be considerable, but he took pains to verify his statements. When

THE HISTORIAN

he erred it was generally because his sources were defective; rarely because he was wilful or careless. No other eighteenth century writer of history (except his pupils) is still seriously discussed by competent historians.

One cannot wholly deny that Voltaire's histories are out of date. Each epoch tends to re-write history from its own point of view and the modern world is now a stranger to Voltaire's epoch; moreover, the discoveries of science, the methodical examination and classification of sources by generations of patient researchers, give modern historians a firm basis of established knowledge which was almost entirely lacking in the eighteenth century. Modern knowledge of the ancient world and of history outside Europe is not only vastly more extensive but much more accurate than was possible during Voltaire's life. In his days the study of pre-history, if it existed, was considered impious; the stone and bronze ages were almost unknown and are ignored by Voltaire; the history of ancient Egypt was a blank or rather a mass of unverified assertions by Greek authors, for no Champollion had then read the Rosetta stone; so little was understood of early Mesopotamia that Voltaire argued on a priori grounds of common sense that Assyria and Babylonia were different names for the same Empire; the existence of Cretan civilisation was unsuspected and knowledge of the Orient was both scanty and inexact.[1] Immense additions have been made to general knowledge even in the history of Europe. In this sense Voltaire's histories are out of date, yet there is not a great deal to be cut away from his *Charles XII* and his *Louis XIV* even if there is much to be added and modified. Even the

---

[1] Which is why the " philosophes " could idealize the Chinese with impunity.

VOLTAIRE

Essai may furnish a modern reader with information and ideas.

Granted that Voltaire's historical work shows defects ; granted that the immeasurably greater knowledge and more accurate methods of modern historians have superannuated him ; we yet cannot treat his work in history as negligible or as defective to the extent indicated by Professor Saintsbury. Some portions of his history are more obsolete than others ; if his surveys of ancient and oriental history are rendered almost worthless by more recent books, his direct contact with the age of Louis XIV gives him an advantage which cannot be contested. If he lacked the privilege of reading Saint-Simon, he had the greater privilege of conversing with Saint-Simon's personages or with those who had known them intimately. Even when he compiled from other than first-hand sources he generally went to good authorities and sifted their information critically. He even renders justice to the successors of Peter ; for though we find him exclaiming sarcastically in one place that " doubtless it was to the interest of Rome that the nations should be imbecile ", he praises Pope Alexander III (1167) for declaring that " all Christians should be exempt from slavery ".[1] Again, when speaking of mediaeval trial by combat and divine proof and of curious religious customs like the Feast of Fools, Voltaire says :

> " Rome a souvent condamné ces coûtumes barbares, aussi bien que le duel et les épreuves. Il y eut toujours dans les rites de l'Eglise romaine, malgré tous les troubles et tous les scandales, plus de décence, plus de gravité qu'ailleurs ; et on sentait qu'en tout,

[1] *Essai sur les Moeurs*, etc.

THE HISTORIAN

cette Église, quand elle était libre et bien gouvernée, était faite pour donner des leçons aux autres."[1]

Voltaire, then, was not wholly prejudiced and fanatical even when dealing with institutions and persons whose influence he considered disastrous to the human race; as a historian, he tried to be just even to " l'infâme ". Contrast Voltaire's *Essai* with Bossuet's *Discours sur l'Histoire Universelle*. One cannot refuse admiration to Bossuet for his vast learning and for that wonderful prose he handled with such dexterity; but as a historian he is negligible. The *Discours* is not a history, it is an eloquent Roman Catholic tract; at every turn " Providence " is invoked to explain the course of events; good kings are rewarded, wicked kings punished; miracles are abundant; Solon and Caesar are "idolators"; " Dieu tient du plus haut des cieux les rênes de tous les royaumes". The supernatural is banished from Voltaire's *Essai*; the facile edification of Bossuet gives place to a rational investigation of human affairs and an attempt is made to expose and to discuss the real motives of the actors in the world's history. The advance is considerable; Bossuet's *Discours* is a pious fairy-tale for children and women; Voltaire's *Essai* is history. However much our historians may have improved upon Voltaire in the philosophy of history, supernatural intervention in human affairs is still tacitly assumed by nations and governments. During the war of 1914-18 all belligerent governments except that of France officially and publicly besought God to come in on their side; they were still intellectually in the period of Bossuet's *Discours*.

[1] *Essai sur les Moeurs*, etc.

VOLTAIRE

An even more important innovation was the intention, expressed in both the *Essai* and *Louis XIV*, to give the history of nations, not chronologies of rulers, to discuss " the great actions of sovereigns which have rendered their peoples better and happier " and to ignore " le vulgaire des rois ". Great universal movements and struggles, like the Crusades, the rise of Mohammedanism, the contest between the Empire and the Church, are explained, not always correctly indeed, but reasonably and with an astonishing ability to reduce to coherence a multitude of facts and confused events. Much as Voltaire objects to the Middle Ages, great as is his impatience with their " barbarity ", their " grossness ", their " superstition," he has an unquenchable curiosity in discovering what were their institutions, morals, customs, how people lived, even what they ate, and how they dressed. He has a sharp eye for the strange anecdote and the picturesque fact which evoke an epoch. He describes the kind of clothes worn by the youthful Louis XIV at the triumphal entry into Paris after the Fronde ; he gives a vivid glimpse of the curious disorder of the Fronde itself by relating how several women of the people gained admission to the Parlement and asked on their knees " that all taxes be abolished."[1] Yet, in theory, at least, he insists on a critical method in accepting or rejecting or repeating historical evidence :

> " To-day we are not allowed to imitate Plutarch and still less Procopius. We only admit as historical truths those which are guaranteed. When contemporaries, like the Cardinal de Retz and the duc de la Rochefoucauld, enemies to each other, confirm the same fact in their Memoirs, that fact is indubit-

[1] *Siècle de Louis XIV*.

THE HISTORIAN

able; when they contradict each other, we must doubt; what is improbable must not be believed unless several trustworthy contemporaries unanimously assert it."[1]

Voltaire's replies to criticisms of the *Essai* and *Charles XII*, though they are slightly more tart and lofty than was necessary, show at least that he had authorities for his defence when he thought criticism unfounded and that he was candid enough to correct errors when they were pointed out to him. Considering the vast scope of the *Essai*, it is remarkable that these inevitable slips were so few that contemporary critics were often reduced to the common straits of misrepresentation and wilful perversity in order to disparage a work they were incapable of producing themselves. Nonotte and La Beaumelle were very free with "corrections"; often in small points of detail they were right, but their criticisms did not invalidate the *Essai* and *Louis XIV*, and for every blunder they set right they themselves made another.

The bulk of the *Essai* is occupied with the period from Charlemagne to Louis XIII; the *Siècle de Louis XIV*, though written earlier, becomes a continuation of the same work, still further but less impartially prolonged by the *Siècle de Louis XV*. The Church of Rome, its pretentions and susceptibilities, were Voltaire's worst obstacle. On the one hand, he was forced to temporize to the extent of inserting numerous remarks to the effect that the history of the Bible is "a respectable miracle" with which he did not presume to meddle,[2] but that he

[1] Siècle de Louis XIV.

[2] Transparent excuses which had no effect at Rome. All Voltaire's works, like most of the classics of Europe, are on the Index.

VOLTAIRE

investigated history by the light of reason alone ; and, on the other hand, his hostility to the Church, his dislike of the " superstitions " of Christianity, seriously misled him in the construction of his enormous chart to the past. He is sound in his attack on the " fable " of the Donation of Constantine, first proved to be a forgery by Lorenzo Valla and now admitted to be such by all impartial writers. He is equally sound in denouncing the supposed letter from Pilate to Tiberius, the false letters of Seneca and St. Paul, but he failed to see that the Apocryphal gospels and *Acts* have a real value for an investigator into the growth of early Christianity. Voltaire saw " forgeries " deliberately performed to deceive, in what was in fact only the literature of the early Christians. In disparaging the martyrs he was at times gross ; yet his description of the miracle of Saint Tecusa and the six other Virgins is as witty and malicious as anything in *Candide*. Voltaire considered that the two great enemies of human happiness were War and Fanaticism ; but he extended Fanaticism to mean all religions which were not akin to Deism and " la saine philosophie " ; he did not observe that Fanaticism is not co-extensive with Christianity but with the spirit of intolerance, which may be discovered in " philosophes " and " rebels " as much as in Christians and in the orthodox. He does dimly see the moral force of the Church during the confusion of the Middle Ages, but he fails to observe the most important fact that from the fall of the Roman Empire to the Renaissance the Church of Rome was the only great civilizing force in Europe. To miss that was a gross blunder, not peculiar to Voltaire. As a reaction against it we now have historians and pseudo-historians who draw impossibly ideal pictures of the Middle Ages

THE HISTORIAN

and would like to persuade us to revive the domination of the Church ; but the Church was at best a palliative to anarchy and social miseries, not a final solution of human problems. Yet even here Voltaire at least attempted to be just. He says of the Benedictines :

> " On leur donna même souvent des terres incultes qu'ils défrichèrent de leurs mains, et qu'ils firent ensuite cultiver par des serfs. Ils formèrent des bourgades, des petites villes même autour de leur monastères. Ils étudièrent ; ils furent les seuls qui conservèrent les livres en les copiant ; et enfin, dans ces temps barbares où les peuples étaient si misérables, c'était une grande consolation de trouver dans les cloîtres une retraite assurée contre la tyrannie."[1]

He laments that history is but a record of crimes, that the nations of Europe exhausted their strength and retarded civilization by fratricidal wars, regrets that there was no international tribunal to judge the disputes of kings. He does not see, when he attacks the suzerainty of the Papacy, that such a tribunal actually had existed and was rendered impotent or a power for evil by the passions of men. The modern effort to create an International Court of Arbitration is in a sense an attempt to create a secular papacy, which will lack the prestige of Rome and of religion ; there is no great hope that it will be any more successful than the Papacy in keeping the peace of the world or avoiding corruption ; for if it becomes powerful it will be the prey of ambition, and if it remains a merely moral force it will be disregarded ; if nations were wise and virtuous it would be unnecessary, and as long as they are the reverse it will be impotent or

[1] *Essai sur les Moeurs*, etc.

VOLTAIRE

liable to corruption. Voltaire under-estimated the positive good achieved by the Church and over-estimated the evil done by ecclesiastics. This hostility puts him wrong both in vast surveys and in trifles; he entirely misunderstands the true purpose of the Crusades and he accepts gleefully the apocryphal " Proud Prelate " of Queen Elizabeth because it provides an opportunity for a " lesson " to Bishops.

Outside Church affairs, which unfortunately for him are half the history of the Middle Ages, Voltaire is often sound. When he traces the secular enmity between France and Germany back to the division of the Empire of Charlemagne, he is stating a proposition conclusively worked out by Sorel. When he points out that the great political ideal of Italy is and has for centuries been the revival of the Roman Empire, he is right; a great nation does not forget its glorious past; the dream of Republican and Imperial Rome was behind the Papacy and behind Rienzi, it is the clue to the Renaissance and the Risorgimento; it is even the moral force of Fascismo. Voltaire's epigram on Feudalism has a large streak of truth in it; he calls it : " Ordonnance pour faire la guerre civile ".[1]

Voltaire excels in rapid summaries of the " state of Europe " at a given time and in brief chapters on the customs of an age. Here he was well served by his clear, orderly mind, his easy style, and his unquenchable curiosity. Such chapters also are made to serve the propaganda which underlies the *Essai*. We can find many of Voltaire's social ideas in these pages, ideas which profoundly influenced the eighteenth and nineteenth centuries. He believed firmly in social amelioration, even though the spectacle of so many centuries of violence

[1] *Essai sur les Moeurs*, etc.

THE HISTORIAN

discouraged and exasperated him. As we read the *Essai* his idea of human happiness emerges slowly. Reason and " saine philosophie " lead us to a belief in a Supreme Being and an orderly universe ; they lead us also to reject supernatural intervention and the immortality of the soul. The only life we know is our life here ; and the object of government is to make that life as tolerable as possible for all men. True liberty is " equality before the laws ", no interference with men's lives by " royal pleasure ". Peace and tolerance are the foundations of prosperity, and prosperity is the foundation of the humane virtues, of sociability, of the arts. With these man's life can at least be made tolerable ; without them he falls into " barbarity ". Luxury is not an evil, because it refines the users and employs many people who would otherwise be idle. It is a reasonable enough view ; but unfortunately Voltaire did not foresee that the perverse ingenuity of man would twist this ideal into " commercialism ", a condition where wealth becomes the sole standard of merit, the sole end of life, and that the struggles of rival kings would give way to the more deadly wars of rival commerces. Nevertheless the misfortunes of the twentieth century have been exaggerated and its advantages disregarded because too well known. Voltaire would have thought us mad to complain and, to an extent, rightly ; most of us would be disgusted and unhappy if transported suddenly to the age of Charlemagne. But in carrying out Voltaire's social ideal Europe has lost more than he could have imagined it would lose and, as always happens, things have not turned out as he hoped they would—the complexity of our civilization has extended its conveniences but greatly increased its fragility. We have more power than wisdom.

VOLTAIRE

The other histories and historical biographies are less ambitious than the Essai, but at least three of them deserve attention. The *Annales de l'Empire*, written for a German Princess as the *Essai* was written for Mme du Châtelet, is perhaps the least successful of Voltaire's prose works. It often repeats the *Essai* in a less happy style, and reads as if composed as a task, without Voltaire's customary energy and sparkle. Yet there are numerous satirical and witty flashes :

"Pour Vencelas, on disait qu'il aurait pu boire avec son pape, mais non négocier avec lui."[1]

But its chronicle form is a serious defect and the narrative too often languishes into a catalogue raisonné of facts ; it reminds one of the " Barebones " of schooldays. On the whole, a book to be avoided ; almost the only work by Voltaire which provides practically no interest and entertainment.

Le Siècle de Louis XIV is a very different affair. The writing of it was no appointed task but a homage to a period which Voltaire sincerely believed to be the most civilized recorded in history. There are more precise and more profound books on this age, but none more entertaining in style, few which give so interesting a survey of its activities and achievements. All writers who are men of letters first and historians afterwards are liable to be prejudiced in favour of Louis XIV, the symbolical embodiment of the age, the central point, as it were, in relation to which the whole nation ranged itself into order. The social order of the age of Louis XIV pleases an artist by its noble symmetry, its clearly-defined

[1] *Annales de l'Empire.*

THE HISTORIAN

hierarchy, its translation into action of a coherent philosophy of life. We, who live in an age of sensationalism and mental anarchy, look back upon the age of Louis XIV with a different sort of respect from Voltaire's; we are not seduced by its "taste" as Voltaire was, but we envy its order and that order may blind us to its defects. With Voltaire the seduction acted differently. He lived in an age which still respected, though to a rapidly diminishing extent, the ordered discipline of the France of Louis XIV and, quite naturally, he prized the good that existed less than the good that might be attained. Voltaire did not despise order; but he did not see that the alterations he proposed to make in the state would destroy the old order of the monarchy. Like all who lived in contact with those who had known Louis XIV he was impressed and seduced by the air of grandeur and nobility with which Louis XIV lived the part of a great monarch. From 1661 to 1715 Louis XIV was his own prime minister; during forty years of that period he and his subordinates raised France to a position it had never yet occupied; wise administration, intelligent official encouragement, stimulated a material prosperity, an intellectual activity, never known to France before; the King himself set an example of manners which made the French the "politest" nation in Europe. All these achievements cannot be denied by the most fanatical opponent of the ancien régime but they were counterbalanced by unnecessary wars of aggression which armed all Europe against France and finally produced the campaigns of Marlborough and Eugene; by a lavish expenditure which over-taxed a country exploited by the disastrous fiscal system of tax-farming. Voltaire, severe enough to these errors in the government of his

VOLTAIRE

own time, was so dazzled by the grandeur of Louis XIV that in his administration they are more than half condoned. Even more than by this, the intellectual Voltaire was seduced by the enlightened patronage of the fine arts and science undertaken by Louis XIV. Chapter XXV of the *Siècle de Louis XIV* contains an enthusiastic eulogy of the King's patronage of letters and of the arts. It is a mere senseless calumny to say that this patronage was ill-directed or that it was disastrous in its effect. On the contrary this stimulus made Paris the intellectual centre of Europe and the institutions created by Richelieu and Louis XIV and revived by Napoleon are of even more benefit to French culture.[1] Moreover (as Voltaire points out) Chapelain, who first advised the government in the distribution of pensions and royal encouragement, though a mediocre poet, was a man of immense erudition and the best critic of his age. The gifts and pensions to foreign men of distinction were another happy stroke of "grandeur" much admired by Voltaire.

These are some of the reasons which disposed Voltaire to look back at the age of Louis XIV with admiration and regret; he considered it to be an age which was truly civilized, imperfect no doubt in many respects, but an immense advance on mediaeval and Renaissance "barbarity", a stage of human development which needed only certain reforms to reach something as near

---

[1] If it be argued that literature and the arts declined towards the end of the reign and the cause be attributed to the official interference of a despot, one must be allowed to point out that the encouragement ceased at precisely that time owing to the expenses of the wars. And it is not true that despotism discourages letters and arts; the mere names of Lorenzo di Medici, Julius II, Leo X, Louis XIV, are a sufficient answer; the true enemy of the arts is not despotism but anarchy and sensationalism.

THE HISTORIAN

perfection as weak humanity can expect. Indeed, when Turgot came into power towards the end of Voltaire's life and actually carried out some of the philosopher's proposals, Voltaire sang sincerely his "nunc dimittis". Chateaubriand is quite right when he says Voltaire would have disapproved of the Revolution ; it was begun by Voltaireans, it was carried to disastrous excess by Rousseau-ites. There is also an important personal factor in his admiration for this age. It will be remembered that when Voltaire was a very young man he was rescued from parental wrath and an office stool by M. de Caumartin. This nobleman, who had known most of the eminent personages of the seventeenth century, not only inspired Voltaire with a cult for Henry IV which resulted in *La Henriade*, but gave him such intimate and picturesque accounts of the early splendours of Louis XIV that Voltaire's mind remained permanently coloured by these vivid images. Several times in the course of the *Siècle* Voltaire mentions the name of M. de Caumartin as his authority ; we may surmise that M. de Caumartin's conversation inspired many other passages and to some extent suffused the whole narrative.

Scientific historians will no doubt have many disconcerting criticisms to offer on *Le Siècle de Louis XIV*. Let us allow their supposed condemnation and see what can be saved from the wreck. If Voltaire's history is compared with that part of Saint Simon's *Mémoires* which covers the same period and personages, it will be found that the general impression from each is strangely familiar, though in temperament and style they are so different and in spite of the fact that they often take completely opposite views of the same occurrence or person. That at least means that Voltaire succeeded in recording the

VOLTAIRE

vague something we call "the spirit of an age". We can add that Voltaire's *Siècle* is the first reasoned, comprehensive survey of an epoch then recent, and that his narrative received little really damaging criticism from survivors of the age. Like all historians of recent epochs he had to struggle through overwhelming masses of detailed information, to sift conflicting evidence, to discover the general aspects of the enormous collection of facts with which he was confronted. Doubtless, the orderliness of the epoch made the task less difficult, but it can hardly be denied that he succeeded admirably in sketching the main features of the age. Moreover, the work is not a more or less skilled compilation from other historians, like the *Essai*. It is original research; the events are often told from narratives of eye-witnesses. And, with all Voltaire's enthusiasm for the age, we can still see him struggling to be impartial. He does not attempt to minimise Blenheim and Malplaquet, though his French heart bleeds at the spectacle of these disasters. He does not magnify the naval raids of Jean Bart and du Gugay-Trouin into great victories and admits regretfully but frankly that the efforts of Louis XIV to wrest naval supremacy from England ended in complete failure.[1] Finally, we can praise the arrangement of the history and the manner in which it is told. Here the theory of "vraisemblance" was of immense use to Voltaire, for it is the keynote to historical accuracy; and here too he was well served by his clear, orderly mind and by his clear, sparkling prose. We may need to correct our knowledge of the period after reading the *Siècle*, but we shall have to

---

[1] This may be thought scant praise, but the absence of Chauvinism or its opposite, anti-patriotism, is not so common in historians as one would like.

THE HISTORIAN

seek long to discover a more interesting presentation. *Le Siècle de Louis XIV* is one of the glories of Voltaire, but as often happens with writers of extreme versatility and fertility, his achievements in several *genres* result in a certain disparagement of all. Without close and expert investigation we are apt to conclude that a man who wrote so easily, so voluminously, and upon so many different topics, must be superficial and diffuse ; we are suspicious of Voltaire's poetry because he was a great prose satirist ; we think his histories must be amateurish because he gave so much attention to belles-lettres. This is not just. Voltaire excelled in many kinds of writing because he had a magnificent brain and matchless energy. Much can be learned and written in three quarters of a century by a man who is never idle. So far from its being true that Voltaire's histories are slip-shod and superficial, modern investigators[1] praise his scrupulous and careful enquiry, his general efforts for accuracy. Voltaire's library at Leningrad contains evidence of his care for historical accuracy in the multitude of notes and documents preserved ; his correspondence also shows him repeatedly enquiring from the Russian Court for confirmation of doubts when he was writing the history of Peter the Great. There is no such thing as a perfect historian ; among all literary works histories are the most apt to fall into desuetude ; we cannot deny that Voltaire's histories have ceased to be generally read, but we can at least assert that no historian of his epoch retains a better claim to our interest and approval.

There is little to be gained by pursuing this analysis into Voltaire's slighter historical works. *Louis XV*, begun in discharge of his functions as historiographer

[1] See Lanson, p. 124.

VOLTAIRE

of France, is less brilliant and comprehensive than *Louis XIV*, but it is a repository of curious and first-hand information about the age, occasionally weakened by too great a complaisance towards reigning grandeur. One fact about the *Parliement de Paris* is worth recording ; le président Desportes, a judge, and no friend to Voltaire, speaks of the book in these terms : " Quoique ce soit un tissu d'épigrammes peu digne d'un pareil sujet, le récit des faits y est d'une grande exactitude." This is one more proof of Voltaire's historical accuracy even when dealing with an institution he disliked.

As a specimen of Voltaire's historical and biographical style, showing his epigrammatic brilliance and power of clear generalization, take this portrait from the end of *Charles XII*, where the King's character and career are briefly summed up :

> " Presque toutes ses actions, jusqu'à celles de sa vie privée et unie, ont été bien loin au delà du vraisemblable. C'est peut-être le seul de tous les hommes, et jusqu'ici le seul de tous les rois, qui ait vécu sans faiblesses ; il a porté toutes les vertus des héros à un excès ou elles sont aussi dangereuses que les vices opposés. Sa fermeté, devenue opiniâtreté, fit ses malheurs dans l'Ukraine, et le retint cinque ans en Turquie ; sa libéralité, dégénérant en profusion a ruiné la Suède ; son courage, poussé jusqu'à la témérité, a causé sa mort ; sa justice a été quelquefois jusqu'a la cruauté, et, dans les dernières années, le maintien de son autorité approchait de la tyrannie. Ses grandes qualités, dont une seule eût pu immortaliser un autre prince, ont fait le malheur de son pays. Il n'attaqua jamais personne ; mais il ne fut pas aussi prudent qu'implacable dans ses vengeances. Il a été le premier qui ait eu l'ambition d'être conquérant

THE HISTORIAN

sans avoir l'envie d'agrandir ses Etats : il voulait gagner des empires pour les donner. Sa passion pour la gloire, pour la guerre et pour la vengeance, l'empêcha d'être bon politique, qualité sans laquelle on n'a jamais vu de conquérant. Avant la bataille et après la victoire, il n'avait que de la modestie ; après la défaite, que de la fermeté ; dur pour les autres comme pour lui-même, comptant pour rien la peine et la vie de ses sujets, aussi bien que la sienne ; homme unique plutôt que grand homme, admirable plutôt qu'à imiter. Sa vie doit apprendre aux rois combien un gouvernement pacifique et heureux est au-dessus de tant de gloire.

XVI

"LE PHILOSOPHE"

In the week that these lines are written Voltaire has twice been described in English periodicals as "a great philosopher". There can be little doubt that he remains in the public memory as a philosopher; and there can be no doubt whatever that he considered himself a "philosophe". But if M. Bergson or Mr Bertrand Russell were asked what they thought of Voltaire's philosophy, the reply would probably be a smile or the retort that Voltaire was not a philosopher at all. To a non-philosophical person there is something mysterious in the remote activities of modern philosophy. Plato complained that poets were never able to give him a rational account of their art and its processes; to the non-expert our philosophers are almost as unsatisfactory. But let us take the old accepted definitions and assume that philosophy is the science of principles, the criticism of all the sciences. Can we say that Voltaire was skilled in these? If not, what does he mean when he calls himself a philosophe? This is worth enquiry because Voltaire as philosophe is the Voltaire who most influenced the lives of human beings, which is recognized by the popular conception of Voltaire as essentially a philosopher. The explanation is perhaps that a philosopher is not the same thing as an eighteenth century philosophe.

When we use the word philosopher we think of a man like Aristotle or Spinoza, one who created a coherent,

LE PHILOSOPHE

rational, and systematic explanation of the universe. Physics, metaphysics, logic, ethics, and aesthetics are the branches or disciplines of philosophy. It might be said that the philosophers of the ancient world were particularly interested in ethics and conduct—hence the popularity of the ethical systems of Stoicism, Epicureanism, and the like—while modern philosophers tend to identify philosophy with deductions from experimental science or with metaphysics. If this be approximately true, then Voltaire was hardly a philosopher at all in the modern sense ; he is only a philosopher in the sense indicated by the ancient writer who said philosophy was learning how to live and how to die. It is quite true that Voltaire dabbled more or less successfully in all the "disciplines", but since he made no discoveries in any he can hardly be called an original philosopher. In point of fact his interests were not speculative but social and ethical. Even there his philosophic ideas and buttresses of argument were copied from others ; Voltaire's innovation was in the manner of presenting them, and that was an artistic not a philosophical originality. Voltaire's philosophy was popular not because he was an original thinker, but because he was a master of clear exposition, satire and witty raillery.

Clearly, then, there is no necessity to conduct a formal enquiry into Voltaire's philosophy as a system ; we are only concerned with the philosophe—a very different thing. Voltaire's physics and mathematics were derived from Newton, Leibnitz, Maupertuis, Clairaut, and Descartes. He confesses himself that his knowledge of these sciences was much inferior to Mme du Châtelet's, though his writings are said to show considerable familiarity with them and his exposition of Newton was

VOLTAIRE

a useful popular work. But none of these writings entitles Voltaire to praise as a discoverer. His ethics and metaphysics were principally derived from Locke, Bolingbroke, and the minor English Deists. Someone said unkindly of his *Traité de Métaphysique* that all it proves is the author's ignorance of his subject. On the contrary, Voltaire shows ability in wrestling with metaphysical abstractions, but his mind was essentially non-metaphysical. He was primarily an artist and there is surely an antithesis between the artist, for whom appearances are reality, and the metaphysician, for whom reality is beyond and apart from appearances. However this may be, Voltaire often expresses a mistrust, almost a contempt of metaphysics. He calls it " the art of reasoning about that which we do not know " ; he says *imagination* is " perhaps the one instrument with which we form our ideas, even the most metaphysical " ; he says that metaphysics is " souvent le roman de l'esprit." These are not the sayings of a metaphysician.

If we deny that Voltaire was in a strict sense a philosopher, we have to admit that he was the greatest and most influential of the " philosophes ". A philosophe might be defined as a reforming publicist of non-Christian ideals ; not a speculative philosopher, but an advocate of " improvement " by means of Reason and material ameliorations. Voltaire himself defines a philosophe as an " amateur de sagesse, c'est à dire, de la verité " ; but this is unconscionably vague, for who would claim that he was a lover of folly and lies ? The assertion that Voltaire considered philosophie chiefly a matter of conduct is proved by the words with which he continues : " All philosophes have possessed this double character ; there was none in the ancient world who failed to give examples

LE PHILOSOPHE

of virtue and lessons of moral truth to men. They may have erred in physics; but physics is so little needed for the conduct of life that philosophers have no necessity for it. Centuries were required to understand a portion of the laws of nature. A day is enough for a sage to understand the duties of man."

Philosophie, then, is largely a matter of ethics and conduct; physics and metaphysics are unimportant. When we are disturbed by questions of the how and why of the universe, the philosophe (leaning heavily upon Locke) bids us consider the order of things and ask ourselves if it can exist without a controlling intelligence. We must therefore respect the First Cause, the Supreme Being, which is God; but if we press our philosophe for something more definite, he slips uneasily into pantheism or artfully evades our queries. The main thing, the philosophe assures us, is social conduct, and the golden rule is to be found in the sayings of Confucius: "Act towards others as you would towards yourself." Philosophie is eminently useful. In England (Voltaire tells us) philosophie destroyed the religious madness which brought King Charles to the scaffold; in Sweden it prevented an archbishop from shedding the blood of the nobles with a papal bull; in Germany it maintained religious peace by showing that all theological disputes are ridiculous. In France it prevented a second Fronde and another Damiens. The philosophe is a wise man, and wisdom is the avoiding of fools and the wicked; therefore a philosophe should live only with philosophes (but, apparently, not in Potsdam). Moreover, a wise man should continually be pointing out that a hundred dogmas are not worth one good action and that it is better to

VOLTAIRE

aid one poor wretch than to "connaître à fond l'abolissant et l'aboli". Finally :

> "I do not think there has ever been a systematic (or system-making) philosopher who has not admitted at the end of his life that he had wasted his time. It must be confessed that the inventors of the mechanical arts have been far more useful to mankind than the inventors of syllogisms ; the inventor of the shuttle " l'emporte furieusement " over the inventor of innate ideas."

Thus far Voltaire himself on the topics of *Philosophie* and *Philosophe* in his dictionary, most of the two articles being devoted to a defence of individual philosophes, an attack on " fanatiques " and a panegyric of Deism. To complete our picture of the philosophe we must go a little further. We have noted that Voltaire's talents were chiefly those of an artist ; he was a consummate man of letters with varied interests, and these interests were largely social, utilitarian, and religious, not scientific or speculative. Poetry led him to the epic and to drama ; the epic brought him to history, tragedy to religion. Philosophie is based upon Deism and an interpretation of history ; for it will be found that much of Voltaire's philosophie is a defence of Deism against other religious beliefs (particularly Christianity), while the rest is an attempt to show how human life and society may be made more tolerable for everyone. The Temple libertins convinced Voltaire of the inadequacy of the Church of Rome as a spiritual and temporal guide ; more, they turned him against pessimism, austerity, and gloom and persuaded him that a wise man " takes the cash and lets the credit go ". After this, the influence of Locke and

LE PHILOSOPHE

Bolingbroke upon him was decisive and confirmed him in Deism. The study of English and of English society did the rest. Here then is the framework of our philosophe.

It seems plain that we cannot consider Voltaire as a "critic of all the sciences" or even as one skilled in the "science of principles". By a line of more or less a priori argument he convinced himself of the existence of a First Cause and agreed to call that First Cause the Supreme Being or God. It is absurd to say that Voltaire was an atheist; he was no more an atheist than Benjamin Franklin. But, since he inclined to pantheism, he did not admit the intervention of Providence in human affairs[1] and he considered it blasphemous to assert the divinity of Jesus Christ or to affirm that God had ever been incarnated in a man. He argues forcibly that Saint Paul never speaks of Jesus as God. Voltaire's opposition to Christianity, and particularly to the Church of Rome and the Society of Jesus, was not the critical opposition of a philosopher but the ardent opposition of a sectarian. Much as he wrote against the folly of sects, one can hardly escape from the impression that his Deism led him into the violence of sectarians. But the God of Voltaire was so mysterious and remote, his own temperament so essentially practical and non-mystic, that his religious views were subordinated to his social and political propaganda. His attitude is that of Pope:

> "presume not God to scan,
> The proper study of mankind is man."

He was not convinced of the immortality of the soul or

---

[1] Yet he does sometimes assert a Deity which rewards good and punishes evil.

VOLTAIRE

even that such a thing as a soul could exist at all independent of the body. He saw no reason why God should not have invested matter with the faculty of thought; indeed, he considered that soul was simply a name that men gave to their mental processes. He ignored the immense force of idealism in Christianity which had made it so powerful; as a pure Deist, he thought Roman Catholic Christianity a gross superstition, and he had more sympathy for the Society of Friends than for any other Christian body, because their faith more nearly approached Deism and because of the high moral character of the Friends themselves. He believed that the domination of priests was founded upon deliberate fraud, that the Church of Rome was an organization compact of tyranny, extortion, and bad faith. In Voltaire's opinion, the Church held mankind in poverty, ignorance, and subjection, in order to further its material ends, while dazzling them with promises of an illusory immortality and numbing their moral sense with superstitious practices. Since God is remote and mysterious; since there is probably no such thing as personal immortality; Voltaire was convinced that men should contemn the promises of Christianity and devote themselves to life in this world.

Voltaire's opposition to Christianity was therefore social and political as well as sectarian. It is incorrect to suppose that his satirical attacks were the result of mere impiety or immorality, that he disowned Christianity in order to palliate vices. Voltaire was not a vicious man; if he had been vicious his propaganda would soon have been discredited. He was not a saint, indeed; but he was not vicious. The turn of his mind was satirical, and he could not help seeing the ludicrous side of Christian belief and practices, or refrain from satirizing them

LE PHILOSOPHE

in a manner which far overpassed the bounds of decent controversy. Carlyle to the contrary, brilliant raillery is a terribly effective weapon, especially with Frenchmen. There is nothing a Frenchman dreads so much as ridicule, and Voltaire made the Church and the Bible and the Saints and the Jesuits appear ridiculous. That is why the Catholics hated him so bitterly; he made converts, he swayed minds away from the Church. Innumerable instances of this raillery might be quoted, for Voltaire seldom missed a chance of crushing the infâme. It is easy to imagine the fury of the Churchmen and Church prelates when they read pleasantries of this sort :

> " Les épicuriens faisaient leurs dieux ressemblants â nos chanoines, dont l'indolent embonpoint soutient leur divinité. . . ."
>
> " La foi consiste à croire, non ce qui semble vrai, mais ce qui semble faux à notre entendement. . . . Nous sommes bien éloignés de faire ici la moindre allusion à la foi catholique. Non-seulement nous la vénérons, mais nous l'avons." . . . !
>
> " L'inquisition est, comme on sait, une invention admirable et tout à fait chrétienne pour rendre le pape et les moines plus puissants et pour rendre tout un royaume hypocrite."

To sample more extensive specimens of Voltaire's verve as a satirist of the Church, the article " Miracles " in the *Dictionnaire Philosophique* and the most amusing *Maladie du Jésuite Bertier* may be consulted. There are unquenchable gaiety and wit in these and a hundred other pieces; they are unanswerable, because only a greater and wittier satirist than Voltaire could answer them and the militia of the Church then furnished no such

VOLTAIRE

champion. The exasperation was increased by Voltaire's affected submission to the authority of the Holy See, an attitude which he exploited with consummate irony. The second of the quotations just given shows one use of this, but he varies the method with inexhaustible wit. Thus, after cataloguing all the horrid crimes committed by the Jews of the royal line of David, Voltaire gravely remarks that only the "respectable authority" of the Church can explain why God chose to be incarnated in one of their descendants. It is incorrect to say that Voltairean raillery is an appeal to prejudice and irreverence; it is an appeal to reason. He often makes his effect and scores his point by stating syllogistically the belief of his opponent and thereby showing it to be false in reason, without any comment. Or he relates a miraculous story with an apparent gravity which only brings its absurdity into relief. Or, while affecting disapproval, he quotes some other author; for example, the extraordinary remarks of Woolston on the New Testament miracles.[1]

Voltaire, then, wished men to leave their vain disputes about celestial and miraculous happenings and to concentrate upon living justly and tolerantly in this world. The study of history convinced him that man is a social animal; that the true interest of the majority lies in co-operation, not in oppression and mutual destruction; that men are happier as they are more civilized, that is, as they are more aware of the true nature of the world, as their laws and institutions are more just and reasonable,

---

[1] It is not the business of an expositor to praise or to condemn Voltaire's criticism of Christianity. M. Lanson says that to understand Voltaire's Biblical criticism we must read Dom Calmet, but life is surely too short to spend weeks on the commentaries of that learned Benedictine.

LE PHILOSOPHE

as their customs are weaned from ferocity and prejudice, as they cultivate intelligently the arts and sciences, as they live peaceably and fraternally with others. Rousseau's paradox—that man is innocent and happy in the state of "nature" and is corrupted by civilization—seemed to Voltaire a piece of prodigious nonsense. How can a man be happy when solitary and without the conveniences and consolation of the arts and sciences? Non-social man is a miserable, helpless, naked biped, exposed to the rapacity of beasts and the elements; ignorant, selfish, contemptible. The complex interests and ameliorations created by civilization are the true triumphs of man; they alone reconcile him to the miseries, vicissitudes, and brevity of life. Voltaire combats Rousseau, who would seduce men to abandon their only consolations for the chimaera or "Nature", as vigorously as he combats the Church which counsels men to neglect material well-being for the sake of the Kingdom of Heaven. Hear Voltaire's condemnation of Rousseau:

> "Il s'est trouvé des esprits assez aveugles pour saper tous les fondements de la société en croyant la réformer. On a été assez fou pour soutenir que *le tien* et *le mien* sont des crimes, et qu'on ne doit point jouir de son travail; que non-seulement tous les hommes sont égaux, mais qu'ils ont perverti l'ordre de la nature en se rassemblant; que l'homme est né pour être isolé comme une bête farouche; que les castors, les abeilles, et les fourmis, dérangent les lois éternelles en vivant en république. Ces impertinences, dignes de l'hôpital des fous, ont été quelque temps à la mode, comme des singes qu'on fait danser dans les foires."[1]

[1] *Siècle de Louis XV*, Chap. XLIII

VOLTAIRE

History, again, convinced Voltaire that the great enemies of human happiness are "injustice and intolerance"; war is the result of both, and war is the destroyer of civilization, the path to barbarity. The intolerance of religion, the greed of conquerers are the foes against which philosophie must direct its forces. "All the collected vices of all ages and all places will never equal the misfortunes produced by a single campaign."[1] "Tolerance is necessary to the stability of governments."[2] The origin of intolerance is mistaken religious zeal, whether Mahommedan or Christian; a fanaticism which converts with swords and defends itself with autos-da-fé. The ambition of absolute monarchs is the most usual cause of war.[3] The whole of the strategy of Voltaire's "Philosopher's War" was based on these ideas. Voltaire's anti-Christian hostility itself verged on fanaticism, but he was perfectly ready to admit a tolerant Christianity with ecclesiastics subject to secular authority, as in England. How far he thought his indecent mockery of Christianity was an example of tolerance one cannot say; his attitude was indeed not conciliatory. He was in general far less energetic in denunciation of despotism, except when personally annoyed or in an expansive mood of Republican virtue; he admitted and praised the virtues of Trajan and Marcus Aurelius, Queen Elizabeth and Henri IV, Frederick the Great and Catherine the Great. He even wrote panegyrics of Saint Louis and Louis XV. In some moods,

[1] *Dictionnaire Philosophique.*

[2] *Traité de Tolérance.*

[3] See *Mémoires de M. de Voltaire* for a significant anecdote of Frederick the Great and the infamous attack upon Silesia.

LE PHILOSOPHE

when he was exasperated with popular stupidity,[1] he inclined to the view that a firm enlightened despotism was the best practical form of government. It must not be forgotten that Voltaire's politics were essentially "capitalist" and "bourgeois"; "Liberty and Property" was his political motto. Freedom and equality meant that all citizens are subject to the Law alone and are all equal in its sight. The "Sacred Right of Property" meant that a man had an inalienable right to all the wealth he could acquire without fraud or force; but taxation should be levied according to a man's wealth, not according to his social position. In the jargon of modern politics, Voltaire belonged to the "Centre", rather than to the "Right" or the "Left".

All the germs of the Voltairean *philosophie* may be found in that miscellaneous collection of notes on England published in 1734 under the title of *Lettres Philosophiques*. The whole literature of social reform in eighteenth century France took its rise from this little book and from Montesquieu's *Esprit des Lois*. The arrangement of the *Lettres Philosophiques* is not systematic, and a number of letters are devoted to literary subjects. The first four letters contain a description of the Quakers; the visit to Andrew Pitt is one of Voltaire's most brilliant and amusing smaller pieces. Though he pokes a little fun at their quaint habits, he is respectful to the Friends' virtues. This exordium is a veiled reproach to Rome for its departure from the simplicity of primitive Christianity. Letter V treats of the Church of England. The first sentence gives us the Voltairean ideal of tolerance:

---

[1] And they were not infrequent; our demagogues would be filled with horror if they ever had time to read Voltaire on the "lie du peuple".

VOLTAIRE

"An Englishman, being a free man, goes to Heaven by what path he pleases." He is delighted at the subjection of the English Church to the State; "The Whigs," says Voltaire, "prefer that the Bishops should derive their authority from Parliament rather than from the Apostles." The letter ends with a shower of satirical shafts against the French clergy:

> "When they [i.e. the English clergy] learn that in France young men, known for their debauchery and raised to the prelacy by women's intrigues, make love publicly, amuse themselves by composing amorous songs, give expensive suppers every night, and from these proceed to implore the light of the Holy Ghost and boldly call themselves the Apostles' successors; they thank God they are Protestants. But they are ugly heretics to be burned to all the devils, as maître François Rabelais says; and so I forebear to meddle with their affairs."

The satire continues in Letter VI, on the Presbyterians —who are not spared his raillery either—but the weighty sentence is this:

> "If England had only one religion, its despotism might be feared; if it had only two, they would cut each other's throats; but there are thirty, and they live happily and in peace."

The next two letters are concerned with the Parliamentary system of Government. Here are two sentences, which alone constitute a declaration of war on the abuses of monarchic France:

> "A man is not exempt from paying certain taxes because he is a noble or a priest; all taxes are voted by the House of Commons."

LE PHILOSOPHE

"The peasant's feet are not crushed in *sabots*, he eats white bread, he is well dressed, he is not afraid to increase the number of his herd or to cover his roof with tiles, for fear his taxes will be raised the next year."

Sharp stabs, these words, against the French system, with its privileged nobles and prelates[1] and miserable peasantry. Letter X is a panegyric of English commerce : "The younger brother of an English peer does not disdain to be a merchant." It ends with a satire on the French Marquis "who gives himself airs of grandeur because he plays the part of a slave in a Minister's ante-room." The next letter is a plea for the use of "inoculation" against small-pox, introduced into England from Turkey by Lady Mary Wortley-Montague. The religious and social views so extensively and warmly advocated by Voltaire are sketched in these opening chapters ; he developed, but did not greatly modify them, even if he was not rigidly consistent.

Letters XII-XVII inclusive are devoted to Bacon, Locke, and Newton. Even a cursory reading will show how deeply Voltaire was impressed by these authors. His direct acquaintance with Bacon's work was probably slight and he considered that the Lord Chancellor lived in an age "which did not understand the art of good writing, still less good philosophy ;" but, chiefly on Bolingbroke's recommendation no doubt, he praised Bacon as "the father of experimental philosophy",[2] by

---

[1] The clergy in France paid a voluntary contribution, but this "fell most heavily on the poorest and most estimable of the body, the parish priests."

[2] Another instance of the loose application of the word "philosopher" in the eighteenth century.

VOLTAIRE

which Voltaire meant systematic, scientific research. He even ventures on the very questionable statement:

> "In a word, nobody before Lord Chancellor Bacon understood experimental philosophy; and there is hardly one of the experiments in physics [épreuves physiques] made after him which is not included in his book."[1]

Voltaire's admiration for Locke and almost complete subjection to that author's views are apparent in Letter XIII, which he begins with the words:

> "Never perhaps was there a wiser and more methodical mind, a more exact logician than Locke; yet he was not a great mathematician."

The last phrase is at once a shaft directed at Descartes and an oblique apology for Voltaire; the latter's knowledge of mathematics is respectable for a man of letters; but is that of an amateur. He devotes more space to Newton than to Locke, but it is plain that Locke made the greater impression upon him. The assertion is not definitely proved but it seems likely that Voltaire was never sufficiently equipped technically to understand in a thorough way either Descartes or Newton; but he was the most intelligent of amateurs. Locke, who is a moralist and whose metaphysics are by no means oversubtle, was much more readily and fully comprehended by Voltaire and influenced him far more.

The remaining nine letters all deal with matters connected with literature. Voltaire's interests were at that time predominatingly literary and they remained so even

[1] i.e. *Novum Organum.*

LE PHILOSOPHE

in the Ferney period of social reform. This revelation of English literature to the Continent has already been mentioned ; strange as it may sound to some quarters, English literature was little prized on the Continent in the early eighteenth century and even now is not unanimously admired as the greatest of all literatures. The letter which concerns us here is that entitled, " Sur la considération qu'on doit aux gens de lettres ". It is at once an affirmation of the dignity of authors, a reproach to French society for the Rohan affair, a justification of Voltaire's political ambitions (whatever they were), a bitter plea for the status of actors occasioned by the indignity offered the body of Adrienne Lecouvreur. There is scarcely any exaggeration in saying that this letter is also a declaration of the principle that the man of culture and enlightenment, the philosophe, is in a civilized state the natural leader of the nation. We can discover from other writings of Voltaire that his social reform had the following idea as one of its main supports. A nation dominated by soldiers will be turbulent and barbarous ; a nation dominated by priests will be stagnant, timid, and poor; a nation dominated by tradesmen will be industrious, wealthy, and unrefined ; but a nation ruled by its wisest and most enlightened men, its philosophes, will be as nearly happy as human life allows and as eminent in the arts and sciences as its genius permits. Voltaire contrasts Addison as secretary of state, Prior as plenipotentiary, Swift as Dean of St Patrick's, with the subaltern position of French men of letters. He is not altogether fair ; he contrasts fortunate English authors with unlucky French ones, he depreciated the Court patronage of letters and the French academies. The rags of young Samuel Johnson and the death of Chatterton are no great honour

VOLTAIRE

to the English people ; but before the long administration of Walpole, men of letters were still encouraged and rewarded in eighteenth century England, though of course the immense, highly-educated and critical audience of the twentieth century did not exist.

No account of Voltaire as philosophe is at all complete without a mention of his schemes of reform for France, and no one can now touch this subject without referring to M. Lanson's admirable study, *La Réforme Voltairienne de la France*—admirable for its learning, wealth of detail, and order. As a reformer Voltaire was an opportunist, not a creator of political theories ; he accepted society and government as facts ; he believed democracy to be the best form of government for small states, monarchy for large states. France was an established monarchy ; it was wise, therefore, to preserve the monarchy but to secure for French subjects the natural liberties of men, which are : Liberty of the person (no slavery) ; Liberty of Speech and Writing ; Civil Liberty (habeas corpus) ; Liberty of Conscience ; Security of Property ; Liberty to work, i.e., to sell one's labour to the highest bidder. War is barbarous and a misfortune, but Voltaire did not believe it would be soon abolished ; he preferred a militia to a standing army, as a smaller temptation to wars of conquest while providing adequate defence. He thought it desirable on principle that education should be a state affair. The lowest classes of manual labourer should not be educated, but craftsmen, artisans, masons, carpenters, farmers, and the like should receive instruction. The Church should be subject to the State, and ecclesiastics should pay taxes like other citizens. Civil marriage should be allowed ; burial in churches forbidden ; the number of church holidays reduced. No glory and

LE PHILOSOPHE

conquest, but economy and peace ; " le régime financier est détestable." Taxes should be proportionate to wealth ; " it is odious to deprive the labourer of part of the bread he has earned." Abolition of feudal rights, " corvées ", and " dimes ". No interference with the liberty of commerce ; protective tariffs if needed, except on wheat ; unity of weights and measures.

Taxes are an element of social order, but should not be wasted by the Court and its parasites. They should go towards the provision of water supply, markets, canals, roads, and the like. Begging should be suppressed, hospitals reformed, new maternity hospitals founded as well as orphanages, alms-houses for the aged and infirm workers. The police should not have the right to open letters as they pass through the post.[1]

The reform of the legal system is imperative. The selling of legal posts should be abolished, the judiciary should be separated from politics. The cost and time demanded by lawsuits should be lessened ; the laws of the whole country should be uniform [2] ; new civil and criminal codes are desirable.[3] Divorce should be permitted by civil law, but the criminal law should only take cognizance of offences " against men and social order ". Justice has not to avenge God ; therefore it is not concerned with sacrilege, sorcery, suicide, heresy, and sodomy.[4] An accused man should be considered innocent until proved guilty ; a man should not be imprisoned

---

[1] " The violation of the secrecy of letters may lose a prince his best friends." Napoleon.

[2] There were many ancient and contradictory local laws under the ancien regime.

[3] Hence the Code Napoléon.

[4] I think M. Lanson is wrong here. At least, Voltaire approves strongly of legal punishment in *Prix de la Justice et de l'Humanité* Article XIX, " De la Sodomie."

VOLTAIRE

upon suspicion ; a prisoner should not be tortured ; secret trials should not be allowed ; the accused should be confronted with the witnesses and should have the right to be defended by counsel.[1]

That, very briefly, is the Voltairean scheme of reform. We, who enjoy almost all these rights without being in the least grateful for them, can only wonder that less than two centuries ago in France it was considered scandalous and impious to propose them. No doubt this scheme of reform could be and was improved upon, but not by Robespierre and Marat. The principles underlying it are those of all wise and good government ; when they are abandoned, whether by a despot, an oligarchy, or a democracy, good government is abandoned with them. Here Voltaire is surely entitled to our praise as a man who saw human affairs clearly and sanely. He is equally removed from the cynicism which worships force and divinizes autocracy, and from the uncritical optimism which seeks the impossible perfection of Utopia. Napoleon Bonaparte, who knew men, told a deputation of cranks ; " The First Consul prefers the good which is possible to the best which is unattainable."[2] There spoke the philosophie of M. de Voltaire.

---

[1] Lanson's *Voltaire* : pp. 180-188.
[2] *Maximes de Napoléon*, publiées par J. K. Frederiks, the Hague, 1922. This book is a remarkable collection of political aphorisms.

XVII

NOVELS AND PAMPHLETS

If the conclusions enounced in the preceding chapter are correct, then the Voltaire who matters to us is not a philosopher but an artist, not an original thinker but a consummate popularizer and expounder of other men's thoughts. It can be shown that his formal philosophical treatises are taken from other writers; his most sustained effort of reasoning, *Le Philosophe Ignorant*, is largely negative, in that its achievement is to show the strict limits of Voltaire's rationalism and hence, by implication, its inability to explain many philosophical problems. To confess ignorance is courageous, in a philosopher especially; but Voltaire's rationalism is surely condemned by the facts that in some cases the knowledge he declares non-existent does exist, that the problems he asserts are insoluble have been, at least provisionally, solved. But we cannot make such objections to Voltaire's art; the art of *Candide* and *Jeannot et Colin* remains, even if the "philosophy" behind them is incomplete and superannuated.

Doubtless, Voltaire would have been astonished and grieved to learn that most of his readers in the twentieth century prefer *Candide* to *La Henriade* and *Jeannot et Colin* to *Zaïre*. One can imagine the restless shade of Voltaire eagerly conferring with new literary arrivals in the Elysian Fields and wringing shadowy hands in

VOLTAIRE

anguish at the decline of " bon goût " in Europe. (Indeed, there would be some reason for this, but not in the way he would mean). The Voltaire we most admire is not the epic poet, the dramatist, the historian, but the charming poet of light verse, the witty correspondent and, above all, the brilliant satirist and prose stylist of the Romans and Mélanges. In the forty volume edition of Voltaire, the Romans and Mélanges fill eight volumes ; and this is exactly four volumes too many. In spite of Voltaire's wit and artistry, his gift of variety in treating the same ideas and topics, many of these pamphlets are redundant and abound in vain repetitions. The explanation is that they were in most cases intended as nothing but journalism, as light skirmishes in the Philosopher's War, " philosophical " propaganda against l'infâme and the abuses of the French political system, a popularization of the *Encyclopédie* for the lower ranks of readers. And since Voltaire knew that truth for such people is that which they hear most often repeated, he indulged in repetition of his main points to an extent which is now tedious.

A reader who knows the Romans and other pamphlets only from modern selections, will no doubt feel inclined to protest against this view ; let him read perseveringly through the whole eight volumes, and it will be surprising indeed if he does not agree. After the fourth volume (and, by the way, the four volumes of the *Dictionnaire Philosophique* might be added to the eight mentioned above) a reader becomes more and more aware of the presence of certain Voltairean clichés. Finally, he gets to know what is coming in the pamphlet from reading only its opening paragraph. He grows weary of raillery at the absurdities, contradictions, and indecencies of the Bible —information largely derived from Bolingbroke, by the

NOVELS AND PAMPHLETS

way. Directly this topic is broached, an experienced Voltairean reader knows that he will get the impostures of Moses, the immoral practices of the Patriarchs, the genealogy of the House of David with remarks on the private morals of this family, the indecent passages in Exodus, Genesis, and Ezechiel (particularly " Oohla and Oohlibah "[1]), the singular commands of the Lord to Hosea. The Jesuits cannot be mentioned without a reference to Sanchez and his grotesque discussion of the relations between the Virgin Mary and the Holy Ghost. For the rest, the romans and pamphlets run upon the topics of the Inquisition, Jesuits, Jansenists and monks, bonzes, fakirs, mages, gymnosophists, the Sorbonne, the Papacy ; Frederick, Catherine, Locke, Newton, the Encyclopédie, la saine philosophie, Deism, advantages of luxury, virtue of Chinese mandarins and North American Indians, fearful calamities, rapes, wars, shipwrecks, autos-da-fé, famines, earthquakes, mutilations, ghastly judicial executions, small-pox, venereal disease, petrified oysters on mountains, the Donation of Constantine, the constitution of England, the magnificence and brilliance of Paris, the trivial causes of wars, the example of Peter the Great, facile and faithless mistresses, imbecility and obstinacy of lawyers, indecency and peculation of monks, corruption of judges, superior antiquity and morality of the Far East, relative smallness of the Earth, insignificance of man, improbability of man's being immortal, rarity of human happiness, characteristics (usually arbitrary and inaccurate) of the nations of Europe ; the frequency of human vanity, perfidy, cruelty, stupidity, persecution,

[1] If Voltaire rallies these ladies once, he does so forty times. It grows mighty wearisome.

VOLTAIRE

sensuality, idleness, levity, inconsequence, drunkenness, heartlessness, calumny ; and rare examples of "saine philosophie", hospitality, wisdom, tolerance, vegetarianism, contentment, righteousness, nobility of soul (usually among Turks, Chinese, brahmins, Indians, philosophers and agricultural small-holders).

This chaplet of clichés might be increased by a methodical compiler ; however, the above list should be adequate for its purpose, which is to show that the romans and pamphlets repeat in popular form the notions and prejudices of the philosophe. But this repetition and a certain superficiality of thought do not destroy the art of Voltaire. He is usually praised as a satirist, and satire is indeed a true description of these innumerable pamphlets; but it is not a vituperative or gross satire. Sarcasm, raillery, irony, wit are the Voltairean weapons ; he rarely breaks into serious denunciation and reproof, and still more rarely loses his temper, though when he does either, his satire loses its force and skill. The mood of Voltairean satire is complex, and is expressed metaphorically in the traditional Voltairean smile of Houdon's statue. That smile is malicious but humorous, sarcastic but not unkindly ; it is that of a tolerant and witty man whose intelligence is prodigiously alert. And these are the qualities of Voltaire's prose satire. Human beings alternately aroused his pity and his mirth ; their crimes and follies exasperated him, but he thought men could more easily be laughed and mocked than reproved and denounced out of them. At times the imbecilities of human conduct and of human systems left him aghast ; but he took pity on us—poor ignorant creatures seduced by priests, crowned fools, stupid ideals, and mad prejudices—and laboured ceaselessly to enlighten us with

NOVELS AND PAMPHLETS

the truths of " la saine philosophie ", though with no great hope of permanently reforming us :

> " Fools will be fools, say what we will,
> And rascals will be rascals still."

" In the name of common sense, act a little reasonably and learn to face facts " is the burden of these numberless diatribes. The personal attacks on his enemies are an invitation *urbi et orbi* not to take seriously the notions of people so unreasonable and foolish. But, on the whole, the Voltairean satire is an encouragement not to look at things and life too solemnly and lugubriously. Let us be reasonable, but let us make life endurable ; we may not be immortal, the world may be and probably is a mass of ills, sufferings, and stupidities, but for God's sake let us crack a jest when we may. Let us, in fact, model ourselves upon the sage of Ferney ; let us be active, industrious, sober, witty, ironic, philanthropic, Deistic, well-informed, and cheerful Rationalists ; the deuce take the Pope and Rousseau, the Jesuits and the Jansenists, Leibnitz and Calvin, all the fanatics and the excessive, gloomy misanthropy and absurd optimism ; let us mind our own business and cultivate our own gardens. Ituriel, the guardian genius of the earth, having received Babouc's report, " resolved to allow the world to go its way ; for, said he, if all is not well, it is all tolerable." This is the " lesson " of many of these brilliant little pieces ; it is madness to hope for the earthly paradise, fantastic to assert that all is well with the world, idiotic to be gloomy about it ; make the best of what you have.

This Rationalist acceptation of the tolerability of life was quite common in the eighteenth century, at least

VOLTAIRE

among the upper classes. It is well put by Lord Chesterfield who in many respects was a living illustration of Voltaire's views and was in perfect sympathy with the Frenchman's philosophie.

> "A wise man, without being a stoic, considers, in all misfortunes that befall him, their best as well as their worst side; and everything has a better and a worse side. . . . It is the rational philosophy taught me by experience and knowledge of the world, and which I have practised above thirty years. I always made the best of the best, and never made the bad worse by fretting; this enabled me to go through the various scenes of life, in which I have been an actor, with more pleasure and less pain than most people."

And again, in a letter to the Bishop of Waterfield, Chesterfield expresses an idea which is the very essence of Voltaire's rationalism :

> "In the general course of things, there seems to be upon the whole a pretty equal distribution of physical good and evil, some extraordinary cases excepted; and even moral good and evil seem mixed to a certain degree, for one never sees anybody so perfectly good or so perfectly bad, as they might be."

Many instances of praise for these short pieces might be cited. One alone must suffice. Voltaire's "frère ennemi", the King of Prussia, who knew him so well, writes to him many years after the Frankfort episode : "You know I have always admired your writing and particularly those collections of short prose pieces called Mélanges." The wit, the gaiety, the diablerie, the clear sparkle, the absence of anything heavy or pedantic in these pamphlets, have kept them alive when Voltaire's

NOVELS AND PAMPHLETS

more serious and ambitious works have fallen into disrepute. The romans especially are still regularly reprinted, and especially *Candide*. It is not unjust to say that thousands of readers know Voltaire only by that jeu d'esprit with which he amused himself in Switzerland. But others among the romans are equally brilliant and the wit of that brief satire on the nouveaux riches—*Jeannot et Colin*—is even more concentrated and amusingly malicious. The consummate art of these pieces has kept them young and fresh for a century and a half. It is not wholly a matter of wit and style, which are indeed almost imperishable when perfect, as with Voltaire they often were ; but he possessed the art of telling a story —l'art de conter—in such a way that whatever he related became interesting and held the attention. We have testimony in abundance to Voltaire's charm of conversation and amusing ability to retail anecdotes. The romans are simply wonderful examples of that charm and ability transferred to paper. The style is that of " polite conversation ", chastened and polished without losing any of its familiarity and ease and without acquiring the least tinge of " literary " affectation and pedantry. The stories of his romans are told as lightly and without effort as he told a fable to young Florian. And just as Voltaire interested a child with the talking animals of a fable, so he interested the larger children of Europe with fanciful and fabulous tales in order to make them absorb his " lessons " while they scarcely knew they had done so. He smeared the rim of the cup with honey, as Tasso says, so that the reader, " deceived, drinks in the bitter juices and from his deceit gains life "—

" Succhi amari ingannato intanto ei beve,
E dall' inganno suo vita riceve."

VOLTAIRE

He drew on his extensive reading as well as on his experience of life for the machinery and setting of these tales ; the old medieval French romances he pretended to despise were levied upon, as well as many books of travel and imaginative literature, from Cyrano de Bergerac to the Arabian Nights, from Gulliver's Travels to Boccaccio. But Heaven forbid that anyone should laboriously seek for the "sources" of Voltaire's tales ! The pure gold of the Romans is all Voltaire's own :

> "Monsieur le baron était un des plus puissants seigneurs de la Westphalie, car son Château avait une porte et des fenêtres. Sa grande salle même était ornée d'une tapisserie. Tous les chiens de ses basses-cours composaient une meute dans le besoin, ses palefreniers étaient ses piqueurs ; le vicaire du village était son grand-aumonier. Ils l'appelaient tous Monseigneur, et ils riaient quand il faisait des contes."

Candide appeared in 1759, under the pseudonym of *le Docteur Ralph* ; but since the style and wit of every paragraph signed it "Voltaire", the precaution was wasted. All the world who read knew that only Voltaire could have written it. The object of attack was the optimistic philosophy of Leibnitz and the no less optimistic statement of Rousseau that "tout est bien." An ingenious modern critic has tried to show that some of the passages of Candide's adventures refer to the career of Baron Trenck, who was arbitrarily imprisoned by Frederick the Great ; it is supposed that Voltaire knew of Trenck's sufferings and used *Candide* as a method of informing Frederick. However this may be, *Candide* is certainly one of the most entertaining prose satires ever penned.

NOVELS AND PAMPHLETS

Its likeness to *Rasselas* is superficial; both Johnson and Voltaire show the misfortunes of man, but Johnson leads the reader to religion, Voltaire to rational acquiescence and a small garden. The manner of the two authors again is dissimilar; a squirrel and an elephant can both pick nuts, but the one does it nimbly and petulantly, the other with solemnity and ponderosity. *Candide* might by an extension of meaning be called "philosophical", because under its gay fiction and satire it combats two philosophical ideas; it attacks the theory of optimism formulated by Leibnitz, that God is the perfect monad, that He created a world to show His perfection, that He chose this out of the infinite number of worlds, that He was guided by the "principium melioris", and that therefore the universe is the "best possible"; and it attacks the optimism of Rousseau, who denied the doctrine of original sin and affirmed that man in a state of nature is wholly good, from which follows the abandonment of rational self-discipline and the paradoxical assertion of the aristocracy of the plebs. Both doctrines are obviously heavy with dangers to human society and both are repugnant and absurd to rational common-sense; their truth, if they be truths, is obviously mystic, and to Voltaire all mysticism was disgusting and barbarous. Vulnerable as Voltaire's Rationalism must be to a concerted metaphysical attack, it was good enough for most people, and he had the skill to bring the laughers over to his side. Nevertheless, the Rousseau paradox of the "domination of the proletariat" has survived Voltaire's "government by the enlightened" as a popular idea; no doubt because it flatters more people and is irrational—an additional proof of Voltaire's pessimistic attitude towards human nature.

VOLTAIRE

The machinery of *Candide* is simple. An ingenuous youth called Candide grows up in the Westphalian home of the Baron Thunder-ten-Troncke, instructed in philosophy by Dr. Pangloss, who taught " metaphysico-theologo-cosmolonigologie ", and proved that all is for the best in this best of all possible worlds. The adventures of Candide, which range from China to Peru, are one long and humourous contradiction of this assumption; they are also a contradiction of the natural goodness of man. Obviously, the art of the narrator lies in the fecundity of invention with which he devises new episodes, his skill in making each arise naturally from those before, and the indefinable gift of the raconteur which makes the incredible acceptable and compels interest. Voltaire's novels and tales are lively parables, not novels in our meaning of the word, and his characters, as we have already seen, are allegorical, well-masked types or embodied opinions. But these parables of philosophie have many of the essential qualities of good fiction and these types are so shrewdly observed and so skilfully portrayed that for all their abstraction and generalization they seem to live. What is true of *Candide* in this respect is true of most of them, though in the less successful romans (the *Lettres d'Amabed*, for instance) the device is too artificial.

In reading steadily through these romans, one is most delighted and entertained by the flashes of wit and satire; the stories themselves are often slight, but the satiric wit of situation and comment is incomparable. Candide thinks Pangloss " the greatest philosopher of the province and consequently of all mankind." He meets an eloquent anabaptist and ingenuously confesses that he had not heard the Pope was Antichrist : " The orator's wife put her head out of the window and, perceiving a man who doubted that the Pope was Antichrist poured on his head a full ... O Heavens! to what excess are ladies carried by religious zeal!" "A lady of honour", says Cunegonde, "may be raped once, but her virtue is fortified by it." When Candide and Martin approach the coast of France, Candide asks what the country is like : "In some provinces half the inhabitants are mad, in others they are over cunning, elsewhere they think they are witty, and in all the principal occupation is making love, the second scandal, and the third talking nonsense." As a more extended example of Voltaire's "admirable fooling" in *Candide*, take this fragment of dialogue :

" ' Apropos,' said Candide, ' do you think the earth was originally a sea, as we are assured by that large book belonging to the captain?'

" I don't believe it in the least,' said Martin, 'any more than all the other whimsies we have been pestered with recently!'

' But to what end was this world formed?' said Candide.

' To infuriate us,' replied Martin.

' Are you not very surprised,' continued Candide, ' by the love those two girls of the country of the Oreillons had for those two monkeys, whose adventure I told you?'

'Not in the least,' said Martin, 'I see nothing strange in their passion ; I have seen so many extraordinary things that nothing seems extraordinary to me.'

' Do you think,' said Candide, ' that men have always massacred each other as they do to-day? Have they always been liars, cheats, traitors, brigands, weak, flighty, cowardly, envious, gluttonous, drunken, grasping, ambitious, bloody, backbiting, debauched, fanatical, hypocritical, and silly?'

VOLTAIRE

'Do you think,' said Martin, 'that sparrow-hawks have always eaten the pigeons they came across?'

'Yes, of course,' said Candide.

'Well,' said Martin, 'if sparrow-hawks have always possessed the same nature, why should you expect men to change theirs?'

'Oh!' said Candide, 'there is a great difference; free will . . .'

Arguing thus, they arrived at Bordeaux."

Amusing traits of this kind are scattered through all the romans. The *Vision de Babouc* is a fable to show the alternate good and evil of mankind and the world; Babouc is sent by the djinnee, Ituriel, to render an account of Persepolis, which needless to say is Paris. One day Barbouc is for destruction, the next for preservation, and so on alternately; finally he decides that there are "de très bonnes choses dans les abus" and, from his report, Ituriel decides to "let the world go on as it is, for if everything is not right, everything is tolerable." *Cosi-Sancta* is not a tale for puritans; it relates the misfortunes which occurred owing to the peevish chastity of a woman, and the good which resulted when her scruples dissolved. *Zadig* shows in a series of witty episodes the disadvantage of numerous estates of life and the misfortunes an honest man has to endure from the world; in short, the rarity and fragility of happiness. *Zadig* contains the famous verse which was sung every day to the conceited courtier by order of the king who wished to cure him of that vice :

"Que son mérite est extrême !
Que de grâces ! que de grandeur !
Ah ! combien monseigneur
Doit être content de lui-même."

NOVELS AND PAMPHLETS

Memnon is a short but extremely clever satire on human prudence. Memnon one day "conceived the absurd project of being parfaitement sage". His fate in Voltaire's hands was assured; for apparently he was a disciple of Jean Jacques. *Bababec* is still shorter but even wittier; it is a satire on "fakirs" and hence upon those whom Voltaire chose to assimilate to fakirs:

> "Some walked on their hands; others swung on a loose cord; others always hobbled. Some wore chains; others a pack-saddle; some hid their heads under a bushel; *au demeurant les meilleurs gens du monde.*"

Micromégas is a "philosophique" tale, inspired partly by Swift's Brobdingnagians and partly by Voltaire's astronomical studies.[1] An inhabitant from Sirius and another from Saturn are dispatched to the world by Voltaire, in order to persuade us of our insignificance and the pettiness of our planet compared with the hugeness of inter-stellar space and the great suns of the universe.

To linger over these romans is to expose oneself to a "damnable iteration" of praise. Yet several others must be at least mentioned. There is *L'Ingénu*, a kind of pendant to *Candide*, where a virtuous Huron is promenaded ruthlessly through the follies and ills of Europe; for a time the reader is anxiously asking himself whether Voltaire is not exposing for admiration one more specimen of the noble savage; but such is not the case, the Huron is an "honnête homme" and does not exhort us to return to caves and reindeer. *L'Ingénu* is filled with amusing traits, like the famous: "l'abbé de Saint-

[1] Directed in part against Maupertuis.

VOLTAIRE

Yves supposait qu'un homme qui n'était pas né en France n'avait pas le sens commun." *L'Homme aux Quarante Ecus* is more nearly related to the political pamphlets and is one of the least interesting to us because it runs upon topics which have mostly lost all actuality. *La Princesse de Babylon* forms another excuse for a vertiginously swift ramble through divers states of the world ; the *Lettres d'Amabed* are a virulent satire on the Catholic missionaries in the East ; *L'Histoire de Jenni, Le Taureau Blanc, Aventure Indienne, Les Oreilles du Comte de Chesterfield* are all amusing for their skill and malice.

Turning from these gems of Voltairean art with their glitter and polish to the huge miscellany of pamphlets, one feels a sense of weariness, almost disgust, before the profuse repetitions of this abounding but limited mind. Take a few of them and the result is wholly pleasing ; the Voltairean charm and wit achieve their effect, but after a time the mind is surfeited with raillery, disgusted with the diffusion and the repetition which are the inevitable mark of journalism. They are the relics of the campaigns of our Philosopher's War, and like all such relics look a little rusty and rather harmless when the war is over. They are ranged together helter-skelter like an unclassified museum of weapons, over-crowded and furnished with too many specimens of the same sort ; any one taken separately will interest, in their disorderly bulk they weary and confuse the mind. In one of his pamphlets Voltaire described himself as a man who has spent his life " à sentir, à raisonner, et à plaisanter." The " sentir " might be disputed, but there can be no doubt about the " raisonner " and the " plaisanter " ; the question is whether these functions may not eventually be abused. There is a quality in Voltairean raillery which is " agaçant "—

piquant but exasperating—as if he said, " Come, let us make fools of all who do not think as we think." The raillery of Voltaire must be intolerable to earnest-minded persons. Even to those who hope they take life more lightly this perpetual tittering becomes an irritation.

No doubt, the reason for this is that we weary of the same mood when it is prolonged beyond our appetite. It is amusing to spend an evening with an irrepressibly humorous man, but what a penance to be forced to live with him. Pass a few evenings over Voltaire's pamphlets, and you will be charmed and entertained ; but read them solidly for a month, and you will be cloyed with raillery and you will turn for relief, as the age after Voltaire's turned, to poetry and sentiment and romance ; you will understand then the immense vogue of Chateaubriand. In order to persuade men to live rationally, to abandon the dreams of mysticism, the " amour de l'impossible " which prevents us from being content with carnal and reasonable felicity ; Voltaire concentrated the clear light of his intelligence upon the pettiness, the inconsistencies, the lamentable failures, the ignominies of mankind. His brilliant shafts flashed through the air and pierced unerringly all aspiring souls in their flight. He brings us back to the hard facts as pitilessly as the family solicitor, though with more wit. There is something almost gross in his utilitarianism, which sensitive minds feel instinctively as an affront. Not so Chateaubriand. Superbly disregarding the useful and the practical, he soars away into an empyrean of poetic sentiment. His works are a kind of Bible of Romanticism, devoted to the extirpation of the Voltairean spirit. Chateaubriand rehabilitated the picturesque, the mysterious, solitude and melancholy, the poetry of wild lonely places, of ruins and fallen grandeur,

VOLTAIRE

of fine sentiment and loyalty—all the ideas and ideals and sentiments which Voltaire had laughed away for half a century. The whole Romantic movement in France was in open hostility to Voltaire ; the battle of Hernani was fought between the rear-guard of Voltaireans and the main body of Chateaubriand's pretorian legion. It was a Pyrrhic victory for the Romantics. Our world to-day is far more the world of Voltaire than of Chateaubriand. Vicisti, Ferniense !

The reaction of which Chateaubriand was the creator (or the mouthpiece) was a failure ; as he lay dying, that dramatic genius which controlled his life wafted into his bedroom the clamour of the Revolution of 1848. Probably Chateaubriand joined battle with Voltaireanism on a false issue ; at any rate, he failed. To us the important reflection is that the modern world of " Democracy and Progress " is to a large extent an awkward alliance of the ideology of Rousseau with the Rationalism and Utilitarianism of Voltaire and the Encyclopœdists. One must insist upon this, because few democratic politicians appear to be aware of their origins ; and the political strife between left and right in commercial countries is often only the struggle between Rousseau's ideology and Voltaire's realism. The Church, which sits at the extreme right, is really hostile to both parties, but is fully aware of what she is contending with ; moreover, the Church is more hostile to Rousseau then to Voltaire. I copy from to-day's *Times* [1] a declaration of the Cardinal-Archbishop of Bordeaux :

> " This programme [of the Government's] is none other than that of the " Social Contract " of Jean Jacques Rousseau, that well-known writer, who was born vicious and died insane, whose apophthegms on

[1] 8th October, 1924.

NOVELS AND PAMPHLETS

the independence of man, individual or collective, who is subject neither to God nor morals, nor any principle whatsoever,[1] have done more harm to France than the blasphemies of Voltaire and all the Encyclopœdists together."

I shall not pursue farther the polemics of the matter, but the Cardinal's heated words touch upon a problem which interests a student of Voltaire. To what extent do writers create public opinion and how far are they responsible for great mutations of the State? Was the French Revolution and all its tremendous consequences, which every one of us still undergoes, " created " by Rousseau, Voltaire, and the Encyclopœdists ; or were they simply the mouthpieces which made audible and coherent a vast inchoate movement which would have been equally effective without them? Men " of the robe ", whether authors or clergy, are inclined to over-estimate the power of the spiritual leader ; as the rest of mankind are apt to rate it too low. There is no possibility of estimating the extent of Voltaire's influence without an exhaustive examination of all kinds of documents by a body of scholars ; and even then the results would be doubtful. Voltaire and Rousseau were only megaphones, if you like, but the advice they shouted gave direction to vast bodies of men wandering in perplexity or sunk in apathy. The rebellion against the Monarchy was an armed protest against misgovernment and despotism, such as the Fronde had been. The rebellion against the Church was the logical outcome of the Renaissance—the revival of pre-Christian Rationalism. The Reformation failed in France when Henri IV became a Catholic and ended the wars of the Ligue ; the Fronde

[1] Is the Cardinal sure of this ?

VOLTAIRE

failed because it was merely a negative disturbance. But between 1789 and the flight to Varennes the French monarchy was faced with a Fronde backed by principles and a Ligue where the antagonists were not Huguenots and Catholics, but Rationalists and Christians. The combined attack was too powerful to be resisted; Monarchy and Church went down together. It seems to me that Voltaire and Rousseau, mutatis mutandis, stand in much the same relation to the French Revolution that Luther and Calvin do to the Reformation; some such movement was perhaps inevitable, given the circumstances, but these great minds set the mass in motion and gave it direction.

In the preceding chapter I attempted to give some account of the philosophie of Voltaire, to show that it was not philosophic speculation or a metaphysical system, but a practical Rationalism, addressing itself to ordinary common sense and proposing in truth only material objects as an aim in life. This Rationalist Materialism, with certain modifications, is the basis of the actions of most people in modern commercial democracies; it is the "philosophy" of the plain tired business man. The immense and indefatigable propaganda of the Ferney pamphlets undoubtedly contributed towards establishing that "philosophy" in France. Such a bombardment of the intelligence is probably unique in history. Think for a moment of the energy, the will-power, the perpetual mental tension, implied by that unremitting discharge of philosophical pamphlets. I have called them journalism and that is what they are—diluted and repetitive thought in a popular form; but Voltaire put something of his genius as well as his energy into every one of them. They are not the mechanical and conventional productions of a

NOVELS AND PAMPHLETS

leader-writer; each had to contain a statement of a principle or principles of philosophie and each had to be entertaining. The eighteenth century public was pitiless, even to the Patriarch of Ferney; if he fell below his own standard they let him know it. All the resources of his wit and invention were drawn upon to the utmost to meet the situation, to continue the flow of propaganda in fresh and attractive ways. Hence the extraordinary variety of forms—sermons, dialogues, speeches, tales, allegories, letters, and a score of others—designed to pique the curiosity and satisfy the taste of innumerable readers. But the correctness and beauty of the prose, the eternal raillery are always there; necessarily, because they were Voltaire's manner and they were what principally charmed his readers.

The greater number of these pamphlets were directed against Christianity, the Roman Catholic Church, and the priests. They may be called blasphemies, if the reader chooses, but Voltaire was not the man to waste his time on mere senseless insults to a religion. Neither was he attacking only a corrupt clergy; for the Church possessed many worthy and good servants in the eighteenth century. For one libertin abbé there were fifty village priests of good morals. No, Voltaire was not merely blaspheming, not merely attacking the clergy; he wished to destroy belief in the divinity of Jesus Christ, the authority of the Old as well as of the New Testament, Protestantism as well as Catholicism. The attacks on the religious orders and the Church were political and a matter of economics; Voltaire wished to remove from the State the financial burden of a considerable non-productive population which controlled an immense income and paid taxes only as a " voluntary contribution ". That end might have been

VOLTAIRE

attained without attacking Christianity. But why this perpetual disparagement of miracles, of the authenticity of the gospels? And why the attack on the Old Testament, which is not fundamental to the Church of Rome? Because, as a Deist and a Rationalist, Voltaire desired to overthrow all sects of Christianity, all revealed religion, especially the persecuting religions, Christianity and Mahommedanism. The purer Deism of Mahommedanism seemed to him preferable to the doctrine of the Trinity. He preferred Confucianism and the thought of a Marcus Aurelius to both. But, above all, the ideas of the incarnation of God in man profoundly repelled him and, whenever he dared touch upon it, he asserted that the belief was blasphemous. In the last analysis his view comes down to this : God exists, but remotely, intangibly, unknowably ; the duty of men is to think and to act rationally. That is the substance of Voltaire's anti-religious pamphlets.

XVIII

CORRESPONDENCE

No account of Voltaire's work can be closed without reference to his Correspondence. This mass of letters, between seven and eight thousand in number, covers three quarters of a century. They form an entertaining and complete revelation of Voltaire's character and a social history of the eighteenth century—" tout Voltaire est là ". Naturally, these letters have been the happy hunting ground of the followers of Saint-Beuve, who are more interested in literary personality than in literature, and the general reader would be grateful to the compiler who would sift about a thousand of the best letters from the prodigious pile. Nevertheless, the literary value of Voltaire's letters is high, and, even if one does not altogether share the admiration expressed by Saint-Beuve and M. Lanson, one would never deny their assertion that the art of Voltaire is conspicuously and amiably displayed in his Correspondence.

Verse, charming light verse, is profusely scattered through these pages ; either in letters to fair ladies or poetic friends or in the carefully composed letters intended for circulation. Voltaire knew that his familiar letters were copied and handed about, were even published in the literary periodicals of the day, and he knew also what a seductive charm his witty gossip exercised over contemporaries. He exerted himself to charm, and rarely indeed did his fertile mind refuse to meet the incessant demands he made upon it. Unluckily, the letters we should most like to read, the eight quarto volumes preserved by Mme du Châtelet, were burned by the husband after her death. We can only guess what charm and sparkle must have characterized his letters to the one woman who touched his heart as well as delighting his intelligence, from the letters to women like Mme du Deffrand and Mlle Quinault, the actress, and from those to old friends like d'Argental, Thiériot, Cideville, Richelieu, and Frederick. Voltaire possessed to the full the art of letter-writing. He is familiar without triviality or feebleness ; he is inexhaustible in the devices of flattery ; his intimate letters are never so slight as to be mere notes, and never so long or so earnest as to be homilies or disguised essays. The consummate man of letters only shows himself in the ease and purity of the style, the mastery of arrangement, the flow of wit. His letters are never pedantic, heavy, self-conscious ; they are what letters should be, rapid and entertaining talk. It must indeed be an austere and unimaginative censor who would reprove Voltaire for the exuberant flattery of his letters ; he knew the men and women of his time and he knew how little they could resist the caressing charm of his personality.

The intellectual energy of Voltaire is displayed in his letters, as in his other work ; but the reader is even more delighted by their variety and appropriateness. He had a feminine intuition of character ; he knew instinctively how to adapt his mind to that of the person he was addressing and to the topic under discussion ; without ever ceasing to be Voltaire. He, not his correspondents, almost invariably set the tone of conversation, to which

CORRESPONDENCE

they half-unconsciously conformed. The domination of his mind over his contemporaries is strikingly demonstrated in these letters. Few escaped it. Even Frederick echoes the style of Voltaire and tries to turn the Patriarch's weapons against himself. Mme Denis, naturally enough, is his sedulous ape. But even Mme du Deffand at a distance and Mme d'Epinay when close at hand succumb to his influence ; they cannot resist, they are Voltaireans, while he is hardly moved at all by their influence. He adapts himself to them ; they imitate him.

More than half these letters belong to the Ferney period when, as Voltaire wrote Mme du Deffand, he defeated the miseries and boredom of old age by multiplying his activities and his interests ; but there is a distinct tendency to redundance and repetition of ideas in some of these later letters. Such perpetual self-renewal as Voltaire exacted of himself was beyond the powers even of his versatility and prolonged maturity. The best of the letters are to be found in the volumes covering the years 1730-1760, though every year provides some masterpieces of the epistolary art. Again, a sensitive taste will prefer the truly spontaneous letters to those consciously composed for publication. Some of the latter, for instance those addressed to Jesuit friends or to the editors of periodicals, would more naturally take their place among the Mélanges, were not that section of his works already over-crowded ; others, particularly the letters interspersed with verse and addressed to literary friends, are delightful examples of Voltairean wit. The letters to Cideville and Formont are alone sufficient to make the reputation of a smaller man. Once more we can notice how the volume and variety of Voltaire's production are actually a handicap to appreciation ; he teaches us to expect so much

VOLTAIRE

in so many different kinds of writing that he almost wearies us with his perpetual glitter. We grow fastidious, and think we detect faults and shortcomings which in another writer we should scarcely perceive or easily pardon. We are unwilling to believe that a man could write so much so well. It is said that when Voltaire was publishing his pamphlets, each was at first censured as inferior to its predecessors and yet each in turn took rank with them. His was a singularly equal genius ; in his books he rarely surpassed himself, rarely fell below himself. The same remark is true of his letters ; and if he had written fewer books and fewer letters he would now be more read and more admired. His energy, which is one of the most precious and admirable qualities of his genius, played him false by urging him to diffusion and over-production.

Voltaire so embarrasses us with his prodigality, that we are forced to make a choice among his letters. The specialist is indeed compelled to read them all, and a student of Voltaire's personality would have to do the same ; but there are many which can safely be neglected by the general reader. Technical letters to Maupertuis and other scientists can be wholly passed over ; complimentary letters to princes, great ladies, prelates, foreign academies, men of letters, need only be absorbed in a few specimens ; the numerous intriguing and protesting letters, the business letters to the abbé Moussinot, Voltaire's financial agent, the innumerable discussions with the d'Argentals concerning corrections to plays, need only be sampled. But even when these excisions are made, there is an immense residue. The correspondence with Frederick the Great would fill a volume by itself, and in those letters Voltaire exerted all his art and his cunning,

CORRESPONDENCE

all his charm and malice. If the earlier letters to the great King are almost monotonously sweet with praise, the irony and innuendo of those written after the Frankfort débâcle are in the highest degree diverting. Frederick is blunter and more directly insulting ; Voltaire more restrained, but with a deadlier thrust of irony.

Despite the—perhaps over-scrupulous—reservations made in the preceding paragraph, one may venture upon the assertion that Voltaire's letters as a whole form one of the most interesting and valuable collections in literature. Like Cicero's, they will always attract cultivated minds in all times and all countries, not only for their historical and personal value, but for their universality and their art. We admire, and rightly admire, the letters of Lamb and Cowper ; but in comparison with Voltaire, Lamb is an amiable and whimsical provincial, Cowper an eccentric recluse. Voltaire's was a European mind ; he disdained the spurious local colour of back-alleys and village ale-houses ; he sought intercourse with his peers, and his peers were the greatest minds, not of Ferney, of Paris, of France even, but of Europe. As the old man sat in his study at Ferney, he held in his hands invisible threads which put him in contact with European life at its most intense and most intelligent. There, one feels, and ventures humbly to assert, is where Carlyle goes wildly astray. He, whose every paragraph in the essay on Voltaire is stamped with the provincial mind, rancorously assaults a European intelligence for its very virtues of urbanity, polish, knowledge of the world and men, delicacy of taste, tolerance, scepticism. How remote this fanatical Scotsman seems, while Voltaire almost thinks and talks like a contemporary, except that he is so much more intelligent, well-mannered, and witty than we are.

VOLTAIRE

" He admires the poetry of England, France, and Italy ", says Voltaire of Bolingbroke, "but he admires each differently, because each is different." Obvious, a commonplace? On the contrary, a lesson ; apply that principle to all human activities and you have the European mind, that culminating point of eighteenth-century culture which the succeeding ages have done so much to destroy. The last and noblest virtue of man is magnanimity ; we must not give that praise to the human Voltaire, who is very far from deserving it ; but to the intellectual Voltaire we can and must. In his mind and by virtue of his immensely extended interests, homo Europaeus erat ; there is no higher praise.

Byron, who was so hated by a provincial age for this very quality, says, in writing to Goethe, "considering you the greatest literary intelligence in Europe since the death of Voltaire ". One feels inclined to dwell upon this aspect of Voltaire, so perfectly revealed in his correspondence. At a time of disastrous nationalism and cant, when those few who strive to become acquainted with " the best that is being thought ", are treated as eccentric, almost obscene, when a flood of desolating vulgarity seems to be engulfing the world ; then, if we can step back a pace, detach ourselves, contemplate that European culture and society of which Voltaire is so brilliant an example, we can at least find an ideal of intelligence to substitute for chaos. Intelligence—how often despised and disparaged, but how rare ; and how pleasant it would be to feel that one might even aspire to possess it !

If these letters are remarkable as an imperishable record of Voltaire's personality and unbounded intellectual curiosity, they charm the modern reader by that effortless and completely controlled use of language which is the glory of French prose. The prose of Montaigne, the prose of Racine, the prose of Voltaire, are three summits of different perfection in French prose style. In Montaigne we find a sinewy vigour, a perpetual felicity of epithet, a raciness of diction dashed with irony and wit. Montaigne's thought was the trunk from which spring the great branches of French scepticism; the manner in which that thought was formed was the matrix of French classic prose. The prose artists of the seventeenth century, in refining upon Montaigne, abandoned some of the most precious qualities in prose, but they made possible the formal nobility of Racine, his beautiful sobriety and measure. Voltaire's prose is the third perfection, so enchanting from its crystal purity and elegance, its point and grace, its rapidity and playfulness, its artful negligence which is the effect of lifelong discipline. The prose of Voltaire's letters is indeed " art become a habit "; the shortest note, the most carelessly penned business orders, are expressed with precision and elegance. " I am convinced ", says Voltaire, " that no work of literature reaches posterity if it lacks method ". Gradually one perceives, and perceiving admires, the method of Voltaire; it orders the structure of the longest and the shortest of his compositions, it ranges and disposes his thoughts correctly and effectively, it directs at every moment the flow of his sentences. Like Montesquieu, Voltaire possessed, either by instinct or by training, that most valuable " tact of omission ", which, in the final analysis, perhaps constitutes the essential difference between a dull and a lively writer. " The art of writing," said Montesquieu, " is to skip the intermediate ideas "; few prose artists have possessed that art more completely and surely than Voltaire.

VOLTAIRE

Neglect or disparagement of style is a mark of the provincial or insular mind. Style is not a mere conforming to a standard of grammatical and syntactical perfection ; it is not something exterior to a writer's thought ; it is the form of that thought, lacking which the thought itself could not exist as we perceive it. If Goldsmith talked like poor Poll and wrote like an angel, the reason is that he thought when he wrote and talked without thinking. The aptest words in the aptest order—that is style. And rarely, or perhaps never, is it acquired without thought and labour. There is a wide difference between the stylistic mastery of *Romeo and Juliet* and that of *Macbeth*. Plainly, the style of verse differs from that of prose, as the form of a tree differs from that of water in a vessel. The form of verse (we are assured) is imposed by the imagination ; of prose, by the intellect. Hence the style of prose has a more regular and formal beauty and is perhaps more consciously directed, little or nothing being left (as in verse) to a sudden flash of spontaneous creation. But woe to the poet who lacks style, who uses words to obtain effects of forced dignity or loose picturesqueness, not as the precise form of thought. We perceive the former vice in Voltaire's *Henriade*, the latter in the degenerate Romantics.

Let us look for a moment at the prose of the three French artists just mentioned, and try to observe by comparison of quotations, the differing perfection of each. Here is the meditative and supple prose of Montaigne :

> " J'aime une sagesse gaye et civile, et fuys l'aspreté des moeurs et l'austerité, ayant pour suspecte tout mine rebarbatifve. Je crois Platon de bon coeur, qui dict les humeurs faciles ou difficiles estre un

> grand prejudice à la bonté ou mauvaistié de l'ame. Socrate eut un visage constant, mais serein et riant ; non fascheusement constant comme le vieil Crassus, qu'on ne veit jamais rire. La vertu est qualité plaisante et gaye. Je hais un esprit hargneux et triste, qui glisse par-dessus les plaisirs de la vie, et s'empoigne et paist aux malheurs ; comme les mouches qui ne peuvent tenir contre un corps bien poly et bien lissé, et s'attachent et reposent aux lieux scabreux et raboteux ; et comme les ventouses qui ne hument et appetent que le mauvais sang."

The order of these words is the aptest expression of Montaigne's humanist wisdom ; only his mind and his thought could have taken on exactly that form, and only a perfection of style like his enables a human voice to speak unaltered across the centuries to a remote posterity. Turn now to the more chastened, austere, and regular prose of Racine, which is indeed less seductive and vivid than Montaigne's, but charms by its noble elegance, that formal and sober beauty of prose which no writer has created so perfectly as Racine :

> "Vous pouvez juger, par toutes les inquiétudes que m'a causées votre maladie, combien j'ai de joie de votre guérison. Vous avez beaucoup de graces à rendre à Dieu, de ce qu'il a permis qu'il ne vous soit arrivé aucun fâcheux accident, et que la fluxion qui vous était tombé sur les yeux n'ait point eu de suite. Je loue extrêmement la reconnaissance que vous témoignez pour tous les soins que votre mère a pris de vous. J'espère que vous ne les oublierez jamais, et que vous vous acquitterez de toute les obligations que vous lui avez, par beaucoup de soumission à tout ce qu'elle désirera de vous. Votre lettre m'a fait beaucoup de plaisir ; elle est fort

VOLTAIRE

> sagement écrite et c'était la meilleure et la plus agréable marque que vous me puissiez donner de votre guérison. Mais ne vous pressez pas encore de retourner à l'étude ; je vous conseille de ne lire que des choses qui vous fassent plaisir sans vous donner trop de peine, jusqu'à ce que le médecin qui vous a traité vous donne permission de recommencer votre travail."

Voltaire's prose, and particularly the prose of his letters, is a refinement upon, and a kind of synthesis of, the prose of these two masters. Voltaire's prose has the familiar ease of Montaigne's and the restraint of Racine's with an additional charm and grace of his own. It has not the raciness, the sinewy strength of Montaigne's prose, but it is purged of Montaigne's faults—the lack of order, the meandering of thought, a tinge of rusticity and grossness ; and, if it lacks the noble sobriety and elegance of Racine's, it abandons his austerity and formality in exchange for a more voluptuous and witty grace. Voltaire's century is the link between the aristocratic art civilisation of the Renaissance and the commercial democracy of our own times ; as a thinker and social reformer, Voltaire anticipated the utilitarian and humanitarian views of the last century, to such an extent that the daring flights of his philosophie now appear as the dullest commonplaces, even as detestable illusions ; but as an artist he was still turned towards the Renaissance. He had the Renaissance respect for classical form, and is guiltless of the incoherence, sensationalism, emotional extravagance, of more recent times. Looking at him as an artist in prose, we might say he was a Montaigne chastened and disciplined by Racine ; or a Racine enlivened and humanized by Montaigne.

CORRESPONDENCE

Here is Voltaire in a mood of compliment and good humour, writing to Mlle de Lubert:

"*Muse et Grâce*, Mme de Fontaines-Martel m'a envoyé votre lettre, pour me servir de consolation, dans l'exil où je suis à Fontainebleau. Je vois que vous êtes instruite des tracasseries que j'ai eues avec mon parlement, et de la combustion où toute la cour a été, pendant trois ou quatre jours, au sujet d'une mauvaise comédie que j'ai empêché d'être réprésentée. J'ai eu un crédit étonnant en fait de bagatelles, et j'ai remporté des victoires signalées sur des choses où il ne s'agissait de rien du tout. Il s'est formi deux partis : l'un de la reine et des dames du palais, et l'autre des princesses et de leurs adhérents. La reine a été victorieuse, et j'ai fait la paix avec les princesses. Il n'en a coûté, pour cette importante affaire, que quelques petits vers médiocres, mais qui ont été trouvés fort bons par celles à qui ils étaient addressés ; car il n'y a point de déesse dont le nez ne soit rejoui de l'odeur de l'encens. Que j'aurais de plaisir à en brûler pour vous, *Muse et Grâce* ! mais il faut vous le déguiser trop adroitement ; il faut vous cacher presque tout ce qu'on pense.

 Je n'ose dans mes vers parler de vos beautés
  Que sous le voile du mystère.
  Quoi ! sans art je ne puis vous plaire,
  Lorsque sans lui vous m'enchantez ? "

In the eighteenth century a dozen letters written with that gaiety and charm and wit earned a man a literary reputation ; Voltaire wrote a thousand such. That letter was written in 1732 ; here are some passages from one written nearly forty years later to amuse Mme du Deffand in her blindness ; and may it be mentioned in

VOLTAIRE

passing that Voltaire was assiduous in his efforts to divert her from the gloom of her blindness and ennui? Mme du Deffand had written Voltaire that it would be " best never to be born ". He replies :

> " Votre grand' maman,[1] madame, doit vous avoir communiqué la *Canonisation de frère Cucufin*, par laquelle Rezzonico[2] a signalé les dernières années de son sage pontificat. J'ai cru que cela vous amuserait, d'autant plus que cette histoire est dans la plus exacte vérité. . . .
> " Je voudrais pouvoir fournir tous les jours quelques diversions à vos idées tristes; je sens bien qu'elles sont justes. La privation de la lumière et l'acquisition d'un certain age ne sont pas choses agréables. Ce n'est pas assez d'avoir du courage, il faut des distractions. L'amusement est un remède plus sûr que toute la fermeté d'esprit. J'ai le temps de songer à tout cela dans ma profonde solitude. . . .
> " . . . . Il vaudrait mieux n'être pas né, dites-vous ; d'accord, mais vous savez si la chose a dépendu de nous. Non seulement la nature nous a fait naître sans nous consulter, mais elle nous fait aimer la vie malgré que nous en ayons. Nous sommes presque tous comme le bucheron de la fable d'Esope et de La Fontaine. Il y a tous les ans deux ou trois personnes sur cent mille qui prennent congé ; mais c'est dans de grands accès de mélancolie. C'est un peu plus fréquent dans le pays que j'habite. Deux Génevois de ma connaissance se sont jetés dans le Rhône, il y a quelques mois ; l'un avait cinquante mille écus de ente, l'autre était un homme à bons mots. Je n'ai point été tenté

[1] Nickname given by Mme du Deffand to the Duchesse de Choiseul, wife of the prime minister.
[2] Clement XIII.

CORRESPONDENCE

d'imiter leur exemple ; premièrement, parce que mes abominables fluxions sur les yex ne me durent que l'hiver ; en second lieu, parce que je me couche toujours dans l'espérance de me moquer du genre humain en me réveillant. Quand cette faculté me manquera, ce sera un signe certain qu'il faudra que je parte."

"Se moquer du genre humain" might stand as the epigraph to a large portion of Voltaire's writings ; but it was at least inconsequent to place dangerous weapons in the hands of such scatter-brained children as Voltaire thought human beings were. But notice how the philosopher of Ferney retained the verve and gaiety of the young Parisian poet, and, above all, how his command of French prose is if anything more complete and masterly. Those who desire to correct as far as possible the vices and inelegancies of style which are the only things most writers have in common under our intellectual anarchy, would find a study of Voltaire's letters a great assistance in attaining clarity and correctness without lapsing into pedantry and archaism. Were it possible to apply the principles upon which Voltaire composed, to the writing of modern English, we might be able to find new prose that would equally delight us. I do not assert that the prose of Voltaire's letters is an ultimate perfection which cannot be surpassed, or that it should be set up as a model for slavish imitation ; but that it possesses qualities which have escaped from many prose of our time, qualities by no means incompatible with modernity of thought and outlook, possibly more suitable to it than the facetious barbarisms and yet more deplorable jargon of our own newspapers. Happy and rare indeed

VOLTAIRE

is the prose writer in our age who avoids both vulgarity and affectation. If we need a Voltaire to redeem us by laughter from our preposterous virtue, we need him also to show us how to write the prose of Swift and Chesterfield.

XIX

CONCLUSION

Were I so criminal as to be extremely rich, I should endeavour to palliate the circumstance by laying out wide and pleasant gardens, rather in the mythological style commended by the Prince de Ligne. Certainly I should imitate M. de Ligne to the extent of planning a secluded Bosquet Voltaire. The tutelary deity should be Houdon's statue, opposite which should be placed some Graeco-Roman Venus, so that M. de Voltaire might seem to smile for ever in his enigmatic way at the emblem of grace, life, and beauty. In his lifetime he admired beautiful forms and, though undoubtedly he made his money by the basest kind of war profiteering, his taste was not affected. If in some respects he appears a forerunner of drab utilitarianism, in others he was a late development of the Renaissance man, if only from his versatility and energy and his respect for what he held to be beautiful. He had a Renaissance gusto for life and he was no puritan ; whatever envy was in his nature was not directed against the pleasures and possessions of others. His rationalism, however much indebted to northern minds, was nevertheless Mediterranean in its recognition of the human right to enjoyment.

A belief in personal immortality was not among Voltaire's convictions ; indeed an opposite belief was one of his crochets, no doubt because of his dislike for

VOLTAIRE

established religion. The extinction of a flaming spirit like his, urged to a perpetual activity by some mysterious daemon, is a painful thought to entertain. Where now is the "fiery particle" which for so many years so unbelievably animated his weak body? If ever toiling hero won a passage to the stars it was Voltaire; but no new constellation decked the heavens at his death and no senatus consultum conferred upon him an honorary immortality. We are reduced to dark speculations and dim fancies. Is there no Bosquet Voltaire in the Elysian Fields, no agreeable corner of Hades where Mme du Châtelet and her lover may carry on their studies without fear of infernal *lettres de cachet*? A placid, resigned, and contemplative Voltaire is hardly thinkable; so well-employed an actor in the human comedy would hardly be reconciled to an immortality of rest. Doubtless he is composing a history of the universe in many hundred volumes, writes madrigals to Son Altesse Royale Mme Proserpine, entertains his friends and is always good humoured and witty, except when those who lost their heads in the Revolution are pleased to be merry at the expense of his social theories. . . .

These are foolish and profitless fancies. All we have is a row of volumes,—most of them neglected—echoes of a great life, memories of a great reputation. We live in a world that has greatly changed since Voltaire inhabited it, and we feel, rather than we can prove, that some of the changes must be credited, or debited, to him. The masses of us are undoubtedly wealthier, better provided with transport, and more comfortable than our eighteenth century progenitors. The compensating losses are less tangible but none the less real. In any case, though we have very nearly hanged the last priest

CONCLUSION

in the garters of the last king, it does not appear that we have acquired more philosophic rulers or that the reign of Justice and Reason spreads a golden peace from Shanghai to Oklahoma. Candides find no warmer welcome now than two centuries ago, and the project of living a life of perfect wisdom is still as foolish as when Memnon was hurled into a sea of grotesque accidents. Let us not blame Voltaire. He did not think we are born perfect and he did not expect to make us perfect; he tried to scold, satirize, laugh, encourage us to be a little more reasonable, tolerant, and just. What more could be done with the vain, quarrelsome, greedy, petulant children that we are? But, though Voltaire despised men, he tried to help them:

> "He avenged Calas, La Barre, Sirven and Monbailly. Poet, philosopher, historian, he gave a wider scope to the human mind.
> He prepared us to become free."

APPENDIX

(I have added here a Chronological List of Voltaire's Works, a list of the best English and French books concerned with Voltaire, and a list of English translations. The Chronological list contains practically all Voltaire's work, only minor poems and prose pieces being omitted; everything of literary or biographical interest has been included. The arrangement is in genres, because one long catalogue of works in prose and verse would have been very confusing. I went carefully through Voltaire's works again to make this list and believe it to be reasonably adequate.

The list of books about Voltaire contains most of those used for this book as well as a number which were not drawn upon, either because they were entirely specialists' books or because they were popular hand-books.

The list of translations was taken from the British Museum catalogue and from other sources. I ought to say that I have not read any of them and therefore do not recommend any).

*Chronological List of Voltaire's Works
arranged according to Genre*

I VERSE

1 PLAYS

1718	Oedipe (Tragedy).
1720	Artémire (fragments) (Tragedy).
1724	Mariamne (Tragedy).

VOLTAIRE

1725	L'Indiscret (Comedy).
1725	La Fête de Bélébat. (Divertissement).
1730	Brutus (Tragedy).
1732	Les Originaux (Comedy).
1732	Eriphyle (Tragedy).
1732	Samson (Opera).
1732	Zaïre (Tragedy).
1733	Tanis et Zélide (T. Mélodrame).
1734	Adelaïde du Guesclin (Tragedy).
1734	L'Echange (Comedy).
1735	La Mort de César (Tragedy).
1736	Alzire (Tragedy).
1736	L'Enfant Prodigue (Comedy).
1738	L'Envieux (Comedy).
1740	Zulime (Tragedy).
1740	Pandore (Opera).
1741	Le Fanatisme or Mahomet le Prophête (Tragedy).
1743	Mérope (Tragedy).
1743	Thérêse (Fragment) (Comedy).
1745	La Princesse de Navarre (C-Ballet).
1745	Le Temple de la Gloire (Opera).
1747	La Prude (Comedy).
1748	Sémiramis (Tragedy).
1749	Nanine (Comedy).
1749	La Femme qui a Raison (Comedy).
1750	Oreste (Tragedy).
1751	Le Duc de Foix (Tragedy). ⎫ Variations on the
1751	Le Duc d'Alençon (Tragedy) ⎬ earlier play Adelaïde du Guesclin.
1752	Rome Sauvée ou Catalina (Tragedy).
1755	L'Orphelin de la Chine (Tragedy).
1759	Socrate (Drame).
1760	L'Ecossaise (Comedy).
1760	Tancrède (Tragedy).

APPENDIX

1763	Le Droit du Seigneur or L'Ecueil du Sage (Comedy).
1763	Saül (Drame).
1763	Olympie (Tragedy).
1764	Jules César (Tragedy). Translated from Shakespeare.
1764	L' Héraclius Espagnole (Tragedy). Translated from Calderon.
1764	Le Triumvirat (Tragedy).
1767	Les Scythes (Tragedy).
1767	Charlot (Drame).
1769	Le Dépositaire (Comedy).
1769	Le Baron d'Otrante (Opéra-Bouffe).
1769	Les Deux Tonneaux (Opéra-Comique). Sketch only.
1769	Les Guêbres (Tragedy).
1770	Sophonisbe (Tragedy).
1771	Les Pélopides (Tragedy).
1773	Les Lois de Minos (Tragedy).
1773	Don Pèdre (Tragedy).
1776	L'Hôte et L'Hôtesse (Divertissement).
1778	Irène (Tragedy).
1779	Agathocle (Tragedy). Posthumous.

(Note: A few of these plays are in prose).

II POEMS

EPICS, BURLESQUES, LONGER POEMS

1722	Le Pour et le Contre
1723	La Ligue (First version of La Henriade).
1728	La Henriade : ten Books (London).
1730	La Pucelle d'Orléans, 21 Books. First authorised edition 1762.
1730	La Mort de Mlle Lecouvreur.
1731	Le Temple du Goût.

VOLTAIRE

1734-37 Discours en Vers sur L'Homme. 7 Discours.
1744   Sur les Evénements de 1744.
1745   Poême de Fontenoy.
1752   Poême sur la Loi Naturelle. 4 Parts
1755   Sur le Désastre de Lisbonne.
1768   La Guerre Civile de Genève.

SATIRES

1714 Le Bourbier.
1736 Le Mondain.
1737 Défense du Mondain.
1758 Le Pauvre Diable.
1760 La Vanité.
1766 Eloge de l'Hypocrisie.
1768 Le Marseillais et le Lion.
1773 La Tactique.
1775 Le Temps Présent.

ODES

Twenty-one Odes, composed between 1709 and 1775.

POÉSIES MÊLÉES

1704? A. M. Duché.
1716   Nuit Blanche de Sully.
1719   A Mlle Lecouvreur.
1723   Les Deux Amours.
1724   Epigramme : " N'a pas longtemps, de l'abbé de Saint-Pierre."
1730   A Mme la Marquise d'Ussé.
1732   Madrigal : " Ah ! Carmago. . . ."
1732   Epigrammes : A Mlle Delaunay.

APPENDIX

1734	Epigrammes : A Mme la Marquise du Châtelet.
1735	A Mme de Flamarens.
1736	Epigrammes : A Mme du Châtelet.
1736	A. M. Bernard.
1736	Le Portrait Manqué.
1738	A Mme du Boccage.
1738	Les Souhaits.
1739	A. M. l'Abbé depuis Cardinal de Bernis.
1741	Sur les Disputes en Métaphysique.
1745	Impromptu.
1745	A Mme de Pompadour.
1745	A Mme de Boufflers.
1747	A Un Bavard.
1748	A Mme du Châtelet.
1749	Sur l'Amour.
1749	Epitaph de Mme du Châtelet
1750	Au Roi de Prusse.
1751	Au Roi de Prusse. } Epigrammes and Madrigals
1752	Au Roi de Prusse.
1753	A Mme la Duchesse de Saxe-Gotha.
1756	Au Roi de Prusse " O Salomon du Nord, etc."
1760	Les Pour ; Les Que ; Les Qui ; Les Quoi ; Les Oui ; Les Non.
1760	Rondeau.
1761	Hymne chanté au village de Pompignon.
1765	Couplets d'un Jeune Homme.
1766	Sur J. J. Rousseau. " Cet ennemi du genre humain ".
1768	A. M. Mairan.
1768	A Une Jeune Dame.
1769	Epitaphe du Pape Clément XIII.
1772	A Mlle Clairon.
1772	A M—— " Croyez-moi, je renonce à toutes les chimères,"
1775	Epitaph de l'Abbé de Voisenon.

VOLTAIRE

1777   A M — "Je le ferai bientôt, ce voyage éternel".
1778   Adieux à la Vie.

STANCES

1740?   A Mme la Marquise du Châtelet
1740   Au Roi de Prusse.
1740   Au Même.
1741   A Mme du Châtelet.
1745   A Mme la Marquise de Pompadour.
1748   A Mme du Boccage.
1751   Au Roi de Prusse
1755   A Mme Denis
1757   Les Torts.
1761   A M. Blin de Sainmore.
1770   A Mme Necker.
1770   A M. Hourcastremé.
1773   A Mlle Lullin.
1773   Les Désagréments de la Vieillesse.

EPITRES

1714   A M. l'Abbé Servien.
1714   A Mme de Montbrun-Villefranche.
1715   A M. le Prince de Vendôme.
1715   A M. l'Abbé de——
1715   A Une Dame.
1716   A Mme de G——
1719   A M. de Genonville.
1720   A M. le Duc de Sully.
1721   A M. le Maréchal de Villars.
1722   A Mme de ——
1725   A Mlle Lecouvreur.

APPENDIX

1729	Aux Manes de M. de Genonville.
1731	Les Vous et les Tu.
1732	A Une Dame, ou soi-disant telle.
1732	A Mlle Gaussin.
1733	A Mme du Châtelet, Sur la Calomnie.
1734	A M ——
1734	A Uranie (two poems).
1734	A Mme du Châtelet.
1736	A Mlle de Lubert.
1736	Au Prince Royal de Prusse.
1740	A Un Ministre d'Etât.
1748	A Mme Denis.
1749	A M. de Saint-Lambert.
1751	Au Roi de Prusse (Three poems).
1755	L'Auteur arrivant dans sa terre.
1759	A Une Jeune Veuve.
1761	A Daphné.
1761	A Mme. Elie de Beaumont.
1765	A Mlle Clairon.
1769	A Boileau.
1769	A M. de Saint-Lambert.
1769	A M. de la Harpe.
1771	Au Roi de la Chine.
1778	A M. le Marquis de Villette.

CONTES EN VERS

1714	L'Antigiton.
1716	Le Cadenas.
1716	Le Cocuage.
1733	La Mule du Pape.
1763	L'Education d'Un Prince.
1763	Gertrude, or l'Education d'une Fille
1763	Les Trois Manières.
1764	Ce qui plait aux Dames.

VOLTAIRE

1764	Thélême et Macare.
1764	Azolan.
1764	L'Origine des Métiers.
1772	Le Bégueule.
1775	Les Finances.
1776	Sésostris.
1776	Le Songe Creux.

II PROSE

HISTORY AND BIOGRAPHY

1731	Histoire de Charles XII.
1751	Siècle de Louis XIV.
1753	Annales le l'Empire.
1756	Essai sur les Moeurs et l'Esprit des Nations (Several earlier incomplete editions).
1759	L'Histoire de L'Empire de Russie sous Pierre le Grand.
1763-68	Siècle de Louis XV.
1769	Histoire du Parlement de Paris.
1764	Commentaires sur Corneille.
1765	Dictionnaire Philosophique (First complete edition, four earlier incomplete editions).

ROMANS

1746	Le Monde Comme il va, vision de Babouc.
1746	Le Crocheteur Borgne.
1746	Cosi-Sancta.

APPENDIX

1747	Zadig.
1750	Memnon.
1750	Bababec et les Fakirs.
1752	Micromégas.
1756	Les Deux Consolés.
1756	Histoire des Voyages de Scarmentado.
1756	Songe de Platon.
1759	Candide ou l'Optimisme.
1764	Le Blanc et le Noir.
1759	Histoire d'un bon Bramin.
1764	Jeannot et Colin.
1767	L'Ingénu.
1768	L'Homme aux Quarante Ecus.
1768	La Princesse de Babylon.
1769	Les Lettres d'Amabed.
1773	Aventure de la Mémoire.
1774	Le Taureu Blanc.
1774	Eloge Historique de la Raison.
1775	Histoire de Jenni.
1775	Les Oreilles du Comte de Chesterfield.
?	Aventure Indienne.
?	Les Aveugles Juges des Couleurs.

MÉLANGES

1728	Remarque sur les Pensées de M. Pascal.
1728	Sottises des deux parts.
1734	Lettres Philosophiques.
1737	Conseils à un Journaliste.
1738	Eclaircissements nécessaires donnés par M. de Voltaire sur les Eléments de la Philosophie de Newton.
1738	Essai sur la Nature du Feu et sur sa Propagation.
1738	Vie de M. J.-B. Rousseau.

VOLTAIRE

1738	Observations sur Mm Jean Law, Melon et Dutot.
1738	Le Préservatif.
1738	Conseils à M. Helvétius.
1738	Remarques sur Des Deux Epîtres d'Helvétius.
1738	Eléments de la Philosophie de Newton.
1739	Mémoire sur la Satire.
1739	Mémoire sur un Ouvrage de Physique de Mme la Marquise du Châtelet.
1739	Réponse aux objections principales qu'on a fait en France contre la Philosophie de Newton.
1739	Vie de Molière.
1740	Exposition du Livre des Institutions physiques.
1741	Doutes sur la mésure des forces motrices et sur leur nature.
1742	Conseils à M. Racine sur son poème de La Religion, par un Amateur des Belles-lettres.
1744	Courte Réponse aux longs discours d'un docteur allemand.
1745	Manifeste du Roi de France en faveur du Prince Charles-Edouard.
1746	Discours de M. de Voltaire à sa réception à l'Académie Française.
1748	Anecdotes sur Louis XIV.
1748	Eloge Funébre des Officiers qui sont morts dans la Guerre de 1741.
1748	Panégyrique de Louis XV.
1748	Anecdotes sur le Czar Pierre le Grand.
1749	Panégyrique de Saint Louis.
1749	Connaissance des Beautés et des Défauts de la Poésie et de l'Eloquence dans la langue Française.
1749-50	Des Mensonges imprimés et du Testament Politique du Cardinal de Richelieu.
1750	Remerciement sincère à un Homme Charitable.
1750	La Voix du Sage et du Peuple.

APPENDIX

1751	Des Embellissements de la Ville de Cachemire.
1751	Dialogue entre Marc-Aurèle et un Recollet.
1751	Idées de la Mothe le Vayer.
1751	Dialogue entre un Plaideur et un Avocat.
1751	Dialogue entre Mme de Maintenon et Mlle de Lenclos.
1752	Sur Mlle de Lenclos.
1752	Eloge Historique de Mme la Marquise du Châtelet.
1752	Pensées sur le Gouvernement.
1752	Défense de Milord Bolingbroke.
1752-53	Histoire du Docteur Akakia et du Natif de Saint-Malo.
1756	Dialogue entre un Brachmane et un Jésuite.
1756	Dialogue entre Lucrèce et Posidonius.
1756	Jusqu'à quel point on doit tromper le peuple.
1759	Relation de la Maladie, de la Confession, de la Mort, et de l'Apparition du Jésuite Berthier.
1759	(Published 1784) Mémoires pour servir à la Vie de M. de Voltaire.
1760	Réflexions pour les Sots.
1760	Dialogues Chrétiens.
1760	Lettre de M. Cubstorf.
1761	Lettres sur La Nouvelle Héloïse.
1761	Anecdotes sur Fréron.
1761	Appel à toutes les Nations de l'Europe.
1761	Rescrit de l'Empereur de la Chine.
1761	Lettre de M. Clocpicre à M. Eratou.
1761	Conversation de M. l'Intendant des Menus en Exercise avec M. l'Abbé Grizel.
1761	Les Car. A M. le Franc le Pompignon.
1761	Les Ah ! Ah !
1761	Entretiens d'Un Sauvage et d'Un Bachelier.
1761	Sermon du Rabbi Akib.
1762	Extrait des Sentiments de Jean Meslier.

VOLTAIRE

1762	Eloge de M. de Crébillon.
1762	Pièces Originales, concernant la Mort des Sieurs Calas et le Jugement rendu à Toulouse.
1762	Mémoire de Donat Calas.
1762	Histoire d'Elizabeth Canning et des Calas.
1762	Idées Républicianes, par un Citoyen de Genève
1762	Sermon des Cinquante.
1763	Relation du Voyage de M. le Marquis Le Franc le Pompignon.
1763	Catéchisme de l'Honnête Homme.
1763	Remarques pour servir de supplément à l'Essai sur les Moeurs et l'Esprit des Nations.
1763	Lettre d'Un Quaker.
1763	Traité sur la Tolérance, à l'occasion de la mort de Jean Calas.
1763	Les Dernières Paroles d'Epictète à son Fils
1764	Discours aux Welches (And Supplement).
1764	Pot-Pourri.
1765	De l'Horrible danger de la lecture.
1765	Conversation de Lucien, Erasme et Rabelais.
1768	Questions sur les Miracles.
1765	Les Anciens et les Modernes, ou la Toilette de Mme de Pompadour.
1766	Relation de la Mort du Chevalier de la Barre.
1766	Avis au public sur les parracides imputés aux Calas et aux Sirven.
1766	Le Philosophe Ignorant.
1767	Les Honnêtetés Littéraires.
1767	Les Questions de Zapata.
1767	Examen Important de Milord Bolingbroke.
1767	Homélies prononcées à Londres.
1767	La Défense de mon Oncle.
1767	Lettres . . . sur Rabelais, etc.
1767	Le Diner du Comte de Boulainvilliers.
1768	Sermon Prêché à Bâle.
1768	Entretiens chinois.

APPENDIX

1768	Conseils raisonnables à M. Bergier.
1768	Profession de Foi des Théistes.
1768	Les Droits des Hommes et les Usurpations des Papes.
1768	Les Colimaçons du R. P. l'Escarbotier.
1768	Le Pyrrhonisme de l'Histoire.
1768	Instruction du Gardien des Capucins de Raguse, à Frère Pédiculoso.
1769	L'A, B, C, ou Dialogues (17 dialogues).
1769	Canonisation de Saint Cucufin.
1769	Le Cri des Nations.
1769	De la Paix perpetuelle.
1769	Dieu et les Hommes.
1769	Réflexions sur les Mémoires de Dangeau.
1769	Préface et extraits des Souvenirs de Mme de Caylus.
1771	Coûtume de Franche-Comté.
1771	Supplique des Serfs de Saint-Claude.
1771	Les Peuples aux Parlements.
1771	Procés criminel du Sieur Montbailli.
1771	Lettres de Memmius à Ciceron.
1771	Le Tocsin des Rois.
1772	Essai sur la Probabilité en fait de Justice.
1772	Il faut prendre un parti.
1772	La voix du Curé, sur le procés des serfs du mont Jura.
1773	Précis du procés de M. le Comte de Morangiés.
1773-74	Fragments historiques sur quelques révolution dans l'Inde, et sur la mort du Comte de Lally.
1773	Fragment sur le procés criminel de Montbailli.
1773	Fragments sur l'Histoire générale.
1774	Lettres à M. Turgot.
1775	Mémoire sur le pays de Gex.
1775	Le Cri du Sang innocent.
1776	Extrait d'un Mémoire pour l'entière abolition de la servitude en France.

VOLTAIRE

1776   Lettres Chinoises, indiennes et tartares.
1776   Commentaire historique sur les Œuvres de l'auteur de la Henriade.
1776   Un Chrétien contre six Juifs.
1776   La Bible enfin expliquée. . . .
1777   Commentaire sur l'Esprit des Lois.
1777   Histoire de l'Etablissement du Christianisme.

CORRESPONDENCE

Œuvres. 7673 Letters to and from Voltaire, between 1713 and 26th May, 1778.
Lettres Inédites. 1064 Letters (with Supplement), 1718-1778. 2 Vols. 1856.
Lettres et Billets Inédits 1887.
Lettres Inédites de Voltaire à Louis Racine. 1893.

PRINCIPAL COLLECTED EDITIONS

Oeuvres Completes de Voltaire. Kehl. Ed. Beaumarchais. 70 Vols. 1784-1787.
Oeuvres de Voltaire. Ed. Beuchot. 1828-1840. 72 Vols.
Oeuvres de Voltaire. Ed Moland, 1883. 52 Vols.
   (The edition used for this book is the Hachette reprint of Beuchot's edition, 40 Vols.).
There are very many reprints, partial editions, re-issues of separate works, and extracts, in existence.

ENGLISH TRANSLATIONS

The Works of Voltaire, translated [nominally] by Dr Smollett and T. Franklin, 35 vols, 1761-69.
The Works of the late M. de Voltaire translated by Rev. D. Williams, H. Downman, W. Campbell, 1779-81.

APPENDIX

Alzire translated by Aaron Hill, 1736.
A Treatise of Toleration, translated by David Williams, 1779.
A Treatise on Religious Tolerance, 1764.
The Coffee-House (L'Ecossaise), 1760.
Candide, 1759.
Candide, 1761.
The History of Candide, 1796.
Voltaire's Candide (H. Morley), 1884.
Candide, (W. M. T.), 1896.
Candide (W. Jerrold), 1898.
Candide (Dorset Chambers), 1919.
Philosophical Tales, 1871.
Zadig and Other Tales (R. B. Boswell), 1904.
Zadig and Other Romances (H. I. Woolf), 1923.
Jeannot et Colin (J. H. L. Hunt), 1806.
The Pupil of Nature (i.e. L'Ingénu), 1771.
The Sincere Huron, 1786.
Micromegas, 1753.
The Ears of Lord Chesterfield, 1786.
The White Bull (J. Bentham), 1774.
Dialogues and Essays, Literary and Philosophical, 1764.
Philosophical Dictionary, 1765.
Philosophical Dictionary, 6 vols. (J. G. Gorton), 1824.
Philosophical Dictionary, selected and translated by H. I. Woolf, 1924.
Epistles on Happiness, Liberty, Envy. (W. Gordon), 1738.
Elements of Sir I. Newton's Philosophy (J. Hanna), 1738.
The Prodigal, 1750.
The General History and State of Europe, 3 vols., 1758.
An Essay upon the Civil Wars of France and upon Epick Poetry, 1727. (Written in English by Voltaire).
The Important Examination of Holy Scripture attributed to Lord Bolingbroke, 1819.
The Civil War of Geneva (T. Teres), 1769.

VOLTAIRE

The Henriade (Daniel French), 1807.
The Henriade (R. G. MacGregor), 1854.
Henriade : an Epick Poem, 1732.
History of Charles XII, 1732.
History of Charles XII, 1802.
History of the War of 1741, 1756.
Mahomet the Impostor (J. Miller and J. Hoadley), 1744
Memoirs of M. de Voltaire written by himself, 1784.
Merope (J. Theobald), 1744.
Metaphysics of Sir I. Newton (D. E. Baker), 1747.
The Orphan of China, 1756.
The Philosophy of History, 1766.
The Age of Lewis the XIV, 1752.
History of the Age of Lewis XIV, 1770.
La Pucelle ; 5 Cantos (Countess of Charleville), 1789.
Maid of Orleans (W. H. Ireland), 1822.
The Questions of Zapata, 1840.
Saul (Oliver Martext of Arden), 1820.
Semiramis, 1760.
Socrates, 1760.
Almida (Tancrède) (Mrs Celesia), 1771.
The Temple of Taste, 1734.
Tragedy of Zara (Zaîre), 1736.
Letters Concerning the English Nation (Thièriot's edition), 1733.
Babouc ; or the World as it goes, 1754.
Critical Essay on Dramatic Poetry, 1760.
Annals of the Empire from the Times of Charlemagne (D. Williams, H. Downman), 1781.
Voltaire in his Letters (S. G. Tallentyre), 1919.

APPENDIX

A SELECTION OF BOOKS DEALING WITH VOLTAIRE

G. Desnoiresterres. Voltaire et la Société Française. [Paris, 1867-76].
A. Pierron. Voltaire et ses Maîtres. [Paris, 1866].
H. Beaune. Voltaire au Collège. [Paris, 1867].
Longchamp et Wagnière. Mémoires sur Voltaire. [Paris, 1825].
Lettres de Mme de Grafigny. [Paris, 1879].
Lettres de Mme du Châtelet. [Paris, 1882].
M. J. A. N. C. de Condorcet. Vie de Voltaire. [Kehl, 1789].
F. M. Grimm. Correspondance Littéraire. [Paris, 1753-1790].
Frederick the Great. Œuvres. [Berlin, 1846-1857].
Duc de Broglie. Frédéric II et Louis XV. [Paris, 1885].
E. Saigey. Les Sciences au XVIIIe Siècle. [Paris, 1873].
C. A. de Sainte-Beuve. Lundis. [1849-1866].
C. A. Collini. Mon Séjour auprès de Voltaire. [Paris, 1807].
E. Deschanel. Théâtre de Voltaire. [Paris, 1886].
H. Lion. Les Tragédies de Voltaire. [Paris, 1895].
J. J. Olivier. Voltaire et les Comédiens. [Paris, 1900].
J. A. A. J. Jusserand. Shakespeare en France. [Paris, 1898].
J. F. de La Harpe. Cours de Littérature. [Paris, 1786,&c.].
Perey et Maugras. Voltaire aux Délices et à Ferney. [Paris, 1885].
Maugras. Voltaire et Jean-Jacques Rousseau. [Paris, 1886].

VOLTAIRE

Harel. Voltaire. [Paris, 1782].
Gustave Lanson. Voltaire. [Paris, 4th edition, 1922].
Nicolardot. Ménage et Finances de Voltaire. [Paris, 1854].
A. R. Vinet. Histoire de la Littérature Française au XVIIIe Siècle. [Paris, 1853].
Bersot. Etudes sur le XVIIIe Siècle. [Paris, 1855].
E. Faguet. Le XVIIIe Siècle. [Paris, 1890].
M. U. Maynard. Voltaire, sa Vie et ses Œuvres. [Paris, 1867].
E. Champion. Voltaire. [Paris, 1892].
J. F. Nourrisson. Voltaire et le Voltaireianisme. [Paris, 1896].
L. Crouslé. La Vie et les Œuvres de Voltaire. [Paris, 1899].
Georg Brandes. François de Voltaire. [Copenhagen, 1916-17].
Thomas Carlyle. Frederick the Great. [1855-1865].
Thomas Carlyle. Voltaire (essay).
John Morley. Voltaire. [London, 1872].
Lytton Strachey. Books and Characters. [London, 1922].
J. Parton. Life of Voltaire. [New York, 1881].
J. M. Robertson. Voltaire. [London, 1922].
S. G. Tallentyre. Voltaire. [London, 1903].
J. Churton Collins. Voltaire, Montesquieu, and Rousseau in England. [London, 1886].
T. R. Lounsbury. Shakespeare and Voltaire. [London, 1902].
A. Ballantyne. Voltaire's Visit to England. [London, 1893].
J. A. A. J. Jusserand. English Essays from a French Pen. [London, 1895].

INDEX

Abrégé de l'Histoire Universelle, 104
Académie des Sciences, 58, 59, 66
Académie Française, 59, 60, 66, 69, 70, 121, 124
Adam (Père), 114
Addison, 33, 109
Aeneid, 140
Aeschylus, 172
Ah ! Ah ! (Les), 112
Ainsworth (Harrison), 160
Aix-la-Chapelle, 66
Akakia, 6, 91, 92, 93, 94
Alembert (d'), 107, 108, 109, 110, 121, 135
Alexander III (Pope), 178
Algarotti, 85
Alsace, 104
Alsatia, 14
Alzire, 59, 131, 166
Amsterdam, 82 note
Amulius and Numitor, 12
Anacreontea, 12
Andromache, 159
Anguesseau, (Chancellor d'), 42
Annales de l'Empire, 96, 175, 186, 186, note
Annecy (Bishop of), 114
Anon, 131
Anthology, 2
Anti-Giton (L'), 17
Apollo, 100
Arabian Nights, 220
Archbishop of Paris, 41
Arcs (Parish of Saint-Pierre André des), 9
Argens (Marquis d'), 85
Argenson (d'), 15, 68, 71, 97
Argental (d'), 46, 71, 84, 104, 105, 121, 234, 236
Argonauts, 141

Ariosto, 140, 145
Aristotle, 157, 194
Arouet (Maître), 10, 11, 12, 15, 16, 17, 20
Arouet (Mme), 9
Arnaud (Baculard d'), 57, 81, 88
Arnold (Matthew), 137
Artémire, 19
Aubigné (Agrippa d'), 35, 141
Auxerre (Château d'), 46
Aventure Indienne, 226

Bababec, 225
Bacchus, 15
Bacon, 33, 207
Bailly (Pierre), 9
Barre (Chevalier de la), 108, 111, 118, 126, 249
Barry (Mme. du), 121
Bart (Jean), 190
Bastille, 6, 18, 19, 23, 24, 45, 46, 72, 81, 83, 108, 131
Baudelaire, 136, 154
Beaumelle (La), 70, 90
Beaumont and Fletcher, 33 *note*
Beaune (Hotel de), 121, 123
Beauregard, 21
Beauvau (Prince de), 122
Benedict XIV. (Pope), 59
Bentinck (Mme. de), 89
Bergerac (Cyrano de), 14, 220
Bergson, 194
Berkeley, 29, 33
Berlin, 6, 64, 65, 66, 82 *note*, 86, 89, 92
Berlin (Academy of), 90, 91
Berni, 145
Bernières (Marquis de), 19, 20
Bertin, 153
Bertinelli, 109
Beyreuth, 66

INDEX

Beyreuth (Margravine of), 82
Bibliothéque Nationale, 124
Blanc (Abbé, Le), 51
Bocage (Mme. du), 109
Boccaccio, 220
Boileau, 11, 71, 149
Boiardo, 140
Bolingbroke (Lady), 28
Bolingbroke (Lord), 19, 23, 26, note, 27, 28, 33, 131, 196, 199, 207, 214, 238
Bolshevists, 164
Bordeaux (Cardinal Archbishop) 228
Boufflers (Chev. de), 110
Boufflers (Mme. de), 76
Bouillon (Mme. de), 15
Bourbier (Le), 17
Bourg-en-Bresse, 120
Bossuet, 176, 179
Bretwitz (Lt.), 95, 101
Brittanicus, 159
Brizard, 122
Broglie (Duc de), 27
Brosses (President de), 109
Brunswick (Court of), 66
Brunswick Lunebourg, 167
Brunswick, (Prince of), 110
Brussels, 65, 66
Brutus, 30, 43, 64, 166
Buffon, 118
Burnet, 33
Bussi (Abbé de), 19
Butler (Samuel), 33
Byng (Admiral), 106
Byron (Lord), 156, 238

Caesar, 155, 171, 179
Calais, 23
Calas, 6, 111, 115, 116, 117, 118, 120, 123, 126, 249
Calmet (Dom), 104, 202 *note*
Calvin, 116, 217, 230
Cambrai, 20
Candide, 6, 31 *note*, 82 *note*, 106, 107, 112, 182, 213, 219-223, inc., 25

Canonisation de Saint Cucufin, 113, 244
Carlyle (Thomas), 7, 49, 176, 201, 237
Caroline (Queen) 31
Casanova, 110
Catalina, 80
Catherine (of Russia), 108, 125, 204, 215
Caumartin (M. de ; Marquis de Saint-Ange), 17, 189
Chabanon, 110
Champbonin, (Mme. de), 53
Champollion, 177
Chancel (La Grange), 21
Chanson de Roland, 35, 140
Chapelain, 188
Charlemagne, 181, 184, 185
Charles I., 197
Charles XII., 43, 175, 177, 181, 192
Charles Edward (Prince), 72, 72 *note*
Chartres (Duc de), 74
Chasot, 85
Chateaubriand, 131, 135, 189, 227, 228
Châteauneuf, (Abbe de), 10-14 inc., 16, 145
Châtelet (Prison), 21
Châtelet (M. du), 44, 49, 53, 77
Châtelet (Mme. du), 6, 40, 43, 44, 47-58 inc., 61, 63, 64 *note*, 65, 66, 68, 70, 72, 73, 73 *note*, 74-80 inc., 87, 145, 154, 195, 234, 248
Chatenay, 18
Chatterton, 209
Chaulieu, 15, 41, 131, 146, 146 *note*
Chauvelin, 79, 109
Chénier (André), 138, 154
Chénier (Joseph), 164
Chesterfield (Lord), 7 *note*, 31, 82, 131, 139, 147, 218, 246
Choiseul (Duc de), 108
Choiseul (Duchesse de), 113 244 *note*

INDEX

Cideville, 15, 42, 55, 234, 235
Cirey (Chateau de), 6, 45, 47, 48-60 inc., 62, 64, 74, 75, 79 *note*
Clairaut, 45, 54, 195
Clairon (Mlle. de), 118, 162
Clarendon, 176
Clarke (Samuel), 29, 32
Classiques Garnier, 153
Clement, 70, 109
Clement, XIII., 244 *note*
Cleves, 65, 82, 108
Coligni, 98, 99, 101, 106
Collège de Louis le Grand, 12
Collins (Anthony), 32
Collins (Churton), 7 *note*, 23 *note*, 24, 28 *note*, 31
Colmar, 104, 105
Comédie Française, 6, 18, 22, 22 *note*, 80, 121, 123, 156, 164
Compiégne, 82
Condorcet, 110, 131, 156, 164
Conduitts (the), 29
Confession de foi d'un Vicaire Savoyard, 82, 103
Confucious, 197
Congreve, 29
Connaissance de la Poésie et de l'Eloquence, 167
Conseils à un Journaliste, 167
Conti (Prince de), 17, 152
Corne de Bouc, 99, 100
Corneille, 11, 19, 160, 173
Corneille (Commentary on), 167
Corneille (Mlle. de), 114
Correspondance (of Voltaire), 167, 233-246 inc.
Cosi-Sancta, 224
Courdimanche, (Curé de), 165
Courtin, 15
Cowper, 237
Coypel, 151
Crassus, 241
Crébillon, 19, 74, 80
Crusades, 85

Damiens, 197
Danäe, 83

Dante, 138, 140, 148
Dantzig, 94 *note*
Daumard (Marguerite), 11
Dauphin, 13, 69
Défense du Mondain, 150
Deffend (Mme. du), 44 *note*, 79 *note*, 234, 235, 243, 244, 244 *note*
"Délices (Les)," 105, 107, 109
Demoulin, 38, 39
Denis (Mme.), 6, 50, 50 *note*, 51, 79 *note*, 83, 84, 86, 97, 99, 100, 101, 105, 122, 235
Denon, 110
Descartes, 83, 195, 208
Desfontaines, (Abbe), 21, 37 *note*, 45, 46, 56, 57, 99
Desforges-Maillard, 58
Desnoiresterres, 7, 7 *note*, 24, 44 *note*, 46 *note*, 79 *note*, 88 *note*, 96
Destouches, 33 *note*
Dictionnaire Philosophique, 85, 108, 110 *note*, 167, 201, 204 *note*, 214
Diderot, 108, 109, 135
Dijon, (Croix d'Or), 120
Discours en Vers sur l'Homme, 145
Discours sur l'Histoire Universelle, 179
Dodington (Bubb), 27
Don Juan, 141, 156
Don Quixote, 142
Dorn, 100, 101
Dresden, 69
Dreyfus (affaire), 117
Drury Lane Theatre, 29
Dryden, 31, 33, 156
Dubois (Abbe and Cardinal), 22
Ducis, 164
Duc (Le), 46 *note*
Duclos, 20
Duncan (Isadora), 147
Dunciad, 42
Dunoyer (Mme.), 15, 16
Dunoyer (Pimpette), 16, 17
Duplessis-Mornay, 31
Duren (Van), 96

INDEX

Ecossaise (L'), 111
Eléments de la Philosophie de Newton, 56, 57
Elizabeth (Queen), 184, 204
Eloge de Despréaux, 121
Eloge de Voltaire, 125
Eloge Historique de la Marquise du Châtelet, 56 note
Emile, 82
Encyclopédie, 94, 107, 110-112 inc., 214, 215
Enfant Prodigue (L'), 74
England, 6, 7, 19, 24-33 inc. 34, 36, 39, 82, 197, 215, 238
Epicurus, 14
Epictetus, 14
Epinay (Mme. d'), 109, 235
Epîtres, 152
Eriphyle, 43
Esope, 244
Essai sur la Nature du Feu, 56, 58
Essai sur la Poésie Epique, 169, 171
Essai sur les Moeurs et l'Esprit des Nations, 85, 106, 131, 175, 178, 178 note, 179, 179 note, 180, 181, 183, 184, 184 note, 185, 186, 190
Etallonde (d'), 118
Eugéne (Prince), 187
Europe et la Révolution Française, 176
Extrait des Sentiments de Jean Meslier, 112

Falkener (Mr ; afterwards Sir Everard), 28, 28 note
Fanier (Mlle.), 123
Faye (M. de la), 50
Ferney, 24, 28 note 82, 93, 104, 107-109 inc, 111-114 inc., 118, 119, 173, 209, 217, 231, 235, 237, 245
Fête de Bélébat, (La), 165
Flaubert, 135
Fleury (Cardinal), 66
Florian, 110, 219

Fontainebleau, 17, 22, 72, 243
Fontaine (La), 15, 244
Fontaine-Martel (Mme. de), 38, 42, 243
Fontenelle, 9, 15, 85
Fontenoy, (battle of), 71
Forges, 19
Formont, 235
France (Anatole), 135, 174
Franciade (La), 141
Francis of Assisi, 142
Frankfort, 93, 94, 94 *note*, 95, 107, 237
Frankfort (Burgermaster of), 97-101, inc.
Franklin, 121, 199
Fronde, 37, 180
Frederick (The Great), 6, 49, 59, 61, 62, 62 note, 63-66, inc., 68, 74, 75, 78-101, inc. 107, 108, 114, 118, 125, 152, 204 note, 215, 218, 220, 234, 235, 236, 237
Frederick William, 62
Fredriks (J. K.), 212 note
Fréron, 6, 70, 109, 111
Freytag, 95-101 inc.

Gassendi, 14, 14 note
Gay, 29
Gazette Littéraire, 167
Geneva, 82 note, 105-108 inc., 116
Génie du Christianisme, 135
Genlis, (Mme. de), 110
Genonville, 20, 22, 42
Gentil-Bernard, 153
George (King), 28
Germany, 34, 61, 65, 68, 103, 197
Gervasi, 19
Gex, 107, 113
Gibbon, 109, 176
Gluck, 121
Goethe, 101 note, 238
Goldsmith, 240
Grafigny (Mme. de), 51, 52, 53 *note*, 54

INDEX

Grasset, 106
Grécourt, 19
Greenwich, 23, 26, 31
Grétry, 110
Grévin, 43 note
Grimm, 109, 120, 156
Guay-Trouin, 190
Guesclin (Adelaide du), 44
Guise (Mlle. de), 45
Gulliver's Travels, 540

Hague, 16, 20, 82 note
Haller, 106
Hamilton, 131, 146, 146 note
Hamlet, 149
Hampstead, 31 note
Harpe (La), 28 note, 110, 156
Hénault (President), 19, 37
Henri IV., 17, 189, 204, 229
Henriade (La), 6, 17, 18, 20, 29 note, 31, 32, 34, 35, 38, 43, 121, 131, 139, 140, 141, 144, 169, 189, 213, 240
Hervey (Lord and Lady), 29, 29 note
Hesse (Margrave of), 110
Hettner, 131
Hirschell, 88
Histoire de la Guerre de 1741, 71 note
Histoire de Jenni, 226
Histoire du Parlement de Paris (L'), 175, 192
History of Charles XII., 7, 30
Hobbes, 32
Hoguère (the Banker), 19
Hohenzollern, 93
Holbach, 109
Holland, 56, 65
Homer, 18, 35, 138-140, 169, 172
Homme aux Quarante Ecus, (L'), 112, 226
Horace, 17
Houdon, 6, 216, 247
Houlières (Mme. Des), 15
Hugo (Victor), 138, 149, 164
Hume, 176

Idylls of the King, 141
Iliad, 169
Ingénu, (L'), 225
Irene, 121, 122, 156
Isaiah, 169, 172
Italy, 34, 238

J'ai vu, 18
Jansenist, 12, 13, 20, 69, 103, 103 note, 215, 217
Jeanne d' Arc, 141, 142
Jeannot et Colin, 213, 219
Jeremiah, 172
Jesuits, 6, 10, 12, 13, 16, 103, 104, 106, 106 note, 133, 215, 217
Job (Book of), 172
Johnson (Dr.), 30, 30 note, 136, 209, 221
Jonson (Ben), 33
Jore, 43, 45, 46, 57, 89
Journal de Politique et de Littérature, 167 note
Julian (Emperor), 83, 92
Julius II. (Pope), 188 note
Jupiter, 83

Kaiserling (von), 64
Keith (Earl Marishal), 85, 97
Koenig, 90

La Beaumelle, 181
Laborde, 109
La Fontaine, 131, 146
Lake Leman, 105
Lally, 117, 125
Lamarre, 57
Lamartine, 139, 154
Lamb, 237
Lanson, (M. Gustave), 7, 24, 44, 45 note, 51, 102 note, 127, 131, 159, 160 note, 169, 191 note, 202 note, 210, 211 note, 212 note, 233
Lausanne, 105, 106, 107

INDEX

Lecouvreur (Adrienne), 20, 22, 40, 42, 124, 209
Levebre, 42
Leibnitz, 45, 55, 195, 217, 220, 221
Leipsic, 92-94, 96, 97
Le Kain, 80, 80 *note*, 106, 109, 162
Lenclos (Ninon de), 11, 14, 15
Leonidas (Glover's), 140
Leo X., (Pope), 188 *note*
Lessing, 87
Lettres d'Amabed, 112, 222, 226
Lettres d'un Quaker, 112
Lettres Inédits, 28 *note*, 69 *note*
Lettres Philosophiques, 29 *note*, 30-33, 36, 37, 45, 55, 63, 64, 78, 110, 169, 205
Libertins, 14, 15
Ligne (Prince de), 110, 156, 247
Ligue (La), 20, 27
Linant, 42, 43, 57,
Lion d'Or, 96-98, 100
Lisbon, 106
Lisbon (Le Désastre de), 106
Livry (Suzanne de), 20-22, 40
Locke, 32, 196-198, 207, 208, 215
London, 14, 23, 25, 26, 28, 29, 45, 47, 64, 82 *note*, 87
Longchamp, 54, 72 *note*, 73, 73 *note*, 75 *note*, 76, 77 *note*, 79, 79 *note*
Longchamp et Wagnières' *Mémoires sur Voltaire*, 50 *note*, 53 *note*, 55 *note*
Lorraine, 38, 39, 46, 47
Louis XIII., 181
Louis XIV., 16, 65, 65 *note*, 71, 78, 82, 135, 168, 180, 186, 187, 188, 188 *note*, 189, 190
Louis XV., 22, 31, 64, 68, 69, 71, 72 *note*, 74, 78, 81, 84, 104, 104 *note*, 118, 204
Louis XVI., 104 *note*, 126
Louis (Saint), 204
Lourdet, 12 *note*
Lowth (Bishop), 171, 172

Lubert (Mlle. de), 243
Lucretius, 14, 15, 20
Lucullus, 83, 92
Lunéville, 74, 76, 77
Luther, 230
Lyons, 82 *note*, 105

Macbeth, 240
" Madame," 19
Mahomet, 59, 131, 163, 166
Maine (Duchesse du), 15, 73
Maintenon, 14
Mainz, 99, 103
Maisons (country House), 19
Maisons (M. de), 19, 42
Maisons (Mme. de), 42
Maladie du Jésuite Bertier, 201
Malta (Knights of), 14
Mancini (Laura),
Marat, 167 *note*, 212
Marcus Aurelius, 83, 92, 100, 204, 232
Marges (Les), 147 *note*
Marianne, 19, 22
Marlborough, 187
Marlborough (Duchess of), 29
Marmontel, 79, 79 *note*, 109
Marot, 131, 147
Mason, 28 *note*
Maupertuis, 45, 46, 55, 56 *note*, 85-87, 90, 91, 99, 195, 225 *note*, 236
Maurepas, 38, 59
Maupeou, 103
Medici (Lorenzo di), 188 *note*
Memnon, 73, 225
Mémoires (of Voltaire), 67 *note*, 204 *note*
Mérope, 59, 166
Metastasio, 165
Mettrie (La), 85, 87
Michelet, 176
Micromégas, 73, 225
Middleton, 33 *note*
Milton, 30 *note*, 35, 139, 170
Mimeure (Marquise de), 19
Moïsade, 12

INDEX

Molière, 14, 70, 167, 173
Monbailly, 117, 126, 249
Mondain (Le), 49, 150
Monrion, 105
Montaigne, 14, 14 *note*, 139-242
Montesquieu, 206, **239**
Moore, 109
Morand, 125
Morangies, 117
Morellet (Abbe), 109
Morley (Lord), 7, 24, 41
Mort de César, 30, 43, 155, 166, 171
Mouhy, 57
Moussinot (Abbé), 236
Musset (Alfred de), 147

Nanine, 123, 165, 166
Napoleon, 126, 135, **188**, **212**
Necker (Mme.), 121
Newcastle (Duke of), 27
Newmarket, 31
Newton, 29, 32, 45, 54-56, 195, 207, 208, 215
Nonotte, 181

Odéon, 156
Odes, 148, 149
Œdipe, 16, 18, 19, 22, 156, 166
Œuvres, 13 *note*, 15 *note*, 23 *note*, 25 *note*, 39 *note*, 42 *note*, 50 *note*, 55 *note*, 56 *note*, 60 *note*, 69 *note*
On the Events of 1744, 69
Oreilles du Comte de Chesterfield, (Les), 226
Oreste, 80
Orlando Furioso, 141
Orléans (Charles d'), 147
Orléans (Duc d'), see *Regent*
Orphelin de la Chine, 166
Othello, 155, 156

Palissot, 109
Palladion, 95
Pandore, 165
Panthéon, 6, 126, 159
Paradise Lost, 140
Paraguay, 106 *note*
Paris, 6, 14, 18-20, 27, 28, 34, 38, 45, 46, 50, 54-56, 67, 69, 74, 81, 87, 92, 104, 104 *note*, 105, 118-120, 123, 159, 180, 215, 237
Paris (Archbishop of), 125
Paris (the financiers), 19
Pascal, 45
Paul (Saint), 182
Pemberton, 29, 32
Penn, 105
Pennsylvania, 105
Peterborough (Lord), 29, 30
Peter (the Great), 215, 175
Pharsalia, 141
Philippiques, 21
Philosophe Ignorant (Le), **213**
Philosophes (Les), 110
Pigalle, 118
Pilate, 182
Piron, 6, 19, 21, 46, 58, **131**
Pitt (Andrew), 31 *note*
Plato, 240
Plombières, 38, 39, 92, 105
Plutarch, 180
Poème sur la Loi Naturelle, **145**
Poisson, 21
Poitou, 11
Poland (King of), 74, 80
Polignac (Cardinal de), 19
Pompadour (Mme. de), 68, 74, 78, 80, 84, 104
Pompignon (Le Franc), 112, 150 *note*
Pope (Alexander), 29, 30, 33, 149, 199
Pope (Mrs.), 30
Porée (Father), 13
Portes, 70
Potsdam, 6, 33, 66, 80-83, 87, 90, 92, 94-96, 98, **197**
Pour et les Contre, 41

INDEX

Preservatif, 57
Prie (Mme. de), 22
Princesse de Babylon, 112, 226
Princesse de Navarre, 69, 69 *note*, 166
Prior (Matthew), 147, 209
Prix de la Justice et de l'Humanité 211 *note*
Procopius, 180
Profession de foi d'un théist, 113
Prometheus Unbound, 165
Prussia, 86-88, 90-92, 94, 96, 98, 100
Prussia (Queen of), 83
Prussia (Queen Mother of), 83
Pucelle (La), 6, 11, 54, 55, 59, 63, 65, 106, 107, 141-145, 171
Puero regnante, 18, 21
Pulci (Luigi), 145, 171
Pultenay, 29
Pyrrhonisme de l'Histoire, 112

Quakers, 105
Quand (Les), 112
Queen (Maria Leszczynska), 20, 22
Quinault, 160
Quinault (Mme.), 234

Rabelais, 206
Racine, 134, 145, 159, 160, 169, 173, 239, 241, 242
Rameau, 69, 70
Raphael, 142
Rasselas, 221
Réaumur, (M. de), 58
Regent (Duc d'Orléans), 17, 18, 20, 21
Rélation du Voyage, 112
Renan, 172, 174
Restauration, 127
Retz (Cardinal de), 180
Revolution, 6, 37, 64, 120, 126, 135, 147, 164
Rezzonico, 244
Richelieu (Cardinal de), 188

Richelieu (country house), 19
Richelieu (Duc de), 19, 22, 39, 40, 45-47, 59, 68, 69, 109, 121, 234
Richelieu (Duchesse de), 16, 51 *note*
Richelieu (family), 11
Rienzi, 184
Robespierre, 212
Rochebrune, 11
Rochefoucauld, (Duc de la), 180
Rochester, 33
Rohan-Chabot, 63
Rohan (Chevalier de), 6, 22, 22 *note*, 23, 24, 27, 31 *note*, 35, 83, 209
Roi, 70
Rome, 200
Romeo and Juliet, 169, 240
Ronsard, 35, 141
Rossbach (Battle of), 107, 114
Rothelin (Abbé), 46
Rouen, 15, 20, 38, 43, 45, 82 *note*
Rouille (M.), 46
Rousseau (J. B.), 12, 15, 21, 21 *note*, 46, 57, 148, 167
Rousseau (J. J.), 82, 103, 103 *note*, 106, 118, 126, 203, 217, 220, 225, 228, 229, 230
Rucker (Rathsherr), 95, 101
Rumpelmonde (Mme. de), 9, 20, 41
Russell (Bertrand), 194
Russia, 37
Ruth (Book of), 172

Saint-Ange, 17
Sainte-Beuve, 34 *note*, 62 *note*, 233
Sainte-Chapelle (La), 11
Saint-Claude (Canons of), 111
Saint-Denis, 126
Saint-Evremonde, 14, 147, 147 *note*
Saint-Germain-en-Laye, 38
Saint-Hyacinthe, 57
Saint-Lambert, 76, 77

INDEX

Saint Paul's, 31
Saint-Simon, 11, 15, 131, 178, 189
Saintsbury (Prof.), 178
Samson, 165
Sancho Panza, 142
Sanchez, 215
Sans-Souci, 84
Saul, 166
Saxony, 89
Scarmentado, 73
Scéaux (country house), 19, 73, 73 *note*, 74
Scellières, 125
Schmid (Councillor), 95, 98, 99, 101
Schmid (Frau), 99
Scott (Sir Walter), 72, 140, 160
Séguier, 110
Sémiramis, 43, 74
Seneca, 182
Sermon des Cinquante, 112
Sermon Prêché à Bale, 112
Servien (Abbé), 174
Shakespeare, 33, 43, 43 *note*, 71, 102, 134, 138, 155, 156, 159, 160, 161, 162, 164, 169, 173
Shaw (Mr. Bernard), 117
Sherlock, 109
Siècle de Louis XIV., 6, 17, 30, 85, 87, 167, 175, 177, 180, 180 *note*, 181, 186, 189-192
Siècle de Louis XV., 175, 181, 191, 203 *note*
Simonides, 172
Sirven, 111, 115-118, 249
Socrates, 24
Solomon, 92
Solon, 179
Song of Solomon, 168
Sophocles, 19, 134, 138, 160, 173
Sorbonne, 58
Sorel, 176, 184
Spinosa, 194
Sporus, 149
Stances, 154

Stendhal, 146, 164
Strachey (Mr. Lytton), 7, 88 *note*
Strasbourg, 104
Suard (Mme.), 110
Sulli (Duc de), 18, 22, 23, 31, 31 *note*
Sulli-sur-Loire, 18
Sundon (Lady), 29
Sweden, 197
Swift, 29, 29 *note*, 31, 33, 52, 209, 246
Switzerland, 105, 107
Synagogue, 31

Tanis et Zélide, 165
Tancréde, 156, 166
Tasso, 35, 140, 219
Taureau Blanc (Le), 226
Tecusa (Saint), 182
Temple, 10, 12, 14, 15-18, 20, 32, 145, 198
Temple de la Gloire, (Le), 71, 166
Temple du Goût, 42
Tencin (Cardinal), 105
Tennyson, 141
Thames, 25
Thiériot, 17, 21, 22, 28, 31, 33, 38, 45, 50, 50 *note*, 57, 105, 234
Tiberius, 182
Thomson, 33
Tories, 31
Toulet (P. J.), 147
Tournay, 107
Tournay (Comte de), 107
Tournemine (Father), 13
Tragiques (Les), 141
Traité de Metaphysique, 33 *note*, 196
Traité de Tolérance, 204 *note*
Trajan, 78, 204
Travenol, 70
Trenck (Baron), 94, 220
Tristram Shandy, 167 *note*
Tronchin, 106, 108
Tu et le Vous, (Le), 40
Turgot, 109, 189
Tryconnel (Lord), 85

INDEX

Universal History, 56

Valla (Lorenzo), 182
Valois, 141
Varennes (flight to), 126
Vanité (La), 149
Vauvenargues (Marquis de), 3, 70
Vaux (country house), 19
Vendôme (Philippe de), 14, 17
Verlaine, 154
Versailles, 27, 47, 63, 69, 113, 120
Vestris (Mlle.), 123
Vigne (Mlle. Malcrais de la); (see Desforges-Maillard), 58
Villars (Duc de), 20, 109
Villars (M. and Mme. de), 19
Villette (Mme. de), 122
Virgil, 18, 35, 139
Vision de Babouc, 73, 224
Voisenon, 153
Voiture, 131
Voix du Sage et du Peuple (La), 82 *note*

Wagnière, 119, 120, 123 *note*, 124
Walpole (Horatio; Brit. Ambassador), 27, 29 210
Wandsworth, 29
Waterfield (Bishop of), 213
Westminster Abbey, 2)
Westphalia, 82
Whigs, 31
Woolston, 32, 202
Wortley-Montague (Lady Mary), 207

Young, 29, 30 *note*

Zadig, 73, 224
Zaïre, 43, 44, 155-158, 166, 169, 213
Zeno, 14

For Product Safety Concerns and Information please contact our EU
representative GPSR@taylorandfrancis.com
Taylor & Francis Verlag GmbH, Kaufingerstraße 24, 80331 München, Germany

www.ingramcontent.com/pod-product-compliance
Lightning Source LLC
Chambersburg PA
CBHW071810300426
44116CB00009B/1266